Founding editor: J. R. MULRYNE
General editors:
JAMES C. BULMAN, CAROL CHILLINGTON RUTTER

As You Like It

Manchester University Press

Already published in the series

Geraldine Cousin *King John*
Anthony B. Dawson *Hamlet*
Mary Judith Dunbar *The Winter's Tale*
Jay L. Halio *A Midsummer Night's Dream* (2nd edn)
Michael D. Friedman *Titus Andronicus*
Andrew Hartley *Julius Caesar*
Stuart Hampton-Reeves and Carol Chillington Rutter
The *Henry VI* plays
Bernice W. Kliman *Macbeth* (2nd edn)
Alexander Leggatt *King Lear*
James Loehlin *Henry V*
Scott McMillin *Henry IV, Part One*
Robert Ormsby *Coriolanus*
Lois Potter *Othello*
Hugh M. Richmond *King Henry VIII*
Margaret Shewring *King Richard II*
Virginia Mason Vaughan *The Tempest*

As You Like It

ROBERT SHAUGHNESSY

Manchester University Press

Copyright © Robert Shaughnessy 2018

The right of Robert Shaughnessy to be identified as the author of this work has been asserted by him in accordance with the Copyright, Designs and Patents Act 1988.

Published by Manchester University Press
Altrincham Street, Manchester M1 7JA, UK
www.manchesteruniversitypress.co.uk

British Library Cataloguing-in-Publication Data is available

ISBN 978 0 7190 8693 9 *hardback*
ISBN 978 1 5261 4350 1 *paperback*

First published by Manchester University Press in hardback 2018

This edition first published 2019

The publisher has no responsibility for the persistence or accuracy of URLs for any external or third-party internet websites referred to in this book, and does not guarantee that any content on such websites is, or will remain, accurate or appropriate.

Typeset by Koinonia, Manchester

For Erina

CONTENTS

	List of illustrations	*page* viii
	Series editors' preface	ix
	Acknowledgements	x
	Introduction: This strange, eventful history	1
Chapter I	Play, parts and players	9
Chapter II	Hunting for Arden in Warwickshire	36
Chapter III	Materials of performance: denim and silk	61
Chapter IV	Between France and Germany	99
Chapter V	At all points like a man	129
Chapter VI	Woeful pageants	159
Chapter VII	As we like it	194
	Appendix Major actors and staff for productions discussed in this volume	208
	References	212
	Index	219

LIST OF ILLUSTRATIONS

1 Frontispiece, Thomas Hanmer's *Works of Mr William Shakespeare*, Volume 3, 1743, The Wrestling Scene, by Francis Hayman. Courtesy of the British Library — page 2
2 Undated postcard (*c.* 1900–19) depicting the stuffed stag. Courtesy of the Royal Shakespeare Company — 38
3 Rosalind (Vanessa Redgrave) and Orlando (Patrick Allen), BBC Television, 1963 — 57
4 Phoebe (Lesley Manville), Rosalind (Juliet Stevenson) and Celia (Fiona Shaw), Royal Shakespeare Company, 1985. Courtesy of Donald Cooper — 85
5 Jacques Copeau as Jaques, *Le Matin*, 13 October 1934 — 108
6 Rosalind (Jutta Lampe), Touchstone (Werner Rehm) and Celia (Tina Engel), Schaubühne Berlin, 1977. Courtesy of Ruth Walz — 122
7 Audrey (Anthony Hopkins) and Touchstone (Derek Jacobi) in rehearsal, the National Theatre, 1967. © Zöe Dominic, courtesy of Dominic Photography — 135
8 Rosalind (Bryce Dallas Howard) and Orlando (David Oyelowo), BBC Films/HBO Films/Shakespeare Film Company, 2006 — 189
9 Amy Cook and Robert Shaughnessy at Shakespeare's Globe, 2015 — 195

SERIES EDITORS' PREFACE

Recently, the study of Shakespeare's plays as scripts for performance in the theatre has grown to rival the reading of Shakespeare as literature among university, college and secondary-school teachers and their students. The aim of the present series is to assist this study by describing how certain of Shakespeare's texts have been realised in production.

The series is not concerned to provide theatre history in the traditional sense. Rather, it employs the more contemporary discourses of performance criticism to explore how a multitude of factors work together to determine how a play achieves meaning for a particular audience. Each contributor to the series has selected a number of productions of a given play and analysed them comparatively. These productions – drawn from different periods, countries and media – were chosen not only because they are culturally significant in their own right but also because they represent something of the range and variety of the possible interpretations of the play in hand. They illustrate how the convergence of various material conditions helps to shape a performance: the medium for which the text is adapted; stage-design and theatrical tradition; the acting company itself; the body and abilities of the individual actor; and the historical, political and social contexts which condition audience reception of the play.

We hope that theatregoers, by reading these accounts of Shakespeare in performance, may enlarge their understanding of what a play-text is and begin, too, to appreciate the complex ways in which performance is a collaborative effort. Any study of a Shakespeare text will, of course, reveal only a small proportion of the play's potential meaning; but by engaging issues of how a text is translated in performance, our series encourages a kind of reading that is receptive to the contingencies that make theatre a living art.

J. R. Mulryne, Founding editor
James C. Bulman, Carol Chillington Rutter,
General editors

ACKNOWLEDGEMENTS

My thanks, first and foremost, to series editors Carol Rutter and Jim Bulman, for giving me the opportunity to write this book, for their patience during the period it took to come to fruition, and for their meticulous attention to the final draft when it eventually arrived. Second, I am grateful to the staff at the following libraries, archives and collections that have provided the material for the stories told in these pages: Akademie der Künste; the BBC Written Archives Centre; the British Film Institute; the British Library; the National Theatre Archive, the Shakespeare Birthplace Trust; Shakespeare-Forschungsbibliothek Munich; the University of Kent Templeman Library Special Collections and the V&A Theatre and Performance Collections. Many colleagues and friends have played their part, especially Fiona Banks, Amy Cook, Paul Edmondson, Peter Holland, Kelly Hunter and John Lutterbie. Very special thanks to Barbara Hodgdon, who has been a source of support and wise counsel, and an inspiration. Material assistance to carry out the archival research was awarded by the School of Arts at the University of Kent, and super-efficiently administered by Dennis Smith; a term of research leave allowed me to concentrate on writing during a crucial period. For help of various kinds I am indebted to Peter Boenisch, Helen Brooks, Krysta Dennis, Tamar Jeffers-McDonald, Mary McNulty and Will Wollen. At Manchester University Press, I am grateful to Paul Clarke for deftly steering the script through the production process. All quotations from Shakespeare, unless otherwise stated, are from *The Norton Shakespeare*, third edition, edited by Stephen Greenblatt (New York: Norton, 2015).

My family are always and everywhere in these pages: Nickie, my co-mate, and companion on the greatest of journeys; Caitlin, Nathaniel and Gabriel. And Erina: this one, with love, is for you.

INTRODUCTION

This strange, eventful history

Even by the standards of Shakespearean comedy, *As You Like It* tests theatrical logic. Opening with one of the most excruciatingly detailed and convoluted expositions of back story in the canon, it moves from a frantically incident-packed first act into a pastoral setting where all sense of narrative urgency almost as precipitately evaporates, where time stands still, and where the wilful insouciance of the title is the order of the day. Unlike other Shakespearean comedies whose structure involves dichotomous locations, furthermore, *As You Like It* does not progress neatly from the court to the green world and then back (as in *A Midsummer Night's Dream*), but moves fitfully between them until the beginning of the third act. Unlike other Shakespearean comedies, comic closure is not compromised by pain, punishment or death; nor does the play return its characters and audiences to a 'real' world in which the fantastic may be put to the test. Centring on a cross-dressed heroine who undertakes a journey into the transformative space of pastoral, it is a drama of conversations and encounters rather than of conflicts, of game-playing, masquerade, verbal set-pieces and song; its conclusion sees no fewer than four marriages, at least two miraculous conversions, and the appearance of a god. Nominally set in the forests of the Ardennes, the play presents a mythical, very English world in which exiled aristocrats living out their Robin Hood fantasies rub shoulders with sheep farmers.

For much of its theatrical afterlife, the play's success has hinged upon Rosalind, whose polymorphous sexual identity has been negotiated in a variety of ways by performers and audiences. Rosalind in our time has been played as both gamine and gender outlaw, a coveted role for leading female performers and, very occasionally, male ones too. The play has also afforded opportunities for performance against the background of, or amidst, greenery and less literal imaginings of Arden as a forest of dreams. Recent commentators on the play have drawn attention to the

1 Frontispiece, Thomas Hanmer's *Works of Mr William Shakespeare*, Volume 3, 1743, The Wrestling Scene, by Francis Hayman

class tensions, the patriarchal imperatives, and the discontents that simmer beneath the play's benign surface; directors have done their best to inject some darkness into it by playing up the violence and totalitarianism of Duke Frederick's court, or by emphasizing a wintry ambience that sooner or later turns to spring. In all of its guises, *As You Like It* has rarely been out of the repertoire.

As this book focuses on the performance of *As You Like It* in the twentieth century, what follows is a brief outline of the prehistory that provides its background and context. Entered in the Stationers' Register in 1600 but not published until the First Folio of 1623, *As You Like It* left no trace of any performance in its own time, and although it was one of the plays acquired by Thomas Killigrew for the new Theatre Royal, Drury Lane, in 1669, it was not among the handful of Shakespeare plays to be revived during the Restoration. The first time anything resembling Shakespeare's comedy was given a documented performance on the London stage was in 1723, at the Theatre Royal, in the heavily adapted form of Charles Johnson's *Love in a Forest*. Johnson brought the text into line with early eighteenth-century standards of elite taste with some radical editing: Touchstone, Corin, Audrey, Phoebe and Martext were all cut, Celia paired up with Jaques (the celebrated Colley Cibber, who, initiating a long-standing tradition, appropriated the First Lord's speech in 2.1), the wrestling match became a fencing bout, and the 'seven degrees of the lie' was replaced by a performance of *Pyramus and Thisbe*. Theatre, for Johnson, 'should support the government', and the piece in his hands propagandized on behalf of the 1723 Black Act, which 'made it a felony to enter a forest under disguise or with a blackened face and to hunt, wound, or steal deer' (Scheil 46, 51). The adaptation managed a run of six performances, but the play was not seen again for nearly twenty years. In December 1740 Charles Fleetwood mounted a production at the Theatre Royal, Drury Lane with the up-and-coming Hannah Pritchard leading as Rosalind, supported by the more established Kitty Clive as Celia and James Quin as Jaques; and, together with the same season's two other cross-dressing comedies *The Merchant of Venice* and *Twelfth Night*, it marked a sea-change in eighteenth-century Shakespearean performance. The staging was to a large extent a response to the popularity of the more recent *travesti* comedies at the other patent theatre in Covent Garden, George Farquhar's *The Recruiting Officer* (1706) and *The Constant Couple* (1700), which exploited the assets of the sex-celebrity Margaret Woffington by putting her in close-fitting breeches and doublet; at this point, the erotic appeal of these women dressed as men was rooted in bodily display rather than sexual ambiguity. Nonetheless, the revival of *As You Like It*, and of Shakespeare's comedies more generally, offered new opportunities for eighteenth-century actors that they were quick to grasp. Woffington herself took on Rosalind in 1741 and played the role for the next 16 years; between her and Pritchard the part became defined as that of a 'spirited hoyden' (Marshall 12).

Among the cast of the 1740–41 production was the painter and book illustrator Francis Hayman (who was listed as playing Silvius), and early in the 1740s his rendering of the wrestling match appeared both in the plate he created for Thomas Hanmer's 1741 edition of the complete works and in a painting apparently based on it (see Figure 1). One of the key players in the development of his century's growing rapprochement between Shakespeare and the visual arts, Hayman worked as a scene painter at Drury Lane from the 1730s to the mid-1740s, and his depictions offer a sense of stage practice and of how the play was imagined at this juncture. Hayman's illustration for Hanmer was executed according to the latter's instructions, which stipulated that Orlando should be 'a handsome young man well-proportioned' and that 'the two ladies show greater joy than all the rest': 'Their figures must be set off to all possible advantage as young and beautiful and of the highest rank' (Allentuck 303). Hayman achieved this in the monochrome illustration, which shows Orlando just having thrown Charles, by placing Celia and Rosalind centrally and framing them with greenery, with the faint outlines of a Palladian structure visible in the background. The sense of a proportionate balance between classicism, femininity, masculine prowess and nature is strengthened in the painting, which completes the detail of the colonnade, substantially embellishes the greenery, and sets the blood-red of the prone Charles's tunic against Celia's blue and Rosalind's white low-cut gowns: though technically inhabiting a scene set at court, the ladies are already halfway to an Arden envisaged as a nurtured and gently regulated aristocratic playground. Woodland and the English countryside, as imagined here and in subsequent stagings of the play, offered the pleasures of spectacle that perfectly accord with the to-be-looked-atness of the heroine, in the course of a century in which the relationship between town and rural environment reflected shifting configurations of class power and ownership, as the wealth of the countryside passed from the landed gentry to the middle classes newly enriched by the industrial revolution. Thus did *As You Like It* begin its history of contribution to what Raymond Williams, in his classic account of the imagined relationship between urban and rural experience, characterizes as a 'contrast between country and city, as fundamental ways of life', a contrast that is articulated as a series of powerful oppositions: 'the idea of a natural way of life: of peace, innocence and simple virtue' versus 'the idea of an achieved centre: of learning, communication, light'; and, also, 'the city as a place of noise, worldliness and ambition' versus 'the country as a place of backwardness, ignorance, limitation' (*The Country and the City* 9).

The eminent tragedian Sarah Siddons was not a success as Rosalind when she attempted the role in 1785, but her contemporary Dora Jordan certainly was. From 1787 to 1814 the role was hers, and she made no attempt to masquerade as masculine when in the guise of Ganymede: James Boaden recorded that her appeal was 'purely feminine' and resided in 'the display of female, not male, perfections'. Should 'the lady really look like a man, the coarse *androgynus* would be hooted from the stage' (Boaden 1 46). Meanwhile, as the less privileged inhabitants of the English countryside experienced the effects of the industrialization of the rural economy, so that, as Williams puts it, 'what happened in the villages to the labourers and the poor was, after 1815, as bad as anything in the long centuries of exploitation and degradation' (*The Country and the City* 221), the forest of Arden, as seen in the factory-scale, increasingly technologically sophisticated theatres of the major cities, became ever more idealized, detailed and three-dimensional. Charles Kemble and James Robinson Planché inaugurated the era of spectacular, historically accurate pictorial realism with their production of *King John* in 1823; producers of *As You Like It* followed the lead. In 1842 Thomas H. Shepherd followed Hayman by depicting the wrestling match; in this instance as it was staged in William Charles Macready's production at Drury Lane. His engraving shows a stage picture that places the combatants in a ringed space semi-circled by a 74-strong crowd of spectators, with Rosalind and Celia distinct in the foreground: in the background looms a vast fairytale castle and the prospect of open countryside. Macready, as was the prerogative of the actor-manager throughout the eighteenth and nineteenth centuries, played Jaques, and caught the favour of Queen Victoria herself, who is reported to have said that he delivered the 'seven ages' set-piece 'beautifully' (Rowell 41).

Macready's Rosalind was Louisa Nisbett, but he would have preferred Helena Faucit, who in the years that followed made the part as much her own as Jordan had done. In the process, she transformed Rosalind into a Victorian ideal of womanhood, characterized by 'dignity and delicacy', 'truth and beauty' and 'passion impermeated with love-breathing sighs, sunny smiles, and delicious tears' (Coleman 1 171). Any possibility of gender ambiguity in her role-playing was decisively dismissed: 'she never falls into the mistake', reported the *Pall Mall Gazette* approvingly, 'so frequently committed by actresses who assume the male manner with the male attire' (10 March 1865). This was not the case with American actress Charlotte Cushman, who when she visited the Princess's Theatre in 1845 was hailed by the *Observer*'s reviewer for a 'transformation' that 'had the same effect on her as on the famed Tiresias': 'Her mind became masculine as well as her outward semblance; and on the assumption of the manly garb she would seem to have doffed all the constraint of her sex and her country. ... She looks every inch a man.' This reviewer says little about the staging other than that it was 'well "mounted"', and that the audience, 'which was numerous and unquestionably intelligent', were 'quite satisfied with the performance' (3 March 1845). Far more detailed comment was occasioned by Samuel Phelps, at Sadler's Wells in 1847, who advanced the cause of spectacle still further by having Hymen enter on 'an ornamental "temple", evidently a pageant wagon' and introducing a deer carcass alongside 'Which is he that killed the deer?' in 4.2 (Marshall 32). By the end of the nineteenth century, producers' and audiences' love of romantic illusion had reached its peak. For their 1885 production at St James's Theatre, John Hare and W. H. Kendal drew upon the illuminations in Froissart's *Chronicles* for their sets and costumes, covered the stage with artificial grass and included natural water features and ferns; in New York and London four years later, Augustin Daly employed 'a revolving panorama of forest, which not only presents a variety of charming pictures, but conveys an impression of great spaces, and suggests in a striking manner the freedom and seclusion of the life in Arden' (Jeanette Gilder, *The Critic*, 28 December 1889; cited in Bate and Rasmussen 118). Ada Rehan was Rosalind, who delighted audiences as she 'never for one moment forgets, or allows her audience to forget, that she is a woman' (*Daily Telegraph*,

16 July 1890), yet displayed a 'restless movement' that 'registered a vigorous style of feminine behaviour', which made her, according to Marshall, 'a precursor of the New Woman' (Marshall 49). By the start of the new century the spectacular tradition was on the wane, though it was briefly revived in 1907 in Oscar Asche's staging at His Majesty's Theatre, which made copious use of real vegetation and prompted the *Illustrated London News* reviewer to wax lyrical about 'this stay by proxy under the greenwood tree, this transference to an ideal world' (12 October 1907).

For some at least, the ideal world of Arden had found its true home in 1879, when the play featured in the first season at the Shakespeare Memorial Theatre in Stratford-upon-Avon. As detailed in Chapter II, this is where the main story of this book begins. Chapter I examines the play as a text for performance on the early modern stage, not by conjecturally reconstructing a performance that may or may not have taken place, but by mining the script for clues as to how it might have been handled by its first players. Barry Sullivan's production was the first to introduce into 4.2 a stuffed stag that returned for every production of the play at Stratford that followed up until 1919, when Nigel Playfair notoriously banished it from the stage. I take this event, and the tradition it confronted, as the point of departure for the first of two chapters examining the long history of *As You Like It* at Stratford, which pay particular attention to three contrasting RSC productions: Michael Elliott's of 1961, which launched Vanessa Redgrave's legendary, epoch-defining Rosalind; Buzz Goodbody's of 1973, and Adrian Noble's of 1985. At this location, the play has often been at its most localized; by contrast, Chapter IV addresses two productions beyond the English (and English-speaking) theatre context. The first of these, seen at l'Atelier in Paris in 1934, is Jacques Copeau's redaction *Rosalinde*; the second Peter Stein's monumental four-hour production for the Schaubühne Berlin in 1977. The latter, described by Dennis Kennedy as 'one of Stein's greatest productions' (Kennedy 261), was a landmark in the history of European Shakespeare; it is also, as I seek to demonstrate, one deeply embedded in the politics and history of its troubled times.

Chapter V focuses on two all-male versions of the play: Clifford Williams's for the National Theatre in 1967, and Declan Donnellan's for Cheek by Jowl in 1991 and 1994. If it goes without saying that *As You Like It* has, throughout its performance history, been implicated in questions of sexual and gender identity, these productions particularly foreground issues of transvestite masquerade and same-sex desire that the tradition of female Rosalinds has largely occluded. This is followed, in Chapter VI, by a consideration of the play's fortunes in the medium in which it has fared least successfully. The first, silent film version of *As You Like It* was released in 1908, initiating a screen history that includes the first British Shakespeare sound feature, Paul Czinner's film of 1936, the BBC/Time-Life Television production of 1978, Christine Edzard's in 1992, and Kenneth Branagh's in 2006. None of these has been particularly well regarded by Shakespeareans, and my aim in this chapter, while not claiming that any of them is an unjustly neglected masterpiece, is to situate them in the context of their original contexts of viewing that might encourage a more sympathetic, or at least less dismissive, response.

The final chapter is the only one to draw substantially upon the first-hand audience experience of a recent production, Blanche McIntyre's for Shakespeare's Globe in 2015. This was the third time that this theatre staged the play in its 20-year history (previously it was seen in 1998 and 2009; the latter production was filmed and released on DVD). Tracking in some detail my own (and my theatre-going companion's) challenging experience of this play at this venue, the chapter does not present the production as noteworthy, accomplished and historically significant in the way that many of the others I discuss clearly are; rather, it embraces the perhaps unique capacity of the space of the Globe to situate its plays and participants within the open-air theatre of ongoing everyday life, the place in which the meanings of *As You Like It*, and the pleasures and occasional frustrations it affords, are ultimately made. The pages that follow contain a number of untold stories, including the experience of the first television audiences of the BBC's productions of *As You Like It* in 1963 and 1978, a German professor sparking a security scare at an airport in 1977, and the hidden history of the stage management of Adrian Noble's RSC production in 1985. This story, at the end of the day, is mine. As I hope to show, the events of an autumn afternoon in September halfway through the second decade of the fourth century of the play's afterlife are part of a history that is strange, eventful, and deeply personal.

CHAPTER I

Play, parts and players

As you like yt / **a booke**

As You Like It was first published in 1623, as the tenth of the 14 plays that make up the first section of *Mr William Shakespeare's Comedies, Tragedies & Histories* (the First Folio). The text had been typeset in William Jaggard's printing shop on Aldersgate Street, nearby London's Barbican, towards the end of the busy four months from April to July 1622. During this period the first 12 of the 36 plays in the Folio were printed; work on the volume was then suspended while the printers devoted themselves to what at the time seemed the more urgent tasks of completing Augustine Vincent's *Discovery of Errors* and his corrections to the York Herald Ralph Brooke's 1619 *Catalogue of Nobility*, as well as beginning to set both the English translation of André Favyn's *Theater of Honour and Knighthood* (subtitled 'A Compendious Chronicle and History of the whole Christian World') and the antiquary William Burton's *Description of Leicestershire*. The Folio *As You Like It* is generally regarded as a straightforward and largely error-free text, its only significant matter of contention being whether certain proper and place names and forms of address (Arden or Ardennes, Monsieur or Master) ought or ought not to be Anglicized (Wells and Taylor 392–5).

One of the 18 plays included in the Folio that had not previously been published in quarto, *As You Like It* was printed from manuscript copy. The general editorial consensus is that this was a transcript of copy used in the playhouse, largely on the basis of its speech headings and stage directions, which are generally regular, consistent, and attuned to staging practicalities, but the evidence is far from conclusive. Its tendency, for example, to mark entrances well ahead in advance, Agnes Latham argues, is sensitive to 'the time it took an actor, entering upstage, to make his way down to the front' (Latham xiii). There are few of the indicative or speculative stage directions that are thought to characterize an authorial draft (the opening of 2.1, '*Enter* DUKE SENIOR, AMIENS, *and two or three* LORDS *like Foresters*', is an exception). The text's division into acts and scenes, a feature of some but not all of the Folio plays, reveals little about its theatrical provenance. The five –act structure, which reflects the need for breaks in the action to allow for the replenishment of candles, is characteristic of plays performed at the indoor Blackfriars playhouse after 1609, but it is also a literary embellishment retrospectively applied to all those performed in the public playhouses prior to this date, possibly by the scrivener Ralph Crane, whose neoclassical tastes significantly shaped the Folio's presentation.

Though there is no record of *As You Like It* being performed at all prior to its publication in 1623, there is evidence that the play was written, if not played, a quarter of a century earlier. On 4 August 1600, the printer James Roberts secured the rights to the publication of four plays with an entry in the Register of the Stationers' Company:

> *As you like yt* / a booke
> HENRY *the* FFIFT / a booke
> *Euery man in his humour.* / a booke
> *The commedie of 'muche A doo about nothing'*
>   a booke /

(Dusinberre 121)

A note in the margin reads 'to be staied', indicating that Roberts was staking his claim to the plays with the intent to confirm publication at a later date (as he had done with *The Merchant of Venice* two years earlier). In the event, three of the four entries were followed by quarto publication: *2 Henry IV* (here misidentified as *Henry V*), *Much Ado* and Jonson's *Every Man in his Humour* all appeared in print soon after, but *As You Like It* did not. Whatever motivated the staying order, Roberts evidently either changed his mind about publishing the play or was prevented from doing so, and the reasons for this reversal have been a matter for speculation. It has been argued that the play never made it into print because it was censored or suppressed, in relation to possible satirical links between Jacques (with its lavatorial echoes of 'jakes') and the courtier Sir John Harington (author of *The Metamorphosis of Ajax*, 1596), or because of suspected allusions to the former Queen's favorite, Robert Devereux, Earl of Essex, whose political career had in 1600 just taken a disastrous turn for the worse following the failure of his Irish military expedition in 1599. If this were the case, *As You Like It* would have had a topicality and direct (not to mention reckless) contemporary allusiveness that was generally uncharacteristic of its constitutionally circumspect and non-aligned author.

An alternative explanation for the fact that almost all of Shakespeare's plays written after the turn of the century were not printed until 1623 is that he either lost interest in, or consciously decided against, publication of anything other than his sonnets. In one version of this scenario, Shakespeare's status as a working playwright and sharer in the Lord Chamberlain's, then King's, Men meant that his priority was to produce scripts for performance with little concern for posterity; in another, his literary ambitions inclined him against putting his plays into print, possibly because he envisaged 'an ambitious collected edition of [his] writings' along the lines of Jonson's Folio *Works* of 1616 (Erne 111). It is also possible that *As You Like It* did not progress beyond the staying entry because it was earmarked as a manuscript presentation copy for an aristocratic recipient. Perhaps, however, the reason why the initially deferred publication led to a delay that extended to over two decades was less a matter of court politics or of literary aspirations than of publishing economics. As far as quarto publication was concerned, 1600 was Shakespeare's peak year; in addition to the plays already mentioned, *Henry V* was published and *Titus Andronicus* reprinted. Thereafter only five new plays were published during his lifetime (*The Merry Wives of Windsor* in 1602, *Hamlet* in 1603 and 1604; *King Lear* in 1608; *Troilus and Cressida* and the co-authored *Pericles* in 1609). All of the other play quartos were reprints of works from the first phase of Shakespeare's playwriting career, none of them comedies.[1] The number of reprints of Shakespeare's two narrative poems, *Venus and Adonis* and *Lucrece* (13 and 6, respectively, between 1593 and 1636) strongly hints that these were more to the reading public's taste than his drama; and it was not until 1619, which saw the unauthorized reissue by Thomas Pavier of six previously published plays, that any of Shakespeare's early romantic comedies were reissued.

Since less than a fifth of the three thousand or so plays that may have been performed between the 1570s and the 1640s were published, and that of these very few were reprinted, this is not that remarkable. What is worth noting, as far as Shakespeare is concerned, is the pattern of play publication considered by genre. Of the 22 plays belonging to the phase of Shakespeare's writing career that extends from the *Henry VI* plays and *The Two Gentlemen of Verona* to *Julius Caesar* and *Twelfth Night*, 14 were published in quarto or octavo, of which 9 are tragedies or histories; the unpublished works in these categories are *Henry VI, Part 1*, *King John* and *Julius Caesar*. During the same period, in addition to *Love's Labour's Lost, Much Ado, Merchant, A Midsummer Night's Dream* and *Merry Wives*, all of which were published in quarto, Shakespeare wrote *The Comedy of Errors, Twelfth Night, The Two Gentlemen of Verona, The Taming of the Shrew* and *As You Like It*, which were not. Risky as it is to draw firm conclusions from such limited evidence, it seems at least plausible that Shakespeare's comedies, even during the period when he was most prolific in the genre, remained unpublished because there was little or no market for them. Perhaps by the 1600s, Shakespeare's pastoralism, his habit of locating his comic intrigues in fantasy worlds elsewhere, and the fondness for cross-dressed boys that he shared with courtly forebear John Lyly in his 1580s heyday, had come to seem rather old-fashioned, especially when set against the emergence of the sharp, cynical, London-set, money-driven civic comedies of Jonson, Thomas Dekker and Thomas Middleton (it may be no coincidence that Shakespeare's last sole-authored quarto comedy, *Merry Wives*, is his closest to the localized genre of citizen comedy). Writing on the 1608 publication of the quarto *King Lear*, Peter Blayney observes that identification of Shakespeare as its author on the title page might have read differently to its first purchasers than it does to us: speculating that although we might like to 'imagine the delighted book-buying public flocking eagerly to the shops to buy the latest master-work from the pen of their favourite playwright', we would be wrong to do so: 'most of Shakespeare's plays had a relatively undistinguished publishing history before 1623' (*Texts of King Lear* 82).

Roberts's monopoly on the publication of playbills (which he ceded to William Jaggard after 1606) afforded him close links with the playing companies, and, in addition to publishing *Merchant* and the second quarto of *Titus* in 1600, he published the second quarto of *Hamlet* in 1604–5; but his involvement in play publication was negligible. Roberts entered a total of nine plays in the Stationers' Register between 1598 and 1603: the publication of four of these (*As You Like It, Merchant, A Larum for London* and

Troilus and Cressida) was considerably delayed; one was lost (*Cloth Breeches and Velvet Hose,* identified as a Chamberlain's Men's play and entered 27 May 1600); and all but two were published by others. It was not Roberts but Valentine Simmes who undertook the printing of *Much Ado* and *Henry IV, Part 2*; *Troilus* was printed in 1609, six years after Roberts's entry, by George Eld; and *Every Man in his Humour* appeared in 1601 without a printer identified on the title page.² The two plays that Roberts printed in 1600 were a sideline to an output which, in addition to his flourishing line in calendars and almanacs, included, for example, a reprint of Robert Greene's 1590 picaresque narrative *Never Too Late*, Sir Edward Dering's pious *Godly Private Prayers* and *A Sermon Preached Before the Queen's Majesty*, and the notorious anti-theatrical pamphleteer Philip Stubbes's tract *A Crystal Glass for Christian Women*.³ Blayney notes that Roberts had a habit of registering plays but then selling them on to other stationers, 'rather than taking the financial risk of publishing them himself' ('Playbooks', 387). Maybe Roberts had second thoughts about committing his printing house to two weeks of compositorial and press work on *As You Like It* because he preferred not to waste the time and expense on another Shakespeare play that might lose him money.

The Arden third series editor of the play, Juliet Dusinberre, states that the 'decision to halt' publication demands explanation 'as the play is so obviously a winner' (Dusinberre 123). Whether it has been 'obviously' anything of the kind during the relatively well-documented centuries of its theatrical afterlife will be for the reader to judge on the basis of the evidence explored in subsequent chapters; for now, the indication that publication was planned, if not implemented, does not necessarily imply popular theatrical success. Legend has it that elements of the play reveal connections with the personnel of the Lord Chamberlain's Men and the 1599 opening of the Globe: Jacques's 'All the world's a stage' set-piece (2.7.139–66) has been linked to the playhouse's alleged motto 'Totus Mundus Agit Histrionum' ('The whole world plays the actor'), despite there being no evidence that this motto ever existed; and the Clown's alias, Touchstone, has been seen as a clue that the part was written for the former goldsmith Robert Armin, who joined the company following the departure of William Kempe. Apocryphally, it has been conjectured that the play is the one for which John Heminges received a payment of £30 from the Revels accounts, on 2 December 1603, for a performance at Wilton

House, the country seat of Mary Sidney, Countess of Pembroke, who hosted the court of King James for two months. According to the nineteenth-century theatre historian William Cory, Mary had written to her son William Herbert to inform him that 'we have the man Shakespeare with us' (Knowles 633), but since Cory failed to produce the letter, the claim has generally been dismissed.

Dusinberre argues that *As You Like It* was premièred at Court before Queen Elizabeth on Shrove Tuesday, 20 February 1599. Using the evidence of a payment to the Chamberlain's Men of £30 in total for three plays, and Touchstone's 'pancakes' routine (1.2.55–70), she claims that an epilogue transcribed by Henry Stanford in his commonplace book, and first ascribed to Shakespeare by William Ringler and Steven May in 1972, 'fits *As You Like It* better than any other play' (Dusinberre 37):

> As the dial hand tells o'er
> The same hours as it had before,
> Still beginning in the ending,
> Circular account still lending,
> So most might Queen we pray,
> Like the dial day by day,
> You may lead the seasons on
> Making new when old are gone ...
> (Dusinberre 351–2)

The implication of this 'occasional' identification is that *As You Like It* is a work designed to appeal to courtly rather than popular audiences. The play's idiom of pastoral, its swains and shepherds who speak like courtiers, seem to bear this out. As Dusinberre points out, the case for regarding *As You Like It* as a play for the elite may be strengthened by the fact that in 1669 it was identified as one of those previously performed at the Blackfriars playhouse in the listings of plays allocated to Thomas Killigrew for performance at the Theatre Royal in Drury Lane (Dusinberre 44–5).

The Folio *As You Like It* is a document whose relation to original conditions and circumstances of performance within, possibly, at least three settings – court, public playhouse, private theatre – is at best uncertain. Included in a volume emphatically pitched to 'the great variety of readers' who are exhorted by its editors, Heminges and Condell, to 'read [Shakespeare], therefore; and again, and again', its place in the Folio is as material for repeated, reflective *reading*, not as evidence of past performance or as a resource for future ones. What, then, can we speculate about its performance on the early modern stages upon which it might have been performed? Generically, it presents a synthesis of a number of ingredients of courtly and popular entertainment, combining the fairy-tale scenario of the feuding brothers, a pastoral fantasy of rural life, the perennially appealing image of the court-in-exile of Robin Hood (the subject of three surviving plays staged by the Shakespeare's company rivals, Lord Admiral's Men, during the late 1590s), and four interweaving love-plots. It offers some violent physical action (the wrestling match in 1.2), a sharp-witted clown with one foot firmly in the playhouse, a good deal of singing, and the recycling of a number of devices used by Shakespeare in previous romantic comedies. These include a structural division between court and country, a green world that is as much as realm of the imagination as a natural environment, and, driving the play's action, a voluble, witty and resourceful cross-dressed heroine.

Rosalind's part

The performative and sexual dynamics of the fiction of a woman, originally played by a boy, masquerading as a man have been much discussed. Rosalind, along with Julia, Portia, Rosalind, Viola and Imogen, belongs to a line of early modern women dressed as men that ranges from the girls-as-boys of Lyly's *Gallathea* (1586) to the Moll Cutpurse (based on the real-life Mary Frith) of Middleton and Dekker's *The Roaring Girl* (1611); and, in the context of a culture in which appropriate attire was a key marker of class and gender identity, it has been suggested that cross-dressing was scandalous, subversive, and so, for theatregoers, beguilingly seductive. Contemporary pamphleteers recurrently denounced the practice, usually refusing to make any distinction between transvestism onstage and off. Philip Stubbes, in his comprehensive catalogue of everyday Elizabethan wrongdoing, *The Anatomy of Abuses* (1583), complains: 'Our Apparell was given us as a signe distinctive to discern betwixt sex and sex, & therfore one to weare the Apparel of another sex is to participate with the same and to adulterate the veritie of his own kinde' (Furnivall 2 73). Stubbes has in mind the practice of actual, rather than theatrical, cross-dressing, but his polemic was echoed by those who targeted plays, players and playhouses, and who found it one of the profession's definitively immoral features. As well as 'making young men come forth in women's attire, like the lewd woman in the Proverbs', wrote John Rainoldes in *The Overthrow of Stage Plays* (1599), plays taught them 'to counterfeit her actions, her wanton kiss, her impudent face, her wicked speeches and enticements' (Pollard 173). The problem, of course, was that transvestism was endemic because there were no women performers: female roles were played by the boys or young men apprenticed to the master-players of the companies.

The theatre's defenders, such as playwright Thomas Heywood, countered that the biblical prohibition of cross-dressing (Deuteronomy 2.5), much cited by the anti-theatricalists, did not apply to stage plays, that the difference between reality and play was widely recognized, and that the theatre's conventions of gender representation were established, accepted and stable: 'they are but to represent such a lady, at such a time appoynted' (Heywood 28). Heywood's proximity to the practice he was defending makes him a more reliable witness than his polemicizing opponents, but this did not stop a succession of scholars (mostly during the 1980s and 1990s) from suspecting that the ambiguous status of the boy-actor placed him at the heart of his culture's deepest conflicts around representation in general and sexuality in particular. Stephen Orgel, somewhat bafflingly, pronounced that 'Everyone in this culture was in some respects a woman' (Orgel 124); Jonathan Dollimore asked: 'Which, or how many, of the several gender identities embodied in any one figure are in play at any one time?' (Dollimore 65); and the boy in skirts has been claimed as a doubled focus of erotic attention, sexy both in what he is and what he is not, and viewed with an interest, as Lisa Jardine puts it, 'which hovers somewhere between the heterosexual and the homosexual around his female attire' (Jardine 11). The plays of Shakespeare and others vary in the extent to which they appear to acknowledge or engage this 'hovering' interest, as well as in the degree to which the representational conventions it involves are affirmed or interrogated within the works themselves; as Kathleen McKluskie points out, the 'fictions of Elizabethan drama would have been rendered nonsensical if at every appearance of a female character ... their gender was called into question' (McLuskie 102). Nonetheless, at the moment when the boy or young man playing Rosalind declared to the boy playing Celia that he, or she, was to 'suit me all points like a man' (1.3.112), even the most credulous of spectators might have suspected that the gender identity of the speaker was not altogether straightforward. Nor would the spectator have considered it insignificant that Rosalind adopts as her alias Ganymede: in classical myth, the beautiful youth abducted by Jove and enslaved as cup-bearer to the gods, and also a contemporary slang term for a catamite.

As You Like It is not unique in Shakespeare in effecting this double transformation. Parallel scenarios are played out in *The Two Gentlemen of Verona*, *The Merchant of Venice*, *Twelfth Night* and *Cymbeline*. In *Two Gentlemen*, Julia assumes the guise of a 'well-reputed page' and is thus prophylactically protected from 'the loose encounters of lascivious men' (2.7.41–3); Portia adopts the persona of Balthasar in order to gain access to the all-male Venetian court; and Imogen dons male attire for similar reasons of self-concealment and self-preservation. In none of these plays does sexual disguise become a source of sexual confusion or danger. Once she has assumed the role of Sebastian, Julia engages in witty banter with a Host, eavesdrops incognito on Proteus's wooing of Sylvia, finds herself enlisted as the emissary of her own betrayal by Proteus, and then engineers Sylvia's refusal of his suit. Throughout, her page-boy guise is impregnable, and none of her interlocutors, male or female, betrays the slightest erotic interest in 'him'. Likewise with Portia as Balthasar: though the uneasy comedy of the exchange of rings generates a play of doubles entendres which forms an uneasy coda to the Shylock plot, her performance of masculinity in the trial scene is almost seamless – though her rejoinder to Bassanio's offer to surrender his wife to deliver Antonio, 'Your wife would give you little thanks for that' (4.1.283), briefly reinforces the audience's double awareness. Imogen is an even paler shadow of her gender-bending forebears, no androgyne but a passive cross-dresser whose essential femininity is exposed through her culinary skills and her propensity to sicken and faint.

In these three instances, cross-dressing may serve to reinforce gender distinctions and hierarchies rather than to interrogate or subvert them. Viola, in *Twelfth Night*, dances to a different tune; as the female lead of the last of Shakespeare's Elizabethan romantic comedies, her role more closely matches that of Rosalind in terms of its play with gender ambiguity. Catherine Belsey, in an influential essay, suggests that *Twelfth Night* 'takes the most remarkable risks with the identity of its central figure', in that Viola 'occupies a place which is not precisely masculine or feminine, where the notion of identity itself is disrupted' (Belsey 185–7). This may be so in terms of what Viola *says* ('I am not what I am'; 'I am all the daughters of my father's house/And all the brothers too' (3.1.132; 2.4.117–18)), but with respect to what she *does* it is less convincing. Compared to Rosalind, Viola is a curiously passive figure, someone who is largely acted upon rather than active: confronted with the conundrum of Olivia's desire for Cesario, her fatalistic conclusion is that 'O time, thou must untangle this, not I. / It is too hard a knot for me to untie' (2.2.39–40).

As James C. Bulman has observed, those who went into the Shakespearean woods looking for 'the extent to which casting boys in women's roles had the power to destabilize gender identity and denaturalize sexual identity' may have been barking up the wrong tree, since 'they applied contemporary hypotheses about gender and sexuality not to performances they had seen, but to historical performances they had only *imagined*' ('Queering the Audience' 565). With this in mind, I leave the job of speculating about the *effect* of a boy-girl-boy Rosalind on early modern audiences (probably as varied and contradictory as that of any staging since) to others, and focus instead on the *means* available to the player to contrive it. I follow the leads of Scott McMillin, Simon Palfrey, Tiffany Stern and Evelyn Tribble, who from different angles have explored the implications of the fact that in the early modern theatre (and, indeed, up until the nineteenth century), actors were provided not with the full text of the play, but with their own parts and (one, two or three-word) cues only. Viewed in the context of the working practices of the Chamberlain's Men, there are two lines of investigation that follow from this. The first, initiated by McMillin, is the relationship between play and part construction and the company's systems of training, rehearsal and performance, and the possible permutations of players that these allowed. The second, developed at substantially greater length by Palfrey and Stern, involves considering the often radical consequences of treating actors' parts as more or less self-contained units written to be studied in isolation and performed moment to moment, in circumstances where the player knows no more about what is said *about* or *to* his character than what is contained in his cues. As none of Shakespeare's players' parts have survived, this involves some reverse textual engineering, in that their form and characteristics can only be hypothesized on the basis of the evidence of those early modern (and later) parts that have survived (primarily, Alleyn's part of Orlando from Robert Greene's *Orlando*

Furioso). The discussion that follows, therefore, is conducted with the proviso that any speculation about early modern performance can be conducted only on the basis of the printed book, and that when I refer to Rosalind's part, I invoke a hypothesis, a fiction, even a phantasm.

Examining the repertoire of the King's Men for the Court performances of 1604–5, as well as a documented performance of *Othello* and *The Alchemist* in Oxford in 1610, and addressing the practicalities of acting work in the context of the company apprentice system, McMillin proposes that some of the variations between the roles for boys in the Chamberlain's/King's Men's plays are due to the varying levels of experience and skill of individual performers at different points in their training. The more skilled the apprentice, the more independently he can work, and the more complex, demanding and rewarding the acting tasks that could be allocated to him. This accounts for the difference between shorter and longer parts – the difference, say, between Mistress Quickly in *Henry V* (63 lines) and Cleopatra (678) – and also informs the structuring of a part's relations to others, most importantly, McMillin observes, in terms of cues. One condition of part-playing is that it demands a high state of attentiveness and mental agility: equipped only with a short cue that is not identified by its speaker, the player (in theory at least) has no idea when his cue will be delivered or from whom it will come. Whereas the seasoned performer could draw upon the advantage of years of craft and shared working practice to handle such an inherently dynamic and unpredictable performance situation, and thus be ready to respond swiftly and creatively to cues whatever their origin, the novice would probably be safer within a narrower range of options.

Given the already considerable feats of memorization, information processing and verbal and gestural action and co-ordination that he is required to undertake, limiting the sources of his cues is one way of managing cognitive load. Distinguishing between 'restricted' and 'wide-ranging' roles in Shakespeare's work, McMillin argues that the first will typically assign a part's cues to one or two speakers, whereas the second may range across the play's dramatis personae, and that a significant proportion of the women's parts are restricted in this sense. In the first category, Mistress Quickly is a restricted role, with 11 speeches cued by Bardolph (3), Pistol (3), Nym and the Boy. In the second, McMillin instances Cleopatra (200 speeches, cued by 18 cue-partners), Portia (117, by 14) and Rosalind (201, by 12). The figures can be finessed further: as McMillin demonstrates, the selective distribution of cues in the restricted roles also accords with the master player–apprentice boy relationship in that, in the context of a system in which group or company rehearsal was virtually nonexistent, it allows the pair to rehearse their scenes together, 'rehearsal' including a strong element of training and tuition. With more than half of the cues that Desdemona receives given by Othello, 'the master actor probably rehearsed the boy-actor one-on-one, teaching the boy how to respond, teaching him enunciation, gesture, and movement' (McMillin 235).

Palfrey and Stern point out that actors' parts and cues establish the foundations of the role in the first scene. This is certainly true of Rosalind, two of whose first three cues ('coz, be merry' (1.2.1) and 'Rose be merry' (1.219)) suggest 'melancholy, stubbornness, and perhaps capricious power' (Palfrey and Stern 409). Rosalind declares that she will 'forget the condition of my estate, and rejoice in yours' cued by 'merry' – 'from henceforth I will', an almost schematic indication of a shift of mood (or pose), from melancholy to merriment, although the Rosalind-player neither knows the full story of the 'condition of [her] estate' (2.1.12), as conveyed by Charles in the preceding scene, nor that 'never two ladies loved as they do' (1.1.98). The affectionate familiarity of 'coz' provides the lead here, and quick skim through the part will alert the Rosalind-player to the fact that he addresses Celia thus ten times during the course of the play, including four times in a row in one speech (4.1.179). He will also quickly note the antitheses: between 'remember', associated with the mildly melancholic state, and 'forget', associated with rejoicing; between 'teach' and 'learn', and between nature and fortune. The terms resonate through the part: Rosalind will act as Orlando's tutor in love, a role that she combines with that of agent of his 'remedy', his 'cure'; which term is set against 'love' (which, alongside 'lover', recurs 68 times in her part; two-thirds of its total occurrences in the play). Other antitheses have a larger resonance within the play as a whole and extend beyond Rosalind's part: nature versus fortune, which operates as a frame of reference within which a range of characters attempt to make sense of their predicaments, in terms of the relations between agency, fate and victimization, between what they are born into and what they can make of it. The play is also sufficiently realistic to acknowledge the part played by the other, financial, sense of 'fortune' in its action, in both the Orlando–Oliver and Corin subplots. 'Merry' implicitly suggests its antithesis, melancholy, which, while remaining as a subtle descant to Rosalind's part, is more comprehensively embodied in the part of Jaques (as he is both self-styled and described on repeated occasions, thus providing the actor – probably Burbage – with the part's own key signature). Addressed as 'Monsieur Melancholy' by Orlando, a riposte to Jaques's 'Signor Love' (3.2.270–3), the line provides both his exit cue and Rosalind's cue to engage, antiphonically, with Orlando as a 'saucy lackey', and to 'play the knave' (3.2. 274–5).

This is the first of two brief encounters between Rosalind and Jaques in the play (and I suspect their inclusion reflects the need to contrive an opportunity for the company's male and male–female star turns to share the stage at least once); the second, at the beginning of Act IV, continues the merry-melancholy duetting but also, as cued by Orlando's entry, affords Jaques a neatly metatheatrical exit line: 'Nay then, God b'wi'you an you talk in blank verse' (4.1.28). Jaques's response to Orlando's formulaically regular pentameter ('Good day and happiness, dear Rosalind!' (l. 27)) is sarcastically extra-metrical, but not anomalous in relation to his part, which is fairly evenly split between prose and verse. Rosalind, however, answers Orlando in prose, which is her part's predominant mode. As Palfrey and Stern point out, Rosalind's shifts between prose and verse furnish the actor with clear cues for passion: the first of these occurs during the wrestling sequence in her first scene, signalling a sudden transition from warily amused detachment to emotional commitment, as 'memory joins with possibility, father with son, a lost love with a future love' (410).

By scripting Rosalind predominantly in prose, Shakespeare adds a further, formidable technical challenge to what is already an unprecedentedly demanding role. As Tribble contends, one of the functions of early modern verse is its mnemonic utility: its metrical and rhythmic structure enables a constelled patterning of words, phrases, lines and thoughts that facilitate navigation of multiple, long and complex parts. The mechanism of the ten-syllable line that provides the basic template for stage speech is a framework within which ordered and retrievable words and thoughts are subject to mechanisms of reinforcement and repetition, built-in predictabilities, ranging from the aural patterning found for example in assonance, alliteration, rhyme and iambic pentameter itself, to the rhetorical devices and structures that not only serve to organize and formalize speech but to shape it as memory material. This is most obvious in the use of rhyme, which in this play is deployed sparingly, and sometimes sententiously, self-consciously or parodically: 'now go we in content/To liberty and not to banishment' (1.3.133–4); 'and you shall say/I'll prove a busy actor in their play' (3.4.52–3); 'We'll begin these rites,/As we do trust they'll end in true delights' (5.4.188–9).

Consider one of Rosalind's more metrically straightforward verse speeches, which marks the moment when she opts to cross-dress:

> Were it not better
> Because that I am more than common tall,
> That I did suit me all points like a man:
> A gallant curtal ax upon my thigh,
> A boar-spear in my hand, and – in my heart
> Lie there what hidden woman's fear there will –
> We'll have a swashing and a martial outside,
> As many other mannish cowards have,
> That do outface it with their semblances.
>
> (1.3.110–18)

The nine lines feature a series of structuring devices and rhetorical techniques that both assist the work of memorization and map the shape and direction of thought. Rosalind's cue is 'assailants' (l. 109), an image of assault that is carried forward and elaborated in her lexicon of weaponry, masculine bravado and violence, to which she responds with a half-line, a rebuttal that is also a change of direction; the eight lines that follow feature, in succession, a rhetorical question ('Were it not better'), *gradatio* (the accumulative argument of the first three lines), *anthimeria*, or the transformation of a noun into a verb ('suit me'), personification and transferred epithet ('gallant curtal ax'; the 'womans fear' that is to 'Lie' within Rosalind's heart), paronomasia (the homonymic double meanings of 'Lie'), consonance ('*swashing*, mar*t*ial – spelt 'marshall' in the Folio – 'manni*sh*'), and paradox ('mannish cowards'). All of these may be seen as *aides mémoires* and pointers towards appropriate pronunciation and lively action. What we also notice is that Rosalind's gender metamorphosis (cued by the physique of an actor who is 'more than common tall') is indexed both to the limbs and organs of the speaker's body (thigh, hand and heart) and to the implements of masculinity (curtal ax, or cutlass, boar-spear) that also serve as its props.

All of this, we may suppose, would have been second nature

to Rosalind's first player. Here, the verse itself is relatively easy to negotiate, familiarly patterned, and metrically and syntactically straightforward: phrase and line are matched, and all but two lines are regular pentameters. The passage is placed towards the end of the only sustained verse exchange between Rosalind and Celia, in the context of one of the three scenes in which verse accounts for more than a handful of Rosalind's lines. As in her first encounter with Orlando, there are moments where the move from prose to verse registers a move into a new emotional register, from game to seriousness (her reaction to the story of Orlando's battle with the lion at 4.3.124–37); alternatively, it may signify closure, as with the symmetrical rhymed couplets of the final scene, marking both the departure of the polymorphously garrulous Ganymede and the moment when Rosalind accepts the heterosexual marital script, and when, as Belsey says of Viola, she 'dwindles into a wife' (Belsey 187):

> To you I give myself, for I am yours.
> To you I give myself, for I am yours.
> I'll have no father if you be not he.
> – I'll have no husband if you be not he.
> – Nor ne'er wed woman if you be not she.
> (5.4.107–8; 113–15)

Nonetheless, she returns in prose for the Epilogue.

Elsewhere, Rosalind ventures into verse when the stakes, at least for her, are not especially high. Her primary verse interlocutors are Silvius and Phoebe, whose end-stopped speech patterns not only seem to place them within an archaic, faintly parodic, idiom of pastoral stage comedy but, for the latter especially, also seem calibrated to the developing skills of a less advanced boy player. It is as though Rosalind (or the Rosalind-player) switches to verse in these scenes for the Phoebe-player's benefit, offering example and instruction in the arts of speech: 'Who might be your mother/That you insult, exult, and all at once/Over the wretched?' (3.5.36–8). Although she delivers one of the play's longest verse speeches (3.5.108–34), Phoebe is, in McMillin's terms, a 'restricted' role, with three scenes, 3 per cent of the play's lines and 20 of her 22 cues provided by two players. One of these is Rosalind; as we shall see, this is not the only instance in the play where Rosalind–Ganymede's adopted role as tutor seems to match her player's role within the Lord Chamberlain's ensemble.

Rosalind speaks a total of 680 lines in the Folio text, of which some 27 per cent are in verse, 73 per cent in prose. Considered in terms of line count alone, Rosalind is not only the longest woman's part in Shakespeare, but also one that is longer than a number of leading male roles (including Coriolanus, Romeo and Prospero). If anything, though, this measure understates the scale of the part; allowing for the relative word density of prose and verse (on average, around 12 or 13 words per line, against 8 or 9), the ratio of prose to verse becomes more like 79 to 21 per cent.

In effect, Rosalind's role is roughly equivalent to a verse part of the order of 900 lines – longer than Brutus, Lear and Macbeth. The predominance of prose in the comedies and histories of the mid- to late 1590s, as well as their progressively more flexible use of the verse line, suggests to Tribble that in this period 'the cognitive work of memory is transferred increasingly from the formal structures of verse to the expertise of the player' (76). Even so, Rosalind's prose is itself formally patterned in order to facilitate the work of memorization and delivery; in its own way, it is as structured, rhythmically patterned, rhetorically heightened and formalized as the verse. This is evident in a passage routinely cut in modern productions on the grounds of its manifest artificiality, the catechistic call-and-response elaboration of the 'time' conceit (3.2.280–307):

> I'll tell you who time ambles withal, who time trots withal, who time gallops withal, and who he stands still withal.
> _____withal?
> Marry, he trots hard with a young maid ...
> _____withal?
> With a priest that lacks Latin ...
> _____withal?
> With a thief to the gallows ...
> _____withal?
> With lawyers in the vacation ...

The invitation is to foreground the artifice, to *display* the schematic quality of the sequence rather than attempt to render it conversationally 'real': hence the sententious personification, the formulaic repetition of the superfluously ornamental 'withal' that epanaleptically begets both the repeated, identical cue and Rosalind's own half-echoing of it ('-*with*al?/ *With* a priest'; '*with*al?/ *With* a thief'), the four-item list of the components of temporal pedestrianism generating an accumulative four-part exposition of these components, the emblematic figures (maid, priest, rich man, lawyer and thief) who serve to illustrate the argument. Cumulatively, this is as close as Rosalind and Orlando get to the kind of verbal tennis that we find in Lyly:

> *Campaspe.* Were women never so fair, men would be false.
> *Apelles.* Were women never so false, men would be fond.
> *Campaspe.* What counterfeit is this?
> *Apelles.* This is Venus, the goddess of love.
> *Campaspe.* What, be there also loving goddesses?
> *Apelles.* This is she that hath power to command the very affections of the heart.
> *Campaspe.* How is she hired? By prayer, by sacrifice, or by bribes?
> *Apelles.* By prayer, sacrifice and bribes.
> *Campaspe.* What prayer?
> *Apelles.* Vows irrevocable.
> *Campaspe.* What sacrifice?
> *Apelles.* Hearts ever sighing, never dissembling.
> *Campaspe.* What bribes?
> *Apelles.* Roses and kisses. But were you never in love?
> *Campaspe.* No; nor love in me.
> (Campaspe, 3.4.30–46)

Shakespeare's dialogue borrows and adopts this model of patterned pertness by incorporating subtle variations that unsettle its predictability. Though the line of the sequence is clear, its players still have to think on their feet, as the sequencing and phrasing of the verbs in her set-up – ambles, trots, gallops, stands still – are re-ordered in his responses: trot, ambles, gallop, stays it still.

Even when Rosalind is not so obviously 'performing', her speech is anything but naturalistic: larger speech units in particular employ many of the prosodic and rhetorical techniques that are operative in the verse. The account of Celia and Oliver's love at first sight is an example:

> For your brother and my sister no sooner met but they looked, no sooner looked, but they loved, no sooner loved but they sighed, no sooner sighed but they asked one another the reason, no sooner knew the reason but they sought the remedy. And in these degrees have they made a pair of stairs to marriage, which they will climb incontinent or else be incontinent before marriage. They are in the very wrath of love, and they will together.
> (5.2.29–37)

Referring to this passage, the director of the 2009 RSC production, Michael Boyd, claims that 'this vivid and moving account' persuades us that Oliver and Celia's 'dash' for marriage is 'the most natural and enviable thing in the world' (Bate and Rasmussen 157). If so, the effect of 'naturalness' is achieved in part by the deployment of rhetorical devices that are entirely conventional. As Katie Wales points out (Wales 285), the speech is a textbook demonstration of the techniques of *anaphora* (the fivefold iteration of *no sooner*), *enthymeme*, or incomplete syllogism, and *anadiplosis* (lexical repetition) in the 'chaining' of *looked – loved – sighed – asked – reason – remedy*, with the lovers' 'climb incontinent' aptly forming the climax of the speech's *gradiato* (aptly, Greek for 'ladder'). There is both parallelism and antithesis (*your brother and my sister; loved – sighed*), oxymoron (*the very wrath of love*), alliteration and assonance (*looked – loved; reason – remedy*), internal rhyme (*pair of stairs*) and, in the succession of three metrically identical seven-syllable lines followed by two metrically varied fourteen-syllable ones, isocolon. The function of the figures is not only to heighten speech above the everyday but also to offer both the player and his listeners the means to navigate it.

Rehearsal and performance

Such is the magnitude of the task faced by the unknown (but presumably more than usually able) young man who was handed the manuscript pages containing Rosalind's part some time around 1599; and such were the linguistic tools that its author provided to enable him to accomplish it. In the pages that follow I consider how this task might have been carried out within the frameworks of rehearsal and repertory; but first, in order to situate Rosalind's role within the larger part-based ecology of playhouse rehearsal and performance practice, and also to emphasize how radical a theatrical experiment it actually was, we need to acknowledge the broader early modern context of part-based playmaking. David Bradley's survey of 265 plays printed between 1497 and 1625 (most of which date from after the opening of the Theatre in Shoreditch in 1576), conducted alongside an examination of the handful of surviving manuscript playbooks and playhouse plots, has established that the vast majority are designed to be performed by a cast of 16, indicating that the standard number of adult actors in the playing companies was around 10–12, with up to 10 apprentices (and very occasionally even more) playing the juvenile and female parts, though the average number of boys per play appears to have been no more than half a dozen. Taking into account the doubling and tripling of roles, and for the recruitment of hired men as mutes and supernumeraries, the 16-strong group, Bradley argues, is adequate to the demands of a corpus of plays with cast lists regularly in excess of 30.

These are the headline figures; behind them, I propose, are shifting subdivisions of labour and responsibility that indicate that, as the sixteenth-century theatre industry developed, the distribution and relative weighting of the leading and chief supporting parts were increasingly designed to maximize efficiency and effectiveness. This was achieved, in the main, through a balancing and spreading of actors' workloads. The groundbreaking plays of the late 1580s and early 1590s – *The Spanish Tragedy*, Marlowe's tragedies, Shakespeare's *Titus Andronicus* and *Richard III* – centred on protagonists whose dominance is absolute: with nearly 700 lines, Kyd's Hieronymo speaks over a quarter of his play; Titus and Richard speak nearly a third of their play's lines; Tamburlaine thunders through over a third of both *Part 1* and of *Part 2*; and the protagonists of *The Jew of Malta* and *Doctor Faustus* commandeer nearly half of their respective plays, with 1,051 and 675 lines apiece. Supporting roles are decisively second-string: Hieronymo's part is over twice as long as that of his antagonist Lorenzo (326 lines), while Titus's role is also twice that of Aaron (357): Barabbas's part is four times the length of that of his nemesis, Ferneze. The parts of Hieronymo, Tamburlaine, Barabbas and Faustus were first Edward Alleyn's, who at the end of the 1580s was still in his early twenties, leading Lord Strange's Men, and in his youthful ascendancy; Titus, possibly, and Richard, more probably, were Burbage's, also in his twenties and moving, with Shakespeare, between the Admiral's, Strange's and Pembroke's. Alleyn was clearly the star attraction at this stage, his stalking and roaring the central factor in Strange's, and initially the Admiral's, marketability: a contemporary commentator wrote that he and Burbage carried any play 'where their Parts had the greatest part' (Stern 99).

In his study of casting, T. J. King has found that, in the vast majority of plays from the 1590s onwards, over 90 per cent of lines are spoken by ten actors, thus enabling 'the leading actors to rehearse the play without the supporting cast' (King 6). Within this figure a further concentration of resources can be detected. In the majority of cases, plays allocate around two-thirds of text to six or seven actors, with the lead afforded anything between 10 and 20 per cent of the total, with up to a half a dozen others sharing between 7 and 10 per cent each of the remainder. Further down the casting hierarchy, the percentages, so far as individual parts are concerned, tend to drop sharply, with the remaining third of the play often delivered by dozens of speakers. Within the 16-strong companies, this meant that a smaller subgroup took primary responsibility for the delivery of a play (though not necessarily the same men every time; presumably this would need to be balanced out across the repertoire and in relation to individual strengths).

Two plays, both immediately contemporaneous with *As You Like It*, are indicative of working practices: Ben Jonson's *Every Man in his Humour*, one of the four plays in Roberts's 1600 Stationers' Register entry, for the Chamberlain's; and Thomas Dekker's *The Shoemaker's Holiday*, performed in 1599 by the Admiral's. In the former, Kiteley's 443 lines account for nearly 17 per cent of the play; once Knowell (12 per cent), Bobadil (11 per cent), Brainworm (10 per cent), Edward Knowell (8 pre cent) and Cob (8 per cent) are added, two-thirds of the play is covered. It happens that, in this instance, the personnel are known; as listed by Jonson in the 1616 Folio, the players were Shakespeare, Burbage, Augustine Philips, Heminges, Condell, Thomas Pope, Will Sly, Christopher Beeston, Will Kempe and John Duke. Precise matching of names to parts is impossible, though it is attractive to speculate Burbage played the pathologically jealous husband Kiteley, a comic mockery of the green-eyed monster that might have fed into his Othello a few years later; and it is likely that Philips's apprentice Beeston might have taken one of the women's roles. With its cast of 16, no supers, and no doubling, *Every Man* is, for its time, a lean and tightly-knit play; *Shoemakers* is, more typically, looser: 16 adult male speaking roles, 6 boys and an indeterminately-sized supporting cast of noblemen, soldiers, huntsmen, shoemakers, apprentices and servants. Nonetheless, most of the speech and action is commanded by six actors: Simon Eyre, who dominates the comedy with 331 lines (15 per cent), Firk (15 per cent), the Lord Mayor (9 per cent), Lincoln (8 per cent), Hammon (8 per cent) and Lacy (7 per cent).

What this implies is that the rewards, challenges and risks of playhouse performance were primarily handled by the company sharers, those professionally best equipped to deal with them. Here is an evolving professional playhouse practice that is also a business model implicated in considerations of the balance between the necessary but intrinsically risky imperatives of innovation, experimentation and diversification and the competing pressures of those practices that provided steady cashflow and financial stability: playing to known strengths and to established tastes, maintaining consistency and continuity of output, and retention and consolidation of existing audiences. For obvious reasons, adult male players tend to dominate the playtexts' core groupings. The majority of plays performed by the Admiral's Men between the mid-1590s and mid-1600s, as well as the non-Shakespearean plays that can be assigned to the Chamberlain's–King's Men, include one boy in the core team, and often none at all. This is the case with *Every Man in his Humour*, which, in characteristically Jonsonian fashion, affords its three female parts, Dame Kiteley, Bridget and Tib, respectively 57, 27 and 32 lines. *Shoemaker's* offers more, but still limited, space to the company's boys, in the parts of Eyre's Wife (115 lines; 5 per cent), Sybil (86 per cent), Jane (75 per cent) and Rose (92 per cent). The last of these, the play's lead female love interest, with just over two per cent of the play's lines, is a lesser part than *As You Like It*'s Phoebe. Line counts and percentages are only part of the picture; a fuller account of the role's significance would also take account of the number of scenes in which the part appears, the amount of time spent on stage, the balance between speech and silence, between verse and prose, and speech and song, and, not least, the extent to which the role is restricted or wide-ranging; and also qualitative matters of dramaturgic function, the level of difficulty of the verbal text, and the range and intensity of the passions that the performer is required to personate. As a headline indicator, however, the figures suggest both the limited nature both of the boys' parts and of most playwrights' interest in them (or ability to script them, as Marlowe and Jonson demonstrate).

With Shakespeare's work for the Lord Chamberlain's Men, but also with the plays he wrote prior to the company's formation, the picture is different. From the very outset, he not only created boys' parts that were qualitatively in excess of those of written by his contemporaries, but afforded them a weighting within their plays' narratives equal to if not surpassing that of their masters: Queen Margaret in the second and third parts of *Henry VI*, dating from the early 1590s for Pembroke's Men, and Joan La Pucelle in the first part; *Shrew*'s Katharina, Tamora in *Titus*. It is probably not a coincidence that their author was a player himself, and the succession of women's parts that proceeds from Julia and Sylvia (*Two Gentlemen*) at the start of the decade, via Princess Katherine (*Love's Labour's Lost*) Constance (*King John*) and Juliet to Beatrice, Portia, Mistresses Page and Ford, and Rosalind, at its end, makes increasing demands on their performers that are unequalled elsewhere.[4]

Two inferences can be drawn from this. First, since Shakespeare would have been unlikely to have created such roles unless he was reasonably confident of the abilities of the Lord Chamberlain's boys to do them justice, the company of the late 1590s included a number of exceptionally able apprentices. Second, however talented one or more of these boys may have been, confidence was not certainty; entrusting (that is, investing in) that talent in the volatile and precarious environment of the public theatre was both artistically and commercially a high-risk strategy. What this may reveal, then, is a certain approach to risk itself, perhaps on the part of a commercially canny playwright, and also on the part of his player peers and mentors, whose previous, current and subsequent business activities – ranging from James Burbage's audacious erection of the Theatre in Shoreditch in 1576 to his sons' legally questionable act of dismantling it just over twenty years later – indicate an entrepreneurial adventurousness that not infrequently expressed itself as sheer recklessness. Aptly imagined by Alexander Leggatt as a 'dangerous' actor, the carpenter's son Burbage might have taught his glover's son writer about the allure of taking risks, each goading the other towards the creation of ever-more 'impossible' parts, ever-more 'unstageable' plays. By 1599, the close relation between risk and opportunity was already familiar to the Shakespeare, who recognized that rewards accrued to those prepared to 'give and hazard all he hath' (*Merchant*, 2.7.9).

The challenge of Rosalind lies not only in the part's sheer length and the range of states and personae that it requires its player to accommodate, but also in the quality and complexity of its interactions with the other parts in the play. Here I turn again to the question of the relationship between the part and its cue partnerships, a relationship which McMillin identifies as key indicator to the player's rehearsal and performance work. Rosalind, McMillin states, is one of the most 'wide-ranging' of Shakespeare's female parts in a numerical as well as a qualitative sense, receiving cues from 12 speakers during the course of the play. Since interpersonal interactions are not evenly distributed, most parts draw the majority of their cues from two, three or four cue-partners; in this case, a third of Rosalind's 198 cues are given by Celia (69), and a further third by Orlando (67). Orlando receives half of his cues from Rosalind, with most of the remainder assigned to Oliver, Jaques and Duke Senior; Celia receives three-quarters of her cues from Rosalind. There is a high degree of efficiency in the organization of cue-pairings; examined scene by scene, this becomes even clearer. Rosalind is at her numerically most wide-ranging in 1.2, where she is cued by six actors; this, not coincidentally, is one of two scenes (the other being 5.4) that might have been afforded a group rehearsal. Otherwise, the majority of her interactions are two- or three-way, with the vast majority of her cues from Orlando concentrated into the two wooing scenes, 3.4 and 4.1, during which Orlando also takes 85 per cent of his cues from her. Celia, who says very little after reluctantly officiating over the mock-marriage ceremony in 4.1 and then observing the remainder of the scene in silence, takes 70 per cent of her cues from Rosalind in three scenes (1.2, 1.3, and 3.2), and there is no scene in which she is on stage and Rosalind is not. As well as accounting for a third of Orlando's part, two-fifths of Rosalind's, and nearly a third of Celia's, 3.4 and 4.1 are a quarter of the play; add Rosalind and Celia's other dialogue sections (the first part of 1.2, 1.3, 3.4 and 4.3), and a third of the play can be rehearsed by just three players.

For Palfrey and Stern, solitary study is the bedrock of early modern rehearsal, as 'actors who were anyway concentrating on solo performance simply did not have the same concern to practise together', although there would have been some 'instruction', in that 'a company style could be collectively maintained, actors overseeing other actors' (71, 67). For McMillin, as we have seen, rehearsal and training are coextensive. Training, however, does not seem to have been a priority with *As You Like It*: the Rosalind-player presumably would need no tutoring by this stage (indeed, it is Rosalind–Ganymede who delivers the instruction), though possibly part of the point of including the Celia-player as a silent witness in the wooing scenes is to give him the opportunity to observe (apprentice-style) two more senior players at work. What we also need to factor in, I suggest, is a further level of challenge in Rosalind's part. Where Rosalind's role differs from comparable Shakespearean roles, both male and female, is in its balance between monologue (more readily mastered solo) and dialogue.

Rosalind has twice as many speeches as Portia; but whereas nearly half of Portia's part (17of 117 speeches) is delivered in speeches of ten or more lines, distributed fairly evenly through the play, Rosalind's 16 medium-length speeches account for a third of her part. Designed to maximize the potential for close-knit rehearsal, the play allows Rosalind to dominate the play but at the same time experiments with the form that a leading role might take: it is as much reactive and interactive as it is active.

Rosalind, Celia and Orlando's study and rehearsal regimes differ from those of the play's other star turns, Touchstone and Jaques. Touchstone's major speeches and scenes, like those of Rosalind, Celia and Orlando, are also amenable to independent small-group rehearsal and solo study. He takes a third of his cues from Rosalind and Celia in three short sequences (1.2.55–125; 2.4; 3.2.95–161), and most of the rest from Corin, William, Audrey and Jaques (who provides the feed lines for the 32-line 'seven degrees of the lie' routine). Touchstone is on stage to be listened to rather than to listen, and in his scenes with the juveniles, most obviously Audrey, his is a strongly controlling role. Audrey herself is a textbook example of a restricted role: appearing in four scenes (3.3, 5.1, 5.3 and 5.4, where she has no lines), she has 19 lines in 12 speeches, most of which are one-liners, and nine of which are cued by Touchstone. Furthermore, Touchstone's cue-speeches are conspicuously contrived in order to provide 'scaffolding' for the novice Audrey, in the form of 'a structure that constrains and enables his activity' (Tribble 138), most obviously, in his repeated use of her name (three times in his first cue, twice in his eighth and ninth) as a means of securing attention and focus. Although Jaques, at 214 lines, is the fourth-largest part, it seems likely that it was Burbage's (Orlando being more suitable for a younger actor, possibly the 22-year-old Henry Condell). Whereas Rosalind's part is defined by relentless interaction, Jaques's is focused and self-contained, with nearly half of its lines delivered in six medium-to-lengthy monologues; Jaques appears in seven scenes (compared to Rosalind's ten) and takes cues from eight performers, with the majority from Orlando and Touchstone. Like Touchstone, Jaques is someone to be listened to rather than someone who listens; his is a part where solo study will take the actor further, where need for small-group rehearsal is minimal or even nonexistent.

This makes sense in terms of what we can surmise of the Lord Chamberlain's Men's workload in 1599. Four plays, in addition to

As You Like It, can be assigned with confidence to the company for that year: *Henry V*, *Julius Caesar*, Jonson's *Every Man Out of his Humour*, and the anonymously-authored *A Larum for London*, a violent chronicle of the 1576 and 1585 sieges of Antwerp, the topicality of which, during a summer of renewed fears of Spanish invasion, is signalled by its title. All are large-scale, resource-intensive works: in contrast to the previous year's *Every Man In* (which perhaps was revived to run alongside its 'sequel'), *Every Man Out* is a sprawling comedy with a cast of more than 30 and an intricate metatheatrical structure which runs to 4,526 lines, about one-and-a-half times the length of the Folio *Hamlet* and more than double that of most plays of the period. The largest part is that of the misanthropic Macilente (characterized by Jonson as a man driven by 'envious apoplexy ... violently impatient of any opposite happiness in another'), which, doubled with Asper in the frame play, gives a combined total of 800 lines (nearly 18 per cent of the play). Heading the Jonson Folio's list of 'comedians', Burbage seems likeliest for this part; he also almost certainly played Henry V (1,031 lines; 32 per cent of the play) and Brutus (722 lines; 28 per cent) during the same year, as well as, possibly, the heroic Captain Stump in *A Larum* (245 lines; 14 per cent of a short play). These are only the known commitments: we cannot even begin to take account of the unknowns, such as revivals of older plays and performances of plays now lost, which perhaps included the *Cloth Breeches and Velvet Hose* that James Roberts entered in the Stationers' Register in 1600. The scripting of the two other Shakespearean roles follows a similar logic to that of Jaques: though massive in terms of their word-counts, both privilege the solo and reduce to a minimum the need for small-group rehearsal. In this context, Jaques is a relatively undemanding part for the Chamberlain's Men's star.

If *As You Like It* is notable for the weight of responsibility it confers upon its Rosalind- and Celia-actors, it is nowhere matched in the other new plays of 1599. The largest women's role in *Every Man Out* is Fallace ('a proud mincing peat', as Jonson puts it), at around 180 lines (4 per cent of the play). *A Larum* has female and juvenile parts (performed, Bradley deduces, by four boys), which, though restricted, present considerable acting challenges, in that they are central to the play's harrowing representations of extreme violence. In this play at least, the parts are small, but the stakes high; but this is not the case with either *Henry V* or *Julius Caesar*.

The former has the highly restricted parts of Hostess Quickly, Princess Katherine, Alice and Queen Isabel, as well as the Boy (the most substantial juvenile part, with 69 lines, or 2 per cent); the latter has Portia (92 lines in two scenes; 4 per cent), Calpurnia (27 lines), and Brutus's page, Lucius (33 lines).

It may be, as McMillin suggests, that repertoire scheduling and planning involved an element of balancing and pacing of commitments: the reason why there were no parts that we know of comparable with Rosalind in 1599 is that this was already at the limits of what its player could feasibly accommodate. On the other hand, it may be that the company had plays in revival that would both showcase the skills of its boys and plausibly complement *As You Like It*: *Much Ado*, probably dating from 1598, but not published until 1600 (suggesting, Knutson infers, that it 'had recently been in production' (Knutson 80)), *Merchant* and *Dream* (both also published in 1600), and *Merry Wives* (published in 1602). We do not, and cannot, know. What we do know is that Rosalind is the longest surviving boy's part of its time, and one that Shakespeare would not attempt to match again until six or seven years later, with Cleopatra. Perhaps there was no other part like Rosalind in 1599 because no boy player could have played it as well as playing Rosalind. Nor was there any part like it in 1600, 1601 or1602, quite possibly, although I have no way of knowing this, because the gift of Rosalind in 1599 marked the end of its recipient's apprenticeship. Perhaps, at this moment, the 'more than common tall' (1.3.109) young man who played Rosalind, who had all along been playing women to learn to play men, was unbound to became a master player in his own right. There would be no woman's part comparable to Rosalind until around 1606, at which point another of the King's Men's apprentices (maybe one of the boys who played Phoebe or Audrey) was ready to take on Cleopatra. Whatever the fate of the young man who first brought Rosalind to life on the Globe stage as the sixteenth century drew to a close, his talents, his history, his body and his potentialities made possible the part with which he can never be conclusively identified. What actors in the modern age have made of that part's possibilities is the subject of the chapters that follow.

Notes

1 These were: *Richard II* (1597, 1598, 1603, 1608, 1615), *Richard III* (1597, 1598, 1602, 1605), *1 Henry IV* (1599, 1604, 1608, 1613), *Henry V* (1600, 1608. 1619), *Titus* (1595, 1600, 1611) and *Hamlet* (1603, 1604, 1605, 1611).
2 Robert S. Miola, in the Revels Plays edition of Jonson's comedy, draws upon the research of J. A. Lavin and Adrian Weiss to identify Simon Stafford and Richard Reid as its printers: see Miola 38–40.
3 Roberts knew his market, having in 1595 acquired the rights to the third top-selling book of the period, Dering's *Short Catechism for Householders*, first published in 1580 and running to 17 editions in a quarter of a century (Blayney, 'Playbooks', 388). Dering would subsequently make his mark in the annals of Shakespearean performance history as the first known adapter of his works, in the form of his 1622 redaction of *Henry IV, Parts 1 and 2*, and as the first known buyer of the First Folio.
4 The juvenile chorister companies require separate consideration which there is not the space to give here, since in some ways the existence of often highly demanding texts and lengthy roles written to be performed exclusively by boys provides a counterbalance to my claim that the Shakespeare–Lord Chamberlain's output was in this respect unique. Briefly, the key difference lies in the very different conditions of training, rehearsal and performance in the playhouse and choir companies, the former operating according to the apprentice system and with rapid turnover of repertoire, the latter conducted within a model of intensive tuition and infrequent performances (see Munro 13–55).

CHAPTER II

Hunting for Arden in Warwickshire

A stag do

It is the classic Shakespeare-at-Stratford anecdote. In April 1919, the Shakespeare Memorial Theatre (SMT) reopened after a hiatus of four years, for its first brief season since the veteran actor-manager Sir Frank Benson had taken a break from leading the company to make an unsuccessful attempt to get himself enlisted. The season was, even by the SMT standards of the time, an eclectic one, with only five plays in total: Shaw's *Candida*, a double bill of abbreviated versions of *Coriolanus* and *The Merry Wives of Windsor*, and two guest productions, *Twelfth Night* and *As You Like It*. The first of these was J. B. Fagan's, from London's Court theatre; the second was directed by Nigel Playfair, who brought his production to Stratford prior to its opening at the Lyric Hammersmith, which Playfair had the year before refurbished and transformed into one of the capital's most exciting venues. *The Times* warned on the day of *As You Like It*'s opening that it would be 'novel to the Stratford revenants' (23 April 1919), consisting as it did of a *mise en scène* based, as designed by Claud Lovat Fraser, on 'some illuminated manuscript of the early 15th century', wherein 'the forest is ruthlessly simplified'. J. L. Styan, who marks the production as one of the milestones on the road to the Shakespeare revolution, describes it thus: 'He represented the leaves of the forest by looped curves', while the 'bizarre' costuming 'in the late French medieval style' boasted an 'uncompromisingly vivid' colour scheme of 'scarlet, lemon-yellow, saffron, emerald-green, Indian pink, crimson, ultramarine-blue, black and white'; the men wore particoloured, 'fantastically slashed' tunics and hose, 'with each leg a different colour', and the women 'high-waisted dresses, tight-fitting across the breast, with long and very full skirts'. Played without the 'customary cuts', the production was fast and full of vitality and exuberance (Styan 127–30); as *The Times* concluded, the 'daring mixture of styles certainly throws up the player against the scene'.

New as all this was to Stratford, it was, as the story goes, nowhere near as controversial as the single artistic decision that set the production violently at odds with the town and its audience's traditions and sensibilities. In the very first season of 1879, the SMT had mounted one performance of *As You Like It*, under the supervision of Barry Sullivan. For the occasion, a stuffed stag, shot in the grounds of Charlecote Park both as an act of homage to the legend of Shakespeare's deer-stealing and as a blood sacrifice to inaugurate the new theatre, was paraded on stage for 'What shall he have that killed the deer?' (4.2.10). Audiences liked it so much that it was brought back on, from display in the Shakespeare Museum, for every revival of the play that followed up until 1915 (see Figure 2).[1] Playfair took a look at a stag that, after four decades of re-use, had clearly seen better days, and vetoed it. Mindful that 'such a piece of iconoclasm, apparently, had never been heard of at Stratford before', he approached the first performance with a degree of trepidation; however, 'we certainly had a record house; and so far as one could tell, the audience approved of the production. There were no boos, no hisses; on the contrary, there was more than the usual amount of applause' (Playfair *Lyric* 54). The trouble, Playfair claims, started later:

> But it was outside the theatre that the storm raged, and it attained a ferocity I should hardly have thought possible. When I came to my hotel I was certainly treated as a 'national criminal': people turned their backs – got up and walked out of a room which I came into. The rest of the cast fared little better – they were cut and cold-shouldered almost everywhere. When Lovat Fraser himself was walking in the street a woman came up to him and shook her fist in his face. 'Young man,' she said impressively, 'how dare you meddle with our Shakespeare!' (Playfair *Lyric* 55)

This version of the reaction to Playfair's innovations has some contemporary corroboration: reviewing the production on tour at the Gaiety Theatre, Manchester, the *Manchester Guardian* reported that 'it is said that persons of taste were fighting on the stairs of all the best hotels in Stratford for some time after Mr Playfair produced this *As You Like It* at the Festival last month' (20 May 1919). It is the version that has been endorsed by subsequent commentators: the reaction of the fist-flailing *grande dame*, Styan

2 Undated postcard (*c.* 1900–19) depicting the stuffed stag

surmises, was to a production that 'denied the traditional idea of Shakespeare' (Styan 127); 'outside the theatre', Sally Beauman states, 'the reaction was one of outrage' (Beauman 66); and, most recently, Jonathan Bate and Eric Rasmussen confidently tell us that 'it was all too much for the conservative local populace' (Bate and Rasmussen 121).

Dennis Kennedy tells us that 'the real problem ... did not lay [*sic*] in the medieval design', but in Playfair's 'adamant refusal to use the stuffed stag' (Kennedy 121), though how he knows this he doesn't say (and even Playfair himself doesn't claim this). The story's appeal is strong because its battle-lines are so clearly drawn and its moral, as it seems to us, obvious: on the one side, the forces of progress and theatrical innovation; on the other, provincial Stratford at its most backward-looking and small-minded. I want to unsettle this simple binary and to consider the reactions of the Stratford townspeople to Playfair's provocations in a different and more sympathetic light. As Kennedy observes, the festival 'had been disrupted, a tradition of forty years violated' (121), and it would have been naïve not to have anticipated strong reactions. Playfair's point is that the reaction was extreme to the point of absurdity, that by cleaving to such a silly tradition and by mourning its loss so violently, the Stratford locals revealed themselves as parochial, petty and foolish. Perhaps; but Playfair's account (taken, as we have seen, pretty much at face value by theatre historians) is particularly self-serving, in that it positions the director against the forces of reaction, personified by an enemy that is all too easy to caricature (the 'serried ranks of godliness' (*Lyric* 51) is his term for the Stratford audience). In his memoirs, Playfair repeated the story: 'It seemed to be a simple enough affair, but the good citizens thought it Bolshevism or something worse' (Playfair *Hammersmith Hoy* 206). In both accounts, however, Playfair provides evidence that the reaction was less polarized. 'I shall never forget', he wrote, 'the speech that Archie Flower [Chair of the Memorial Committee] made at the end of that festival: '[H]e tentatively began, "What shall I say about *As You Like It*?" – expecting, very naturally, to be guided by a storm of cheers and counter cheers. Instead his question was received with a deadly silence as from the grave. And so he merely said nothing or at least nothing very much to the point' (*Hammersmith Hoy* 206–7).

When the history of the stuffed stag tradition is examined in more detail, it becomes apparent that its omission in Playfair's production was an act that (to use Kennedy's term) 'violated' a far more significant network of local sensitivities and social relationships than the director acknowledged. As stated earlier, the stag made its debut in the first-season production of 1879; what Playfair did not mention, and perhaps did not know, was that it did not make its entrance unaccompanied. As well as displaying the stag, 4.2 was the opportunity for the performance of the glee, 'What shall he have', by local singers, members of the Stratford Choral Society; and this was the scene, the *Stratford-upon-Avon Herald* considered, that 'must not be dismissed without special notice ... . [I]ts full significance ... is hardly possible to over-estimate' (9 May 1879). The *Herald*'s reviewer reported that the glee 'was sustained by the gentlemen of the town in such an able manner as to make an encore inevitable'. A moment that jubilantly exceeded the bounds of both the scene and play, the glee was also a climactic act of celebration of the town's own contribution to the festival, not least, the *Herald* recorded, in 'the services rendered by the ladies and gentlemen of Stratford, who took upon themselves the duties of supernumeraries'. 'The glee was encored, the stag was encored', reported the celebrated American journalist Kate Field in the *New York Daily Graphic* (date unknown), 'and Shakespeare's youthful escapade was lived over again in the minds of all present.' From the outset, the ritual of the stuffed stag embodied a specifically local, emotional investment in the SMT festival as a type of community performance, one that took place for a clearly demarcated and time-limited period each year, and one that bridged the gaps between amateur and professional performers, and between residents and visitors.

Charlecote's owner, Spencer Lucy, who personally shot the deer that he gifted to the SMT, also supplied 'two beautiful deerhounds'; the following year, their numbers had swelled (according to the *Birmingham Daily Gazette*, 3 May 1880) to 'a pack of fine deerhounds', and the stag and the glee had likewise grown in significance. In 1881 the glee was again 'one of the features of the evening' and was 'enthusiastically cheered, and not undeservedly' (*Herald*, 6 May 1881); in 1882, it was 'undoubtedly' the 'most effective scene' and an encore was duly demanded and delivered (*Herald*, 5 May 1882); in 1884 it 'created the usual fervor on the part of the audience' (*Herald*, 25 April); and in 1885 'the glee ... did so much to please that it had to be repeated' (*Herald*, 1 May 1885). This performance saw the Stratford debut of the American star Mary

Anderson as Rosalind, who, the *Leamington Spa Courier* revealed, herself subscribed to the increasingly entrenched mythology of the stag by persuading Spencer Lucy 'to supply her with a buck from his famous herd' (29 August 1885). 'What a *furore*', speculated the *Courier*'s reporter, 'a real deer from Charlecote and a brace of deerhounds will create on the American stage!'

The glee was still in place in 1914, and was described as 'delightful' by the *Herald*: the 'unaccompanied part singing ... added much to the atmosphere of the play' (8 May). Clearly the stag and its attendant rituals had more than enough of a history to warrant local anger at Playfair's 'meddling' with it; indeed, I suggest, the rituals were an important means through which the Stratford audience imagined itself, through 'our Shakespeare', as a community, however ridiculous or infuriating these might appear to metropolitan outsiders. But perhaps there was a further dimension to the anger that was directed towards a director and a designer perceived as metropolitan interlopers. The last time that the stag had performed its encore on the SMT stage had been in August 1915; the years since then had seen the playing-out of a war from which a great many men of Lovat Fraser and Playfair's generation had returned either profoundly and permanently damaged, or not at all. At the age of 41, Playfair was just old enough to avoid conscription when it was introduced in 1916; Lovat Fraser joined up in 1914 but was invalided home, suffering from shell-shock and gas poisoning, in 1916. One of the reasons Benson invited Playfair to Stratford was because he barely had a company: ten of his long-serving actors had died in France (and he was deeply affected by the loss of his only son in action in September 1916), and others were, in April 1919, still to be demobilized (Trewin 221–2). Benson had offered to volunteer at an early stage of the war even though he was in his late fifties, and he spent the last years of the conflict as an ambulance driver with the French Red Cross. The day that Playfair's production opened, Benson gave a talk in Stratford about his wartime experiences. The *Daily Sketch* (22 April) reported Benson's account of the atrocities he had witnessed: 'there were orders one day not to indulge in heavy fire because the Germans had massed the remnant of the civilian population in front of their guns. An old man came out of a house in No-Man's-Land with a little baby in his arms. Crack! crack! went the German machine-guns, and down fell the man and child.' 'Sir Frank', the report continues, 'told of the job he had to find Passchendaele ... now represented by a quarter of an iron lamp-post.' Incredibly, Benson found some ghastly reasons to be cheerful amidst the carnage: 'against the bank lay a Belgian cavalry officer with a smile on his face, typical of the happy warrior'.

The title of Benson's talk, the *Manchester Guardian* noted, was 'The Song of the Shrapnel', and the reporter wondered if Benson 'probably feels what he spoke about far too deeply to give it satisfactory expression', since 'it amounted to little more than a long discourse on the merits of the British and Allied troops who had won the war' (22 April). Stratford-upon-Avon had sent its own share of men to the front who did not return (the town's war memorial, in the Garden of Remembrance in the Old Town, lists 235 names). Who knows whether, among them, were the sons, brothers and husbands of the furious women who found themselves in the streets accosting those young men who seemed to be maliciously assaulting everything they held dear? Is it any wonder, in the circumstances, that the Stratford audience looked to the first SMT festival in four years in the hope of finding a reassuring continuity with its past?

Changing seasons

History was on Playfair's side in the long run; 1919 also saw the appointment of William Bridges-Adams as director, who made some modest and more diplomatic attempts during his 15-year period of tenure to free the SMT from the burden of its own traditions. *As You Like It* reappeared in 1920 and at regular intervals thereafter, but the stag did not, and Playfair's theatrical modernism became part of the mainstream of staging practice at Stratford, as it did elsewhere. Some have read the story of the stuffed stag, apparently an emblem of all that was moribund about Stratford theatre-making and theatregoing in its time, as a victory of theatrical innovation, creativity and good sense over the forces of reaction and parochialism; but this misses some deeper problems that it both obscures and epitomizes. As the subtitle of Kennedy's account suggests ('The stuffed stag and the new look'), the stag is set in opposition to novelty, innovation, adventurousness, urgency; that is, to the modernity that the Shakespearean theatre, from Granville Barker onwards, has habitually sought to embrace. When Cynthia Marshall describes *As You Like It* at pre-Playfair Stratford as 'encrusted with tradition, of which the stag was emblematic', not just 'an increasingly moth-eaten prop' but 'a relic linked to Shakespeare himself' (Marshall 53), she identifies the problematic of localism and ritual reiteration that is not just confined to this play but is endemic to the Stratford enterprise. I have argued elsewhere that the original SMT's 'architectural and etymological affinity with Victorian funerary monuments' suggests 'a close, if unconscious, connection between bardolatry and ... ritual disinterment or resurrection' (Shaughnessy, 'On Location' 88), and in this respect the ceremonial parading of an animal corpse is a vivid reminder that a memorial theatre dedicated to an annual cycle of festival performances (often, in the 1920s and 1930s, of virtually identical productions) is itself implicated in a culture of backward-looking commemoration. The stated aim of successive directors at Stratford has been to treat Shakespeare's plays as if they were written yesterday, and thus capable of making immediate and urgent claims upon their audiences' attention; and yet, because of Shakespeare's long-standing near-monopoly on the main stage, almost every play has had, until recently, to be performed at least once every five or six years. This means that every new production, no matter how determined to make a fresh start, is already caught up in a cycle of iteration and haunted by the ghosts of its performance history.

In his account of *As You Like It* at Stratford, Robert Smallwood writes of how taking a long view of its performance reveals how much productions are in dialogue with previous ones, and how much they are linked by continuities of personnel; and he decides that 'there has been little of the repetitive about the treatment of *As You Like It* at Stratford in the past half century' (Smallwood, *As You Like It* 3). Surveying the same era, I am not so sure; I am struck less by the productions' variety than by how similar, even interchangeable, they are, a characteristic that has also been noted by other long-term observers. Reviewing David Thacker's 1992 production, Smallwood himself reported that it was 'agreeably lively and by no means unengaging', but since it had 'little to offer by way of fresh thought about the play', offered little that was 'worth recording about it in the pages of a journal to be preserved in the libraries of the world' (Smallwood 'Shakespeare at Stratford-upon-Avon' 347). A decade later, Michael Dobson voiced similar concerns in the pages of *Shakespeare Survey*: remarking the similarities between Gregory Thomson's RSC Swan production and Peter Hall's, he wondered whether 'the remarkable amount which they had in common demonstrated the extent to which this play is currently languishing in something of an interpretative rut' (Dobson 'Shakespeare Performances in England, 2003' 266).

The story of Smallwood's *As You Like It* volume begins, inevitably, with the stag, and he concludes from it that the 'traditionalism and provincialism' of Stratford theatre 'effortlessly survived the onslaught of Playfair's production' (Smallwood, *As You Like It* 2). During Bridges-Adams's period, there were six productions of *As You Like It*, none of which made much of an impression. In 1933, Bridges-Adams directed a 'completely conventional' production (*Birmingham Gazette*, 20 April), which was 'a repetition, in essentials', of his 'dainty production last year' (*Birmingham Mail*, 20 April). Bridges-Adams was succeeded in 1935 by Ben Iden-Payne, whose innate conservatism set the Stratford clock even more determinedly back to the Victorian era: Balliol Holloway's production for the 1939 season restated the play's immediate affiliations with what the *Manchester Guardian*'s Ivor Brown identified as a 'local woodland of Arden' of 'realistic forestry' (8 April 1939). When it was revived in 1942, the same reviewer found that the production had 'surprisingly grown younger with the years', its forest 'a spring-time glade again with Miss Margaretta Scott's Rosalind as its goddess of enchantment' (*Manchester Guardian*, 19 April). Two years previously, the *Times* reviewer had written that for visitors under the spell of 'a few green days and quiet nights in Warwickshire', so far as this play was concerned, 'Brilliance of production is not among the requirements of the occasion': Holloway's 'new production is in the old tradition, and that is just what was wanted' (25 April). The *Yorkshire Post* (25 April) concurred: the play, it stated, 'opens in a world as brutal as our own, but does not stay there long'. As an example of the thriving genre of wartime pastoral, this Arden was an eloquent reminder to Stratford audiences of what they were fighting for.

The 1946 season, Sir Barry Jackson's first as artistic director, included an *As You Like It* directed by Herbert Prentice, a production which, despite the *Times* reviewer's speculation that 'possibly it will turn out to be among the pleasantest things of the festival' (3 June 1946), was completely overshadowed by the season's unexpected hit, the Stratford debut of Peter Brook with *Love's Labour's Lost*. Revelling in his own status as iconoclast, Brook characterized the Stratford of the time as one in which 'every conceivable value was buried in deadly sentimentality and complacent worthiness – a traditionalism largely approved by town, scholar and Press' (Brook 51). Meanwhile, readers of *The Times*, turning the page from its favourable notice of *As You Like It*, would learn that Charlecote Park had on Saturday 1 June been handed over to the National Trust 'on behalf of the nation'. The occasion, which marked the nationalization of an asset that the Fairfax-Lucy family could no longer afford to maintain, included a speech by Jackson in which, rather tactlessly in the circumstances, he invoked the legend of Shakespeare's 'poaching' and attempted to assuage fears of what public ownership and common access might entail: 'under no circumstances would he be guilty of despoiling what was given for his delight by thoughtlessly scattering litter and rubbish ... . He begged everyone to follow his example.'

The article informs its readers that admission to Charlecote Park cost 1s 6d. By 1952, the next time that *As You Like It* was staged at Stratford, this had become 1s for admission to the grounds only; 2s for the house and grounds. As advertised in the *Stratford-upon-Avon Official Guide* for that year, this was less expensive than the cheapest seats at the SMT, which began at 2s 6d, rising to 12s 6d; visitors undecided about which of these attractions to taste first were informed that while Charlecote Park promised 'an interesting collection of portraits and furniture', the theatre offered a not dissimilar hierarchy of attractions in the shape of John Gielgud, newcomers Ralph Richardson and Margaret Leighton, Anthony Quayle ('the versatile director of the theatre'), and 'many capable, if less distinguished, supporting players'. Alongside the Shakespeare Birthday Celebrations on 23 April, the 'Principal Events' of the year identified by the *Guide* were the Conference of the Women's Gas Federation (22–25 April), the National Folk Dance Festival (2–16 August), and no fewer than three dog shows hosted by the Stratford-upon-Avon Canine Society (5 April, 9 August and 29 November). Stratford in 1952 (population: 14,800) boasted one cinema (the Picture House on Greenhill Street), five car parks, and twelve places of worship; early closing day was Thursday.[2]

This was the world in which Jackson and Quayle, as Brook put it, began 'a true search for true values' (Brook 51). In his own work, this search in the short term yielded ground-breaking productions of *Measure for Measure* in 1950 and *Titus Andronicus* in 1955; *As You Like It*, meanwhile, remained in more cautious hands. The 1952 production, directed by Glen Byam Shaw, was generally well received as an example of what T. C.

Worsley, writing in the *New Statesman and Nation*, identified as the 'recipe' concocted by Quayle, 'luxurious décor, large-scale production in the Guthrie tradition and star actors for the main roles', accounting for 'the "House Full" notices extending a long way through this season' (10 May). This was a staging notable for a *mise en scène* that marked the transition from court to forest as a movement from winter to spring, from snow underfoot to grassland, and for Margaret Leighton's Rosalind and Michael Hordern's Jaques, the former appreciated by *Punch*'s Eric Keown as 'boyish from the start ... a tomboy, but one of such gaiety and charm that she wins us as completely as she does Orlando' (14 May). The play continued to occupy its special niche in the heart of Stratford's deep England; and when Byam Shaw revived a slightly reworked version of the production in 1957, it opened in a week in which, Worsley reported, 'the town of Stratford was drenched in the smell of wallflowers, and a matching freshness and lyricism was to be enjoyed in the theatre' (*New Statesman and Nation*, 13 April).

Redgrave and redwood

When Peter Hall assumed control of the Shakespeare Memorial Theatre in 1960 and began the process of rebranding it as the Royal Shakespeare Theatre and its employees as the Royal Shakespeare Company, he too had an eye on the complacent traditionalism and self-referential localism that the benignly bucolic performance history of *As You Like It* at Stratford especially embodied. Modelling his plans for the new company on the example of the great permanent European theatre companies (the Moscow Art Theatre, Berliner Ensemble, and Théâtre National Populaire), Hall from the outset envisaged an organisation with a forward-looking, cosmopolitan character and international reach. Moving at impressive speed, Hall in his first year acquired the Aldywch theatre as a London base, instituted three-year actors' contracts, commissioned new plays from up-and-coming writers, and radically redesigned the Stratford stage, 'with a rake, a new false proscenium arch, and an apron stage that jutted fourteen feet into the auditorium' (Beauman 239). He also took a gamble with the first season's choice of plays. In 1957, the *Times* reviewer had written that *As You Like It* was a play that 'more than any other of the comedies, has a way of engendering a mood of gentle acceptance' (3 April 1957), and it might have seemed a natural and safe choice for a season of comedies. Instead Hall launched the new company (on 5 April) with his own production of *The Two Gentlemen of Verona*, a play that had last been staged at Stratford in 1938 and had only been seen six times in the theatre's history. The opening was, according to Colin Chambers, 'a disaster'; it was followed by John Barton's *The Taming of the Shrew*, for which Hall was forced by a mutinous cast to take over as director (Chambers, *Inside* 16–17).

Hall's better-received *Twelfth Night* was followed by his and Barton's *Troilus and Cressida*, Michael Langham's *The Merchant of Venice* and Peter Wood's *The Winter's Tale*, and by the end of the season the company had begun to find its feet. Hall declared himself committed to the idea of ensemble, but the company had some real star power too: the 48-strong company included Peggy Ashcroft as Katharina, Peter O'Toole as Shylock and Petruchio, and Jack McGowran as Autolycus, Christopher Sly, Speed and Old Gobbo. Planning the second season, Hall built the programme around one acting legend (John Gielgud, who played Othello in a catastrophic production directed by Franco Zeffirelli) and a nucleus of rising or established younger stars, including Ian Bannen, Peter McEnery, Ian Richardson and Dorothy Tutin. Among them was Vanessa Redgrave, an actor whose only previous exposure on the Stratford stage (apart from watching her father from the wings as a child) had been in the 1959 season as Helena in Hall's *A Midsummer Night's Dream*, and as Valeria and unnamed parts in his Olivier-led *Coriolanus*. Rosalind was her only role during the Stratford run (Bannen, by contrast, combined Orlando with Hamlet, Mercutio and Iago[3]). *As You Like It* (directed by Michael Elliott) was the fourth production in a season that also included *Much Ado*, *Hamlet*, *Richard III*, *Romeo and Juliet* and *Othello*, and it was the first to be received as an unqualified success. *Shakespeare Quarterly*'s Robert Speaight, a writer not usually given to hyperbole, described it as 'not only by far and away the best production of the play that I have seen', but also 'one of the most richly satisfying Shakespearian performances in all my fairly long experience' (Speaight 'The Old Vic and Stratford-upon-Avon, 1960–61' 432).

To a very large extent the production's appeal and significance were due to Redgrave's winning performance. First, however, I turn to another key factor, the production's positioning in relation to traditional Stratford discourses of pastoral. On first inspection, this production's Arden was deeply and reassuringly familiar. A drop-curtain was in place as the audience took their seats; when it was removed, they were faced with the spectacle of a steeply-raked stage dominated by a vast single tree, 'more redwood in girth than greenwood', on 'a mound of grass which looks as though it has a slope of one in seven' (Gerard Fay, *Guardian*, 5 July 1961). As for the tree, Bamber Gascoigne wrote in the *Spectator*: 'branches jut from it like elephant tusks, supporting flat palettes of leaves', lit to serve as a multi-purpose indicator of setting: 'patterns could be projected on to the ground; the grille of an iron gate in a courtyard, the dappled pattern of sunlight through the leaves of the forest'; this was a golden world, a realm of russet, leafy green and cool shade. And as for the rake, 'characters could converse lying flat on their backs – which (quite apart from its theatrical novelty) is precisely what one does in a forest glade'. Gascoigne was in no doubt that 'this was the knoll where I would pitch my ideal picnic. And what better definition could there be of Arden?' (*Spectator*, 14 July 1961). Other critics agreed: describing the show as 'gay and magical', Michael Hand in the *Oxford Times* noted how '[t]he sunshine filtered through [the tree's] boughs to bathe the stage in a kaleidoscope of light from dawn to sunset, from season to season' (5 July). The *Stratford-upon-Avon Herald*, determined as ever to reassert the local connection, marvelled at the 'vast oak, the great west door to a cathedral of trees', and insisted that 'it has been said a thousand times before: we know exactly where we are with *As You Like It*. For all its thin veneer of disguise, the Forest of Arden is rural Warwickshire, and the snake and hungry lioness but escapees from a passing circus. Once in the forest we are in Shakespeare's own country, where the purest of love reigns' (7 July).

For some, though, this was an Arden in which the prospect of picnics was not untouched by the more troubling aspects of rural life, manifested most obviously in a staging of 4.2 which saw the Stratford stage revisiting a relationship to blood sports that had lain dormant since 1919. Half a century earlier, and in the decades preceding that, the trophy display of a long-since sacrificed stag had, far from being controversial, been a focus of community fellow-feeling and the occasion for a jolly sing-song; now, within an English culture of hunting that centred on the pursuit and slaughter of the fox, the killing of the deer was a matter of horror. As one historian of the practice documents, hunting had steadily expanded throughout the 1950s, attracting increasing numbers of aspirant members of middle classes and women into the hunting fraternity. Meanwhile, the first public opinion poll canvassing views on hunting was conducted in 1958; it found that 65 per cent of respondents favoured a ban on stag-hunting, and 53 per cent one on fox-hunting (Griffin 191). How this spectrum of opinion was reflected in the audiences that gathered in the theatre of a town that lay at the heart of the territory of the mighty North Warwickshire Hunt is impossible to say; some of the critics, at least, were left a little queasy by Elliott's staging. 'In the excitement of the chase', Gascoigne reported, 'these courtly foresters show a streak of savagery which is out of keeping with the spirit of Arden' (*Spectator*).

J. W. Lambert in the *Sunday Times* went further: 'Mr Elliott exercises his sole touch of director's licence – fully justified, for Shakespeare must have written that strange little scene of the foresters, the slaughtered deer, and the brooding Jaques with something more in mind than filling another five minutes. By staging the stalking of the prey, Mr Elliott gives point to Jaques' wincing – and suggests a reason for his melancholy, the old nightmare of the horns' (9 July 1961). The relatively graphic staging was an attempt both to introduce a note of realism and to subtly darken the tone of a play that, at this address, had always inhabited a largely shadow-free green and golden world. The promptbook conveys the sense of a bloody macho ritual, specifying five of the forester-lords emerging from the orchestra pit as the 'deer' (stuffed, presumably) trundles from stage left to right; one forester raises a bow, fires an arrow, and 'Deer leaps in air' (quite how this effect is achieved is not clear). The deer is tied to a pole offstage (accompanied by 'shouts') as Jaques enters downstage; the lords re-enter, two of them hoist a third onto their shoulders, and Amiens crowns the deer-slayer with the horns of the kill (Promptbook 36). Observing all this, Jaques (as the television film of the production shows) is quietly appalled: 'Which is he that killed the deer?' (4.2.1) is an accusation; 'Let's present him to the Duke' (l.3) an ironic indictment.

This kind of treatment quickly became the norm: the next production of the play, directed by David Jones in 1967 (and described by Irving Wardle as reliant on 'echoes of past productions that take the place of original invention' (*The Times*, 16 June 1967)), had the exiled Duke's courtiers 'shivering in sheepskins in the snow' and repeated the hunting ritual: 'When they kill a deer, they smear blood on their faces, leeringly. Not much fun here' (D. A. N. Jones, *New Statesman*, 23 June 1967). Touches of bloody realism in Arden have become as *de rigueur* as the stuffed stag once was, perhaps the most graphic instance being in Michael Boyd's 2009 production, when the show's second half opened with the dialogue between Touchstone and Corin in 3.2, during which Geoffrey Freshwater's phlegmatic shepherd skinned and gutted a real rabbit before the clown's (and audience members') fascinated-appalled eyes. As Carol Rutter commented: 'And the point of this was? That "we're" ruining Arden – planet-wrecking killers who make deer sob and Nature weep? Or that visitors had better get used to blood because there are no Waitrose home deliveries in the forest?' (Rutter, 'Shakespeare Performances in England 2009' 346).

The heart of Elliott's production was Redgrave's Rosalind. In a volume published in 1964 that charted the company's first three years, the RSC reprinted Bernard Levin's *Daily Express* review: 'The naturalness, the unforced understanding of her playing, the passionate, breathless conviction of it, the depth of feeling and the breadth of reality – this is not acting at all, but living, being, loving. ... If the word enchantment has any meaning, it is here' (quoted in Goodwin 181). This passage is quoted with evident disapproval by Jonathan Bate and Eric Rasmussen, who furnish it as evidence of the reviewers' sexism, and who counter its sentiment by citing Penny Gay's claim that what Redgrave 'was demonstrating on the Stratford stage was literally "actresses'" liberation' (Gay 135). They take the critics to task for 'fail[ing] to mention how Redgrave's performance forced the audience to recognize' this 'liberation', though how they know the audience experienced this recognition they do not say (Bate and Rasmussen 134). With respect to Redgrave's disguising as Ganymede, certainly no one found any hint of androgyny, nor any subversion of gender stereotypes, nor anything to trouble a straightforwardly heterosexual rendering of the central relationship. Indeed, the actor and her director took repeated opportunities to keep a very feminine Rosalind well in view: the *Daily Telegraph* recorded that 'she was allowed from time to time to snatch off her cap and let her hair flow loose so that she could appear for the moment as a girl indeed' (5 July), a gesture also spotted by the *Birmingham Mail*, which transposed the 'quality of sunlight' in Arden with the captivating moment when she was allowed to 'take off her boy's cap and shake sunbeams from her hair' (5 July). Redgrave was 'richly feminine, rosily impetuous, and incontestably in love', wrote Robert Muller in the *Daily Mail* (5 July), 'and one can only marvel how Orlando and Phoebe could have been fooled for so long over the question of her gender'. Barefoot, in cropped knee-breeches and oversized man's shirt, and sporting a rakishly-angled grey cap, Redgrave was a gamine Dickensian urchin with a dash of Audrey Hepburn chic, and to a man (and they were all men) the critics loved her for it.

Levin's breathless prose style was, for once, entirely representative of the prevailing view. When the Stratford *Herald*'s Edmund Gardner wrote that 'Any male who does not fall in love with Miss Redgrave for this performance alone must be as insensible as a plastic acorn', he was franker than most, but he articulated that which was barely latent in Levin's review. The recurrent theme of the reviews is spontaneity, impulsiveness, innocence, youth and *naturalness*: Redgrave's Rosalind was as at home within this golden world, as was the great tree in whose dappled shadows she skipped and sprawled. Redgrave, wrote the *Oxford Times* reviewer, was the embodiment of nature itself, 'a magical compound of vernal sprightliness and midsummer moonshine by an actress with springtime in her heart, her gait and her voice' (7 July); while the *Nottingham Evening Post* (5 July) found that 'her emotions burst from her in little waves and rainfalls, not tempests or thunderstorms'. Much of the appeal of her performance lay in its apparent artlessness: for the *Times* reviewer (5 July), 'her sudden involuntary tendernesses' were 'quite unaffected and most touching'; and for Alan Brien (*Sunday Telegraph*, 9 July), 'Her emotions seem to be chiming with those of the characters she plays almost by accident .... Her voice, warm as fur in the sun, strokes her words as unthinkingly as one fondles a cat. And yet it never misses an emphasis nor inserts a false punctuation. She moves with the lanky unselfconsciousness of one who has never been watched except by animals and children. And yet she stumbles into grace and is embarrassed into beauty.' 'I found her open-mouthed eagernesss irresistible,' confessed Caryl Brahms (*John O'London's*, 13 July), 'words tumbling down, arms outflung, she would share her sudden love with the whole earth and skies above it.' The perceived lack of guile, of Rosalind (and perhaps Redgrave) not being able to contain her feelings, was both part of her allure and perhaps the stimulus for the reviewers to respond, lyrically and even rhapsodically, in kind.

Redgrave's charms did not win everyone over. T. C. Worsley (*Financial Times*, 5 July) conceded that she 'carried it off with natural high spirits and gawky charm' but put her firmly in her place: 'charm however gawky and spirits however natural are no substitute for style'. Redgrave's inexperience, the rawness of her craft, were similarly targeted: 'if she loses her dignity she has nothing but schoolgirl gaucherie to put in its place' (*Leamington Spa Courier*, 7 July); 'Miss Redgrave ... is often too exuberantly skittish in her enjoyment of the game, as if Arden were the school playing-fields' (*Stage and Television Today*, 6 July). The suspicion that a more dangerously adult Rosalind might be having too much of the wrong kind of fun was voiced in even more strongly gendered terms by the *New Statesman*'s reviewer: 'she could hardly stop herself from eating Orlando alive ... [and] she could no more disguise her state than if she were drowning. This may be *Venus toute entière* and a credit to the laws of nature; but it struck me as being unfeminine and unShakespearean' (14 July). For this critic, femininity is incompatible with emotional openness, vulnerability and the frank display of desire; for others, they are its very essence. On one thing most agreed: Redgrave was, as Eric Keown put it, 'an entirely modern Rosalind'. For him, this meant that '[s]he might be any one of our daughters ... and it is a pleasure to watch her' (*Punch*, 12 July); for the *Birmingham Mail*, reviewing the Aldwych transfer, it was to see Rosalind as 'a twentieth-century gamin, a fantasticated Bisto kid, a terror of the lower fifth' (11 January 1962). The reviewer concluded: '*As You Like It* has had to wait until the 1960s for someone to appreciate that this is what Rosalind is.'

Possessed of a spirit of play that carried more than a whiff of subversiveness, this Rosalind was more a woman of her time, or ahead of her time, than the reviewers realized. For Redgrave herself, the theatrical was both personal and political. By the end of the Stratford season, Rosalind's persona, her disposition to total commitment, had become inseparable from Redgrave's own politics of emergent feminism and established anti-nuclear activism, and, as she understood and experienced it, of life and love. In her autobiography, she revealed that Michael Elliott had taken her for lunch on the day of the première. Expecting bland words of thanks and encouragement, she was in for a shock: 'Vanessa, the whole production is going to be a failure. You won't give yourself up to the play and to what is happening. You are refusing to give *yourself* over, you are holding back. You've held back all through rehearsals, and if you don't go on stage tonight and give *all* of yourself to the play, the actors and the audience, we will have failed totally' (Redgrave 93). 'I doubt', writes Redgrave, 'whether any other director would have had the courage, or the wisdom, to speak to me as he did only hours before the first performance'; but, as we have seen, it worked: 'I threw myself into the moment of Rosalind's life, into Orlando's eyes, into the Forest of Arden' (94). 'As I had made a leap as an actress,' she continues, 'I took an irrevocable decision to make a leap into political life as well' (95). Having accepted an invitation to join the Campaign for Nuclear Disarmament's Committee of 100, she wrote to her father, Michael Redgrave:

> The only thing we can do for the future is to do all we can to make sure there is a future. I want to act as well and as continuously as possible all my life, no holds barred ... unilateral disarmament for Britain is a *must – must, must*. And is the only minute hope we can have for a *beginning* which could conceivably make possible an ultimate world disarmament ... my work in the theatre and 'real life' have now marvelously become one. When I play at night I not only feel happy, as I have always done, because I enjoy acting ... but I feel a far greater joy, a longing to share everything with the audience, to give them all I can. I feel almost in love with them. (Redgrave 95–7)

Small wonder that, with a performance and a personality this disarming, Redgrave's Rosalind earned the notices that it did.

So total was Redgrave's dominance of the reviews that the other major roles received less than their usual share of attention. Ian Bannen's Orlando suffered a little from the role's perceived lack of definition: Bamber Gascoigne (*Spectator*) thought that 'if Ian Bannen's Orlando seems palely romantic beside Miss Redgrave, that is partly Orlando's fault. The tree-spoiler is a conventional wooer unworthy of the girl.' Bannen was 'somewhat questionable', according to *The Times*: he 'looks the part but ... lacks the noble innocence of heart that draws Rosalind to him'. Mindful of Bannen's not particularly well-received Hamlet of the same RSC season, J. C. Trewin noted 'a lank figure with a weary eye, looking like someone from a contemporary novel who has lost his way in the forest. Or, shall I suggest, like an *avant-guard* [sic] dramatic critic who is not much enjoying a performance' (*Birmingham Post*, 5 July). Finding him 'strangely haunted, like all his heroes',

J. W. Lambert wondered why Bannen seemed 'to respond much more eagerly to the apparent boy than to the dream of the lost girl' (*Sunday Times*). Kenneth Tynan was particularly spiteful, dismissing Bannen as 'a swarthy weakling' (*Observer*, 9 July). Being rude about Orlando is something of a critical habit, and one wonders whether on this occasion it betrays a touch of envy: why *him*, rather than me?

More to Tynan's taste was Max Adrian's Jaques, who 'speaks his lines with sardonic relish'; Adrian was admired by the *Guardian*'s Gerard Fay for bringing 'an edge to Jaques which cuts through the sententiousness'. Judging Adrian as giving 'the most subtle reading of the part that I remember', Speaight reported that 'he wandered off at the end like Marcel Proust retiring to a monastery' (434). Lambert could 'hardly praise too highly' Adrian's performance, for 'its restraint, its cankered pathos'; reviewing the Aldywch transfer, he recorded him 'furred like a Muscovite', trailing 'terribly behind him that refusal of joy ... the deadly essence of sloth' (*Sunday Times*, 14 January 1962). Smallwood refers to the 'astringency '(143) of Adrian's performance, also an apt term for Rosalind Knight's Celia. Noticeably smaller and darker than Redgrave, Knight is an intriguing presence in the production photographs and in the television film: her speaking marked her as an amused, sceptical and detached observer of the wooing, and as noticeably more upper-crust than her cousin. If Adrian's Jaques was Thanatos to Redgrave's Eros, Knight countered Rosalind's abandon with Celia's guardedness. Lambert saw in her performance a 'devoted shrewishness' in Stratford and a 'dark, pert and loving' devotion in London which 'never fails to make a point and never tries to steal a scene'. For Tynan, this self-effacement produced only 'a prim little nobody', while the *Tatler* reviewer (9 July) declared that Knight was 'something too much of a mischievous witch', although 'the uncovenanted touch of cynicism does no harm'.

Arden in black and white

Speaight hoped of Redgrave's 'magical' Rosalind that she 'will go on giving it for years' (Speaight 'The Old Vic and Stratford-upon-Avon, 1960–61' 433), but she gave her final stage performance of the role at the Aldwych on Saturday 2 June 1962. An audio recording, directed by Howard Sackler, was made for the Shakespeare Recording Society and released on vinyl in 1962 (it is now freely available online), and a cut version of the stage production was filmed, under the direction of Ronald Eyre, for BBC Television towards the end of the same year, and screened on 22 March 1963. This was the second of a planned series of BBC broadcasts of RSC productions, under the terms of an agreement which gave the television company exclusive rights to televise two of the RSC's productions a year (the first was *The Cherry Orchard*, screened in April 1962). *As You Like It* was billed as event television: in the *Radio Times* (16 March), Eyre wrote of the stage production as 'something of a legend' and predicted that 'this production would have the largest audience of any Shakespeare play on television', whilst acknowledging that its audience 'has never seen the play before'. The *Daily Mail* trailed the 'king-size' broadcast with the statement that the BBC 'takes an audience gamble tonight on Shakespeare. It is hoping that most viewers will like *As You Like It* for two hours 15 minutes' (22 March 1963). The next day, the paper's reviewer clearly thought the gamble had paid off, concluding that the BBC had successfully adjusted the production to the rhythms of its medium: 'the play transferred well too, because it cleanly divides in incident and mood into two halves, allowing better than almost any other for the necessary news interval' (23 March). Eric Shorter, writing in the *Daily Telegraph*, likewise reported that 'this triumph from the stage' made 'pure television' (23 March).

Surprisingly, given the high profile of the screening, the respectable viewing figures (six million) and the evidence of the BBC's own audience research, which recorded a highly favorable response, the recording was never repeated and has only recently become generally accessible. A copy is held in the RSC archive at the Shakespeare Birthplace Trust; given the BBC's haphazard approach to programme preservation during the period, we are lucky it was not lost altogether (in 2016, the programme was added to the newly-launched BBC Shakespeare Archive Resource, where it is available to subscribing educational institutions). The BBC's Audience Research Report, marked 'confidential', signed 'MSA/BML', and intended solely for internal circulation, is dated 17 April 1963 and runs to two single-spaced typed pages. It records the estimated size of the audience (derived from the results of the Survey of Listening and Viewing) for both parts of the broadcast (12 per cent of the UK population for Part I, 10 per cent for Part II) and records respondents' ratings on a six-point scale: A+ (46 per cent), A (37 per cent), B (10 per cent), C (6 per cent) and C- (1 per cent). It notes that the 'very good' aggregated reaction index of 80 'has only been reached twice before in the history of televised Shakespeare' (this was for the second part of *Richard II* and *Richard III* in the 1960 *An Age of Kings* serial; the BBC's previous attempt at *As You Like It* in 1953 has scored 57 on its first showing, and 70 when repeated). The enthusiasm of the BBC viewing panel's lay respondents matched that of the theatre reviewers. As quoted in the report, the viewers thought that the 'generally enchanting effect' of the production was due to 'delightful' sets which gave 'the maximum effect of space', to the 'beautifully smooth' camerawork and 'brisk' continuity, and to the central performances, whose highlights included a 'stylish' Jaques and a 'strong and vivid' Celia, performances which were marked by 'verve and a perfection of diction' as 'the words fell like jewels from the actors' lips'. Above all, there was Redgrave with her 'lissom appearance' and 'lovely speaking voice': 'no Amazon, but a vulnerable and appealing girl … whose rapier-like wit made piquant contrast with her essential femininity'.

What are we to make of this? Confidential or not, the report is hardly a dispassionate evaluation of the evidence, which, it concludes, demonstrates that the programme, 'an "excursion" into Shakespeare of calibre and distinction', 'brought out the Spring-time gaiety of Shakespeare's inspiration in all its freshness and vitality'. The questionnaire sample (a total of 114, or 17 per cent of the viewing panel) was relatively small and possibly self-selecting: the report noted 'the frequency of such comment as "this has always been my favorite comedy; we know the Jaques' speech by heart"', and, as a way of contextualizing the observations, categorized its respondents by profession and social status, citing a Solicitor, an Editorial Assistant and a Housewife. But it is the only evidence of audience response that we have, and in places it is refreshingly direct, perceptive and nuanced. For one respondent, this was a evening of 'rather tiresome punning, together with people wandering round the forest in inadequate disguises'; praise for Redgrave was qualified by the recognition that she delivered a theatrical rather than televisual performance, 'with facial expressions that bespoke "a wonderful technique" in conveying swift changes of emotion, but proved "too prominent" for close-ups'. In contrast, Patrick Allen, who had taken over the part of Orlando during the Aldwych run, 'seemed more aware of the requirements of TV'.

When I viewed this half a century after it was screened – in the reading room of the Shakespeare Birthplace Trust one July day in 2015 – I thought the recording had stood the test of time remarkably well. In some obvious ways the programme reveals the limitations of its conditions of making: filmed over two days in a studio set that preserves the essentials of the RSC staging as it attempts to meet the conventions of the medium half-way, the production seems uncertain whether to flaunt or to camouflage the artifice of its *mise en scène*. The central fixed feature is the large tree, around which scenic elements come and go to effect shifts of location: providing the backdrop to the confrontation between Orlando and Oliver (to a soundtrack of clucking chickens), it is then glimpsed through the latticed windows of the shadowy, claustrophobically low-ceilinged cottage (introduced for the television version) where Oliver plots with Charles. During the wrestling, a brutal scrabble that Orlando at first looks in serious danger of losing, the tree remains at the centre of a space, now enclosed by forbiddingly high brick walls, crowded with half-heartedly ad-libbing supers (again, added for the screen version). Rosalind and Celia's first scene takes place in an echoing panelled room dominated by a grand staircase, which is also the location for their banishment, a scene underscored by the slow ticking of a grandfather clock.

3 Rosalind (Vanessa Redgrave) and Orlando (Patrick Allen), BBC Television, 1963

In Arden, the walls disappear, the space begins to breathe, and the tree remains in shot most of the time, supplemented by scattered items of monochrome greenery planted around the studio perimeter. At first, this seems a bleak and inhospitable place, marked by the silhouettes of leafless trees and the cries of gulls and ravens ('Well, this is the Forest of Arden' (2.4.11) voices massive disappointment). In this artificially natural world, where (after the interval for the news broadcast halfway through) the onset of spring is heralded by birdsong and the first hints of foliage, the cast give camera-scaled versions of their stage performances, among them, notably, Knight's compellingly gimlet-eyed and sharp-witted Celia and Adrian's mesmerizing Jaques. Adrian is as visually striking as he is vocally distinctive: with a delivery dry as bones, wrapped in black from head to foot, he casts a shadow across the screen, snarling his way through the 'seven ages' as a flickering campfire illuminates his bared teeth and narrowed eyes. Acting as a background auditor to Orlando's subsequent dialogue with Duke Senior, thanks to the limitations of cathode-ray technology, Adrian is transformed by the low-resolution image into an out-of-focus black smudge, more death's-head (seen through a glass, darkly) than living human face. Patrick Allen's Orlando is quite unlike Ian Bannen's. With a rich, caressingly authoritative baritone that subsequently became the basis of a long career as a voice artist for innumerable commercials, documentaries and public information films, Allen is a genial, warm and laid-back foil for Redgrave, though far from a conventional romantic lead (see Figure 3).

The programme, like the stage production it commemorated, rested on Redgrave's Rosalind. Reviewing the broadcast the next day, the *Daily Mail*'s Michael Gowers wrote that she was 'blinding': 'radiating and sparkling, soaring and swooping, tender and pert by terms, boyish without being principally boyish, uninhibitedly woman' (23 March). I can only agree. Redgrave is captivating: this is a performance radiant with life, generosity and longing. As she dances through the play, the viewer's gaze is directed by a camera that (often in big close-up) seems unable to tear itself away from her face. The effect is winningly, sometimes almost uncomfortably, intimate: as Rosalind and Orlando roll on the ground during 4.1, I imagine them tumbling from the screen onto the carpets of the nation's living rooms.[4] The medium of close-up enables numerous subtle touches and grace notes, as when Redgrave briefly catches

Allen's hair with the chain of her necklace as she places it round his neck on 'Wear this for me' (1.2.215); when she hangs back, hesitant, on the staircase while Celia, confident and commanding, offers her hand on 'Now go in we content/To liberty, and not to banishment' (1.3.133–4); and when she dreamily traces with her finger the large 'R' that Orlando has carved into the bark as she asks after the 'man who haunts the forest that abuses our young plants' (3.2.330–1). Moments earlier, as Orlando and Rosalind share a laugh at the lawyers who 'sleep between term and term' (305–6), she catches herself, glances downwards, appears suddenly aware of the breasts beneath her man's shirt, then returns Orlando's gaze for 'Where dwell you, pretty youth?' (308). The 'old religious uncle' (316–17) is an inspired – or desperate – improvisation, fearful as she is that she has blown her cover, but Orlando appears not to notice. Rosalind's 'coming-on disposition' (4.1.98) is even more sexually charged: on 'love me, Rosalind', she swoons backwards on the floor, wringing a delicious innuendo from 'Yes, faith, will I – Fridays *and Saturdays*, and all' (101).

The Rosalind–Orlando scenes are shown pretty much in their entirety; even so, the total running time of two hours and fifteen minutes is a drastic redaction of a stage show that ran to three hours. The deepest cuts occur in the second half: the Phoebe and Silvius subplot is reduced to the bare minimum, as are Touchstone's routines and his scenes with Audrey. The epilogue, too, disappears, the credits rolling over the final moves of a stately pavane performed by the four pairs of lovers. I will return to the televisual context and circumstances of this broadcast in Chapter VI, where I explore the screen history of the play. For now, let it stand as an abiding memory of a Rosalind that lodged in the hearts of the thousands who experienced her in the theatre, and of the millions who glimpsed her on the small screen, for decades to come.

Notes

1 The production was revived in 1880, 1881, 1882, 1884 and 1885 (twice, in April and for a benefit performance for the Shakespeare Memorial Fund in August). Benson took charge in 1886, and the play was not revived again until 1894, when he and Constance Benson, respectively aged 38 and 30, played Orlando and Rosalind. It was revived in 1895, 1897, 1899, 1900, 1901, 1904, 1905, 1906, 1907, 1908, 1910, 1911 (twice), 1912 and 1913, when it formed part of the Benson company's first tour of the United States. It was twice revived in 1914, and again in 1915.

2   Compare Stratford-upon-Avon in 2017 (population 25, 505, according to the 2007 census): one cinema (the Stratford-upon-Avon Picture House in Windsor Street, which opened in 1997), 11 car parks (plus a park-and-ride in Bishopston Lane), five churches, and early closing – in a town served by six open-all-hours supermarkets – a distant memory. Tempting as it is to think of Stratford then as a reactionary and isolated backwater, it is worth noting that everyday life had its redeeming features. The Public Library on Henley Street made it known in the *Guide* that 'books may be borrowed by visitors presenting any Public Library Ticket in England and Wales'. As a culture in which the mere possession of a library ticket vouchsafed one's trustworthiness, the Stratford of 1952 is in some ways as unimaginable as that of 1592.

3   In a 59-strong company (43 men, 16 women), Redgrave was one of five female leads, alongside Peggy Ashcroft (Emilia), Edith Evans (Nurse), Geraldine McEwan (Beatrice, Ophelia) and Dorothy Tutin (Desdemona, Juliet). Redgrave took over Katharina from Ashcroft when the *Shrew* transferred to the Aldwych. The distribution of labour can be illuminatingly compared with that of subsequent seasons addressed in this chapter. In 1973, the company numbered 45 (35 men, 10 women); Eileen Atkins took only one part (Rosalind), as did Maureen Lipman (Celia) and Brenda Bruce (Lady Capulet). David Suchet combined Orlando with Tybalt, Tanio, and bit parts in *Richard II*; Ian Richardson Jaques with Berowne, and Bolingbroke and Richard II in Barton's double-cast production. In 1985, there were 48 men and 14 women in a company of 62; Juliet Stevenson played Cressida, Rosalind, and Madame Tourvel in Christopher Hampton's *Les Liaisons Dangereuses*, and Hilton McCrae, never an RSC lead on any other occasion, Orlando and Patroclus. This company served four productions at the RST and two at The Other Place. In 2013, the year of the most recent RSC *As You Like It* at the time of writing, a core group of 20 actors (7 women, 13 men) performed *Hamlet*, *As You Like It* and *All's Well* at the RST while completely separate companies delivered eight plays at The Swan.

4   Among them, perhaps, was that of my ten-month-old self, for I was born in a house with the television always on. I will never know whether I spent that evening in front of it, mewling, puking or sleeping in the arms of my mother, Kathleen Shaughnessy (née Stratford), but I like to hope that the programme brought some joy into a life that would be cruelly cut short barely a year later.

CHAPTER III

Materials of performance: denim and silk

A woman's place

In 1973, Buzz Goodbody made her main-stage solo directorial debut with a production of *As You Like It* that was led by Eileen Atkins as Rosalind and Richard Pasco as Jaques. Goodbody had joined the RSC in 1967, the year of the RSC's second production of *As You Like It* and the National Theatre's first (see Chapter V), when she was appointed by director John Barton as his personal assistant. Goodbody came to the company as a communist and active feminist and went on to found the Women's Street Theatre Group in 1971. She was also the first woman to direct at Stratford since Dorothy Green in 1946 (*Twelfth Night*), and, as Chambers puts it, she was 'the first to survive the RSC obstacle course – periods of unemployment, waiting for something to turn up at the RSC and intense internal competition – and to establish a regular presence in the male-dominated company' (Chambers, *Inside* 67). From 1967 to 1972 Goodbody worked with Barton and others on small-scale touring productions that operated under the umbrella of Theatregoround, as well as acting as assistant director on the *Romans* cycle in 1972; she also directed two productions at the company's London studio, The Place, in 1971, Trevor Griffiths's *Occupations* and the devised docu-drama *The Oz Trial*. She played a central role in the foundation of the RSC's Stratford studio space, The Other Place, in 1974. *As You Like It* proved to be her last main-stage production.[1]

In setting and costuming, the production was contemporary. Perhaps taking his cue from Ralph Koltai's pop-art settings for the National Theatre six years earlier (see Chapter V), designer Christopher Morley rendered Arden non-realistically: for some reviewers, by what appeared to be organic material, in the shape of 'hanging wooden poles' (Michael Billington, *Guardian*, 13 June), 'a grove of bamboos or an assortment of organ pipes' (J. C. Trewin, *Birmingham Post*, 14 June), 'a grotto made of bamboo' (Frank Marcus, *Sunday Telegraph*, 17 June); and for others, by decidedly non-organic 'hanging metallic tubes' (Irving Wardle, *The Times*, 13 June), a 'pattern of dangling metal pipes' that 'suggests that someone has disembowelled the Albert Hall organ above the stage' (Jeremy Kingston, *Punch*, 20 June). For John Elsom, the court was a 'casino', while Arden 'looks as much like an empty boutique as a respectable forest' (*Listener*, 21 June); while Benedict Nightingale felt that the 'aluminium glades', announced by 'a resonant, echoing clang as long thin metal tubes are lowered from the flies, casually buffeting together as they drop', created, not altogether helpfully, the ambience of 'a chi-chi Chinese restaurant' (*New Statesman*, 22 June). Clearly, the intent was to suggest a world of artifice and surfaces and to dispense with traditional images of pastoral; as Goodbody saw it, the denizens of Arden were 'not really country people' but 'art college drop-outs who live in the country and have mummies and daddies in town with big incomes'. Observing that '[h]ardly anyone seems to do any work', she stated that her aim was 'to set up *worlds* for them to live in', which meant placing the play's characters 'in a convincing social context' (*Birmingham Post*, 9 June).

At the same time, much of the staging was rampantly, crowd-pleasingly theatrical (not so pleasingly for some reviewers). The court was furnished with candelabra, gilt chairs and parquet flooring, which remained in place for the forest scenes; courtiers smoked and drank cocktails as they watched an extravagantly prolonged freestyle wrestling match choreographed by the professional wrestler and television personality Brian Glover, who played Charles (Peter Thomson noted his 'finger-stretching gestures' and 'the wicked relish with which he punched a fist into his other hand' (Thomson 148–9)). Clement McCallin's Duke Fredrick smoked fat cigars, sported a melodrama-villain's black eye-patch and velvet-lapelled black jacket and reminded one critic of 'some seedy Greek colonel' (David Nathan, *Jewish Chronicle*, 15 June). His forest counterpart, Duke Senior (Tony Church), wore a faded smoking jacket, smoked a pipe, and sat with his exiled lords at a picnic table consuming cold chicken and red wine. Maureen Lipman's Celia was given a hammock to doze in through much of the show's second half, and Oliver Martext, played by Richard

Mayes as a stage-Irish whisky priest, was equipped with a pram and a wedding cake.

The song-and-dance numbers, arranged as soft rock by composer Guy Wolfenden, were vamped up for all they were worth; Goodbody, Nathan concluded, had 'conducted the play as if it were an opera – treating the great set scenes ... the speeches like "All the world's a stage" and, of course, the songs themselves, as arias demanding – and getting – a round of applause' (*Jewish Chronicle*). The *Daily Telegraph*'s John Barber Eeyoreishly pronounced that, as a 'specialist in yesterday's bright ideas' Goodbody was 'over-anxious to make Shakespeare *fun*' (13 June); Kenneth Hurren complained in the *Spectator* that 'this twee little romp ... is as depressing to attend as *any* party at which everyone is tipsy except oneself' (23 June). For Wardle, as for a number of other reviewers, the eclecticism was 'erratic', noticeably and jarringly so when, for 'the first Orlando–Rosalind interview', the abstract forest setting was invaded by 'three stagehands with a realistic log' (*The Times*). Similarly, Thomson found in the introduction of this item 'a conflict of styles for which there seemed no explanation': 'with the old-fashioned reality of a pantomime ground-row', the log was at once all-too-prosaically real and all-too-cheesily theatrical.

Nonetheless, Thomson thought, the design created 'a seedy, Chekhovian elegance' that was 'surprisingly apt' for 'the histrionic misanthropy of Richard Pasco's brilliant Jaques' (Thomson 149). Most critics agreed, and many likewise evoked the Russian doctor-dramatist, his compatriots and his contemporaries, in relation to Pasco's portrayal. Billington, who considered Pasco's 'brilliant' Jaques 'the one triumph of the evening', saw 'a stooping, sottish almost Chekhovian figure in whom bitter self-hatred has turned to misanthropy' (*Guardian*); Wardle reported that Pasco 'seems to have wandered into Arden from the pages of Dostoevsky', as he 'gazes sourly at the merrymakers through steel-rimmed spectacles ... trembling with something between passion and incipient epilepsy' (*Times*); Kingston recorded 'a thick-lipped exile from *mittel-europa* in a white mac, surely a victim of the bone-ache' (*Punch*), Barber 'an arrogant dandy of the old Café Royal' (*Daily Telegraph*). The performance's effectiveness was due in part to the sense, both dramatic and metatheatrical, that Pasco's Jaques was a man haunting the periphery of this Arden's with-it world ('peering at the action with beady distaste through rimless glasses', as Robert Cushman characterized it in the *Observer* (17 June)), that he was, as these comments suggest, out of time and out of place, 'speaking for an older generation of theatregoers', as Thomson put it, 'in his dislike of what was going on around him':

> His white suit and hat had seen better days. He smoked without evident pleasure, wore glasses with cheap frames, and walked with his knees bent in a strange, small-stepping slouch. He has the air of a man faced with the alternative of alcoholism or indigestion. Not only did he know that his breath smelt vile, but also that no one would dare tell him ... . Left alone at the dining-table, Jaques wheezed his way into a long belly-laugh – at the Duke, at life, at us – which became, in effect, the beginning of the interval. (Thomson 149–50)

Uniquely, the one performance in the production that met with near-universal acclaim (Elsom excepted, who saw in Pasco's 'poised disdainful wrist' a 'bad attack of the Muggeridges'[2]) has survived for posterity. Five years after Goodbody's production, Pasco gave a near-identical portrayal in the BBC Television Shakespeare version of the play, in a performance that, save for the costuming (which is early rather than late modern, and which includes neither rimmed nor rimless spectacles), preserves both the outline and the detail of the Stratford incarnation (down to the laugh at the end of 2.7): a world-weary cynic with an entrenched drinking habit, Jaques now looks like one of the BBC production's rare strengths.

In what has become a familiar tactic in productions of this play, the strict, tightly-buttoned formality of the court scenes lent them a vaguely Edwardian rather than contemporary flavour, while the move to Arden released the lords and lovers into a more easy-going, casual-contemporary style. This was evident in the most remarked-upon of the production's costume decisions, its liberal use of denim: along with the other slumming-posh young inhabitants of the forest, Orlando and Rosalind were both clad in hip-hugging flared jeans. For one reviewer this was all too much: 'by all means wear jeans for painting sets, manning switchboards or sweeping the stage, but – please – let our Rosalinds and Violas be togged out in natty suede, or ever-so-slightly tatty tweed and not looking as if they were en route for the latest student "demo"' (*Oxford Times* 29 June 1973). As this comment suggests, this element was more than a matter of costuming; it was one of deliberate theatrical and cultural positioning. In broad terms, the generational and class divisions around jeans were, in 1973, as sharp as they had ever been: the affectation of what some still regarded as workwear for manual labourers by middle-class youths was an act of insubordination associated with free love, pop music, drug-taking, radical politics and general fecklessness. Denim on the Stratford stage conveyed an attitude of casualness, and of ordinariness, that was at odds with the spirit of the space. This was not the first time the RSC had staged a comedy in modern dress: that distinction belongs to Brook's *A Midsummer Night's Dream* and Robin Phillips's *The Two Gentlemen of Verona*, both in 1970. In both of those productions, however, the costuming was marked by a heightened theatricality that set it apart from the everyday: in *Two Gentlemen*'s case, in the flamboyant high camp of unfeasibly tight shorts, thigh-length boots and skimpy beachwear; in *Dream*'s, in the tie-dyed shirts and loose slacks of the lovers and the flowing, baggy silks of the fairies. David Waller's Bottom, in that production, wore a string vest, but even among the mechanicals jeans were nowhere to be seen. Rosalind's and Orlando's jeans, by contrast, were just clothes; in production photographs, Eileen Atkins and David Suchet might just as easily be rehearsing as performing. This did not necessarily work to their advantage: Wendy Monk, for example, liked Suchet's 'good, strong acting' and 'well-defined speech', but lamented that 'in those dreary jeans he must fight a visual battle' (*Stage and Television Today* 21 June).

For Eileen Atkins's Rosalind, the ostensible liberation of denim imposed restraints of a different kind. For most reviewers, the unisex nature of jeans meant that Ganymede was, if anything, even *more* conventionally – and alluringly – feminine than the Rosalind who appeared in her first scene in a severely formal black frock and, in her second, in a loose nightdress. As a result, Billington wrote, 'any hint of sexual equivocation is knocked on the head .... Indeed, with her headband, fringed blouse and crutch hugging jeans, she is even more seductive as Ganymede than before' (*Guardian*). At one level, comments such as this (which is very much of its time) make us thankful that male critics' licence to pass judgement on actors' sexual attractiveness has long since been revoked; at another, they candidly convey us to the heart of spectatorial desire for Rosalind in a way that the reticence of reviewers before and since does not. Kingston broadly agreed: 'The sexual ambiguity of Orlando's courtship of the disguised Rosalind passes for nothing since Eileen Atkins in her blue trouser suit continues to look exactly like a 1973 woman.' This hardly mattered, though, since 'these scenes ... draw from her a quicksilver succession of amused glances and jokey voices based on a delicate oscillation between laughter through tears and sorrow in smiles' (*Punch*). As far as the man act went, Speaight doubted that she was even trying: 'Most Rosalinds are tempted to swagger too much; Miss Atkins might have swaggered a little more, and coaxed an extra affectation of virility into her voice.' Nonetheless, 'the delicacy of the performance was beyond praise' (Speaight 'The Stratford-upon-Avon Season' 403).

In contrast to Redgrave's fresh-faced youthfulness and innocence, Atkins presented to some a more knowing, sceptical persona: 'no exponent of springtime romance' for Wardle, 'she expresses the wary defensiveness of someone who has seen too much to have Rosalind's emotional self-confidence' (*The Times*). 'Her evident depression and boredom at her uncle's court', Nightingale speculated, 'marks [*sic*] her out as a woman of more than average capacity for feeling'; a capacity that finds its imagined manifestation in a vivid flight of critical fantasy: 'she can't always prevent that bony face from breaking into a look of extraordinary longing, as if she might suddenly do something unexpected and embarrassing, like clutch Orlando by the bicep or buttock and kiss him' (*New Statesman*). For Penny Gay, the overall effect of both the jeans and the actors' performances was to 'normalise' the play's fluid sexualities and to put in their place 'an uncomplicated heterosexuality, modern and uninhibited' (Gay 67). It seems a fair judgement – though one that could equally apply to virtually every production of the play, with or without jeans, to have been seen at Stratford since the RSC was founded.

While there are few signs that Goodbody was interested in pursuing a queer reading of the play, there are plenty to confirm that she had in mind a feminist one. Gay states that the production was 'to reclaim the play for women' following the National Theatre's 'reactionary experiment' of casting the play exclusively with men (64–5), and some aspects seemed to indicate this. The poster for the production displayed a rear view of Eileen Atkins (in jeans), beside a quotation from Martin Luther: 'Women ought to stay at home … for they have … a wide fundament to sit upon, keep house, and raise children.' The sentiment of this mildly Dadaist juxtaposition of patriarchal imperative with sexually liberated womanhood is obvious enough, and perhaps there was some scope for a queer viewing of the image, since this slim young denim-clad bum could, at a push, have been male *or* female. The programme featured excerpts from Virginia Woolf's essay 'Shakespeare's Sister', from David Young's 1972 study *The Heart's Forest* (significantly including his mild-mannered attempt to annex the play's concerns to those of contemporary eco-politics, of 'a time when we are faced with the need for a searching re-examination of our own attitudes toward our environment' (Young x)), and from John Berger's recently published treatise on gender representation in the visual arts and the male gaze, *Ways of Seeing*: 'Men look at women. Women watch themselves being looked at' (Berger 47).

The programme also included a short essay by Anne Barton, 'A Woman's Place', which sought to locate the play's gender politics historically. The women in *As You Like It*, Barton argued, 'contain within themselves the values which will prove to be those of the comedy as a whole and which the masculine world needs, painfully, to acquire: values of tolerance, courtesy and kindness, of realism, honesty and self-control'. For any critic or theatregoer anxious at the prospect of a 'women's lib' production, there was little to fear here: this was an ameliorative, regenerative and conciliatory feminism which taught that, at the end of the play, 'Arden must be exchanged for the court, the liberty of doublet and hose for the confinement of skirts, but at least [Rosalind] and Orlando have met in the greenwood as equal human beings and can never forget this fact.' As a communist first and foremost, Goodbody was at least as exercised by the play's concern with class and economic status as by its gender politics. 'It is perhaps interesting', read a programme note, 'that in the opening lines of the play, Orlando speaks of being bequeathed 1,000 crowns. At that time, according to Peter H. Ramsey, '1,000 crowns was equal to £250 which, allowing for the inflation of four centuries, would be the equivalent of £6,000 now.'

Goodbody was certainly keenly aware of the gender dynamics of her role as director, and of how they were implicated in the power relations and working practices of a heavily male-dominated branch of the 1970s cultural industries. Interviewed in the *Daily Telegraph* (13 June), she was frank about the potentially exploitative relationship between the director and female actor, and about the implications of this for her own authority: 'Actresses are in a paradoxical position because they are more independent than most women, but they are used to, if not sleeping with the director, at least flirting with him, because he is a man and they are used to having him boss them around ... I have to convince them that

I have a different kind of strength.' As Chambers records, it was impossible for Goodbody not to internalize the contradictions of her position: she 'blamed herself when things went wrong, and felt that is she were successful they would say "what a good director", but if a failure, "the women can't do it"' (Chambers *Other Spaces* 12). The RSC at this point in its history thrived on a punishing, overwhelming macho work culture in which Goodbody had no choice but to participate: 'I was working a 19- or 20-hour day for six weeks. We'd go through from 10 a.m. to 5.30 p.m. with a half-hour break, then work on till 10 p.m.' For the time being, she claimed, this not just tolerable but positively enjoyable: 'I don't need the relaxation – I just never unwind'; but as the interview's author put it, 'this deceptively delicate looking young woman has put a firm limit on her future as a director'. 'By 35 or 40' (she was 27), Goodbody predicted, 'you can't take the strain any longer in a company like this ... You haven't got the physical stamina any more.'

Goodbody's gender was mentioned by some of the reviewers, a few of whom also picked up on the feminist elements. But claims that her *As You Like It* was, as Sheila Hancock put it, 'viciously attacked' (Hancock 172) by the male critical establishment are not borne out by the evidence of the reviews themselves. Herbert Kretzmer of the *Daily Express* (13 June), a paper not renowned for feminist commitments, declared that 'women directors are rare on the British stage ... the production struck not only a mighty blow for women, but for the theatre too'. The production, he urged 'must be brought to London later this year. I cannot recall a happier evening by the Royal Shakespeare Company since Peter Brook's *Midsummer Night's Dream*.' John Elsom titled his review 'Rosalind's Lib', drew attention to Barton's programme essay, and wrote that with the 'focus on Rosalind as a modern liberated woman', Eileen Atkins 'fits this particular bill perfectly' (*Listener*). Benedict Nightingale facetiously suggested that Atkins 'reminds you less of a boy than of Vanessa Redgrave on her way to address a meeting for shepherdess's lib, ban-the-crossbow, or somesuch' (*New Statesman*). For Elsom, the approach was 'misconceived', a 'scamper through an enchanting play in pursuit of an anachronistic moral'; for Nightingale, 'In no way does it penetrate to the essence of Shakespeare ... Still less does the production make fresh, interesting points about "a woman's place" in society.' Gay reports Michael Billington remembering that 'They had great problems with the final scene, because Buzz Goodbody said "I don't believe this'". How do you direct something if you don't fundamentally subscribe to that ideal?' (Gay 65). One solution might have been to have directed deliberately against the grain of the text (as happened at Stratford five years later with Michael Bogdanov's incendiary *The Taming of the Shrew*), but there is little in the critical responses to suggest that Goodbody's treatment of the ending, and of its closing offer of monogamous heterosexual union, was in any way interrogated or subverted. Indeed, some felt that the final scene was, if anything, marked by an excess of positivity; as Robert Cushman saw it, Goodbody 'clearly recognizes the importance of the marriage-theme, but her methods of underlining it are tired. Grinning supers fling confetti into the house, and the audience gamely grins and wishes it would all go away' (*Observer*, 17 June). Perhaps this overstatement was meant to be ironic; if so, the point seems to have been lost.

The one truly discordant note at the end of this production was provided by Pasco's Jaques, who had been a glowering presence throughout. Peter Thomson records that, 'having watched the modern frenzy of the wedding from off the raised stage, he spat out "so, to your pleasures" disconcertingly. It was only with some difficulty that Duke Senior recovered sufficient poise to restart the dance.' 'Against the strength of Pasco's Jaques', Thomson concludes, 'the Duke seemed dangerously sentimental' (Thomson 150). Perhaps this moment also registered some of Goodbody's own reservations about the 'pleasures' afforded by a play whose ending she could not bring herself to believe in, but had not the heart to directly confront.

As a garment that allegedly erases distinctions of class as well as of time and geography, a pair of blue jeans connects performers and audience in a way that costume trousers do not. This sense of a play still rooted in the workaday worlds of its on- and offstage participants bears the imprint of the work that Goodbody had developed with Theatregoround in the previous decade, and would be further developed in the productions at the RSC's new studio theatre, The Other Place, which opened (on 7 April, with Goodbody's *Lear*) the following year. Importantly, the style had not just to do with making Shakespeare contemporary, small and simple, but also, it was hoped, genuinely accessible and popular. The belief that the RSC should reach out, as Peter Hall had delicately put it in 1964, to 'the masses who buy paperbacks' (Hall 48) had been central to the company's mission from the beginning; and in

1974 Trevor Nunn restated this: 'I want an avowed and committed popular theatre ... a socially concerned theatre. A politically aware theatre. In reality not in name' (Addenbrooke 182). By the early 1970s, nonetheless, the sense was widespread that the RSC was both artistically and financially at a low ebb, and that unless it succeeded in cultivating the younger and more socially diverse audiences that Nunn (and Goodbody) saw as vital to its long-term viability, the work would atrophy still further. Outlining the feasibility of a studio theatre in an RSC internal report in December 1973, Goodbody wrote that its 'primary concern' should be 'its development of a wider audience for classical theatre' (Chambers *Inside* 67). Acknowledging that 'we play to an audience largely drawn from the upper and middle classes', she declared: 'We have to broaden that audience for artistic as well as social reasons. We know it'll take years. Unless we make the attempt – classical theatre will become like Glyndebourne' (Chambers *Other Spaces* 34).

Although Goodbody's legacy has been identified with The Other Place and with the studio-scale work that followed in its wake, the one main-stage production for which she was afforded sole directorial credit may be the most achieved instance of the kind of popular (though not political) Shakespeare that she hoped for. Perhaps this was far more achievable (and, to an extent, achieved) in the 1,200-seat RST than in its 200-seat alternative just up the road, and in this respect the production was significant less in relation to the stage history of the play itself than to the RSC's staging of Shakespearean comedy in late 1970s and early 1980s. Goodbody's eclectic opportunism, cheerful vulgarity and liberal appropriation of the conventions of musical theatre created a template that would be developed to much greater effect in the subsequent directorial work of denim-loving Nunn, and that would serve the company well in the increasingly marketized environment of the 1980s. Nunn had absorbed the lessons of Goodbody's *As You Like It* and, in the years that followed, beginning with a contemporary musical-comedy version of *The Comedy of Errors* in 1976, he and others put them into practice. Even those reviewers who disapproved of Goodbody's populism admitted that it was to taste of its (first night) audience, and subsequent attempts to reclaim Goodbody's production from its (alleged) bad press have reiterated this; Gay records that the show 'delighted audiences but dissatisfied critics' (Gay 69), and Dympna Callaghan quotes the *Nottingham Guardian Journal* (14 June 1973) to this effect ('this is pop Shakespeare, and as such will be enjoyed by the non-Shakespeareans in the audience'), concluding: '[t]hat non-Shakespeareans enjoyed the play was no doubt exactly what Goodbody had intended' (Callaghan 170).

If 'no doubt' is itself doubtful, such claims made on behalf of the show's audiences are perhaps less so, given the evidence of audience responses furnished by the reviewers. Gordon Parsons (*Morning Star*, 14 June) found the audience's reaction 'more spontaneous' than that of his colleagues, leaving 'no doubt of their enthusiasm'; *Berrow's Worcester Journal* (14 June) reported that the song-and-dance finale 'provoked such storms of approval that Eileen Atkins had to command silence to deliver the epilogue'. Hurren, however, saw it differently, noting that 'the assembled players, in a final outburst of bizarre jocularity, heave handfuls of confetti over the cringing spectators in the stalls' (*Spectator*), and Cushman, as mentioned, also detected awkwardness and embarrassment rather than unalloyed joy in the audience's 'gamely' grinning (*Observer*). 'This is tourist Shakespeare', wrote Wendy Monk, 'In the coaches and the restaurants it will be talked of. The attractive songs ... and dances ... will be enjoyed by all those non-Shakespeareans who enter the Theatre because it is part of their package tour or day trip to Stratford' (*Stage and Television Today*). Even so, unlike Barton's *King John*, Nunn's *Macbeth* and Peter Gill's *Twelfth Night*, the production did not transfer to the Aldwych, and it closed on 8 December after 59 performances.

This was probably just as well, for the production was dogged by misfortune and appears not to have been a happy one. Suchet only bagged the part of Orlando because he was understudying the 'much more conventionally good-looking' Bernard Lloyd (Gay 67), who injured his ankle in the wrestling match during previews and never returned. In interviews, Goodbody did not refer to her working relationship with Atkins, but, Chambers records, 'her terms of reference were different from those of her leading actress', and two did not get on (Chambers *Other Spaces* 30, 33). When they were interviewed jointly just before the production opened, Atkins declared: 'I don't believe in productions having an "overall conception" or a "line of attack". I just take a part and do it. The most important thing a director can do is to choose the cast and then let them get on with it – although obviously he [*sic*] is responsible for orchestrating the production as a whole .... Stratford has a reputation for "conceptions!"'(*Birmingham Post*, 9 June).

This sideswipe at what was becoming known as 'director's Shakespeare' occurred in the context of growing divisions between actors, directors and scholars over questions of ownership and authority, and of the legitimacy and limits of directorial licence. In 1974, John Russell Brown published his manifesto for a directorless Bard, *Free Shakespeare*, in which he specifically targeted the practice of an RSC intent on reducing 'the baffling to the comprehensible, the old to the new, the complicated to the simple', and advocated an actor-centred alternative 'unfixed by detailed rehearsal and direction' wherein 'the drama would be held together by the structure of its action' (Brown 12, 85). Nunn eventually hit back: '"Free Shakespeare! Banish conceptions. End the tyranny of Directors Theatre. Let the plays speak for themselves." I disagree with these essentially academic slogans' (*Sunday Times* 28 March 1976). Goodbody thought of herself as an actor's director rather than a conceptualist, and she stated that '*As You Like It* is not a piece which is well served by a strong idea. It wouldn't take, let's say, a Brechtian interpretation.' Atkins, however, had a more personal axe to grind. 'I'm getting a bit of a name for being difficult', she confessed, 'I don't think that's quite fair. I'm very good when I'm being directed properly. It's when I'm not, that I get a bit angry.' Whether or not she felt that Goodbody was directing her 'properly' can only be guessed at.

The situation worsened when Atkins tore a ligament during the preview performance on 7 June, and in an interview published three weeks into the run (titled 'Why I was so awful on the first night'), she made her dissatisfaction with the production, with the RSC, and perhaps with Goodbody, evident. 'I thought I was dreadful', she confesses; 'I was appalled by my performance but you cannot give everything when you are in pain.' Because of her injury, Atkins missed three previews, so that she had only given one performance before the first night. 'I like about seven or eight run-throughs of a play before it gets on stage. We had one here. It is just the way they work. It is certainly not the way I work.' Atkins recognized that she was therefore out of sync with the rest of the cast, who were all geared up for a first night that she was unprepared for, and facing an impossible choice between 'going on in a bad way or throwing everyone else out ... I did and took the rap.' Atkins's discontents were not confined to the misfortunes surrounding the opening. The parquet flooring was 'unsafe ... too bouncy, the carpet is too thick', and 'just about everybody' in the company hated it. It epitomized everything that was wrong with the production: 'I like a base that is firm and solid. Actors need that kind of base.' At this point, her interviewer reports, Atkins stamped on the floor and 'knots up a feminine fist. It is an action that is to appear time and again.' She also had some astringent words for her colleagues. 'Everybody is too keen on liking everybody and caring too much about being liked', she stated, 'I know three brilliant directors who are not getting work because they are not nice to everyone' (*Birmingham Sunday Mercury*, 1 July).

Interviewed two decades after the production closed, Atkins's ire was undiminished. Modern dress, she stated, 'is a nightmare for Rosalind': 'The first time I did it in 1973, it was set in a sort of hippyland. Impossible. I kept looking at boys and girls on the street and I decided the only difference was that boys had sideburns and an Adam's apple ... Peggy Ashcroft came to see me to sympathise: "My dear, you can't play Rosalind without a hat and a tree" she said' (Sarah Hemming, *Independent*, 15 April 1992). The sentiment appears to have been taken on board. In the next two productions at Stratford (1977, directed by Nunn; and 1980, directed by Terry Hands, with Susan Fleetwood), hats and trees were once again very much in evidence as the play was sent decisively back in time. In Nunn's production (designed by John Napier) this took the form of pastiche of late seventeenth-century baroque opera that set Kate Nelligan's Rosalind against a backdrop of 'a dotty fairyland of toy bridges, painted brooks and round holes for fishing, and daintily gartered shepherds' (John Peter, *Sunday Times*, 11 September 1977) and equipped her with 'lace and ruffles, floppy boots and a huge feathered hat' (Gay 71). Hands created an Arden 'filled with sky-seeking birches and vulpine howls' (Billington, *Guardian*, 5 April 1980) in which Fleetwood gave the first Rosalind in twenty years to compete with memories of Redgrave.

Well, is this the Forest of Arden?

In 1973 *As You Like It* was marked, as it had been in 1919 and 1961, by an innovative treatment of the stag hunt, one that established another long-standing Stratford performance tradition. Following her 'And I'll sleep' (4.1.191), Celia dozed off in the hammock where she had spent most of the third act, and a 'deerhunt dance' followed, 'neatly presented', according to Jeremy Kingston, one of only two reviewers to mention it, 'as a vision ...

dreamed by Maureen Lipman's Celia' (*Punch*). Kingston did not read anything into this sequence, but Elsom, fleetingly, did: it was a 'fertility dance' that compensated for 'an uninspired treatment of Hymen's arrival' (*Listener*). This was the moment when, Smallwood observes, Goodbody launched 'this apparently innocuous little scene on a career which would give it a place of increasing significance in Celia's psychological, and sexual, development' (Smallwood *As You Like It* 84). It was an isolated moment of theatrical abstraction in a production otherwise predisposed towards realism. Twelve years later, the scene would be given a more pointedly metaphorical colouring in Adrian Noble's production, which was led by Juliet Stevenson as Rosalind, Fiona Shaw as Celia and Alan Rickman as Jaques. This time, the sequence was not so easily missed. Referring to 'the apparent pursuit and shooting of Celia by the huntsmen though she emerges unscathed a few minutes later', an unimpressed Martin Hoyle complained that 'Dream sequences are always a cheat, and here an irrelevance' (*Financial Times*, 25 April 1985). His *FT* colleague, Michael Coveney, thought rather better of it when the production transferred to the Barbican in December, judging 'the foresters' deer hunt' to be 'brilliantly appropriated as a metaphorical "death" of Celia' (18 December 1985).

This was, according to Roger Warren, 'the production's clearest idea': 'The brief hunting episode ... was interpreted as her dream. Jaques drew a bloodstained sheet across her as she slept, and the lords then pursued her around the stage as if she were the hunted deer. She had obviously had an erotic dream, a sexual awakening, and was therefore especially receptive to Oliver on his arrival, a point reinforced by the little laugh of sexual shock at his reference to the snake from which Orlando had saved him' (Warren 116). For Smallwood, this is an example of director's Shakespeare at its most egregious, and he notes that Shaw and Stevenson, in their 'otherwise comprehensive' *Players of Shakespeare* essay on the production (of which more below), are 'curiously ... silent about the episode' (Smallwood *As You Like It* 90). But what is there to say of the gender politics of a sequence that associates an adult woman's sexuality with the onset of menses and with the loss of hymen, and that evidently regards these as a ritual initiation at the hands of 'naturally' predatory men? Given that, as Smallwood records, some reviewers thought 'the scene depicted a gang rape', perhaps Shaw and Stevenson's silence is not curious at all.

The dream sequence was of a piece with a production that, to the irritation of many reviewers, strived hard to advance a strongly conceptualized reading of the play. Addressing the Third Congress of the International Shakespeare Association in Berlin in 1986, shortly after the production closed, Noble attempted to articulate it. Taking as his cue Rosalind's 'Well, this is the Forest of Arden', he states: 'we must ask ourselves what does Rosalind see when she says that line, and what does the audience see?' The beginnings of an answer, Noble suggests, can be found by explicitly disaffiliating the play from its traditionally implied locale: 'So what sort of place is this? It doesn't really strike me as the kind of countryside that those of us who live and work around Stratford-upon-Avon know and love. It's not really Charlecote Park, it's not Chipping Campden' (Noble 335–6). Noble is clear about what his Arden is not ('logs and trees with slightly different lighting effects'), but less forthcoming about what it is: it 'did not simply become a place, but became a process, an idea'; 'this is adolescent country. This is country [sic] where we have terrifying dreams, where we believe that if the girl or boy doesn't love us, we will die' (339). Modesty forbids Noble from claiming outright that, by drastically defoliating and desentimentalizing the play, he had attempted as radical a reinvention of *As You Like It* as Brook had achieved with *Dream*, but the insinuation is in the air.

Noble mentions that the production opened 'to what can certainly be called a controversial press', while claiming that by the time it closed 'it had created for itself a very unusual and loyal audience' (335). The production was, at Stratford, certainly much disliked, both for its strong directorial vision and, as its means of delivering it, its refusal to grant the visual pleasures traditionally associated with the play. As the audience took their seats, they were faced with a court that consisted of a bare stage equipped only with a grandfather clock, some high-backed chairs, and long white sheets, and dominated by a large circular mirror-frame set into the upstage wall. While waiting for the play to start, there was plenty to ponder in the programme, which laid out the production's announced terms of reference in the form of a collage of excerpts and quotations overlaid onto moody monochrome shots of the principals (title: 'The Forest Within'). Where the programme for the 1961 production is simply informative and that for 1973 carefully expository, this is, like the set, allusive, imagistic and suggestive. Early modern texts (Robert Greene, Thomas Lodge,

Thomas Campion, Robert Herrick, *Venus and Adonis*) are juxtaposed with works of canonical modernism (T. S. Eliot's 'Burnt Norton'; Robert Frost's 'The Road not Taken') and extracts from Marina Warner's study of Joan of Arc (on cross-dressing) and Jan Kott's 'Shakespeare's Bitter Arcadia'. Prominent amidst this collage is a quotation from Jung:

> The dream is the little hidden door in the innermost and most secret recesses of the psyche ... There are indications that at least a part of the psyche is not subject to the laws of space and time ... [W]e must face the fact that our world, with its time, space, and causality, relates to another order of things lying behind or beneath it, in which neither 'here and there' nor 'earlier and later' are of importance. (Jung *Collected Works* 9 123)

The programme also cites Jung on the concepts of persona ('that which one in reality is not, but which oneself as well as others think one is') and, in attention-grabbing capitals: ANIMA and ANIMUS, or, respectively, 'PERSONIFICATION OF THE FEMININE NATURE OF A MAN'S UNCONSCIOUS' and 'PERSONIFICATION OF THE MASCULINE NATURE OF A WOMAN'S UNCONSCIOUS' (Jung *Memories* 211). The world of this production was certainly not Chipping Campden, and there was more than enough to alert the spectator to an emphatically non-literal reading of the play, to one that dealt in emblem, abstraction and archetype rather than the default position of mainstream Shakespearean performance, then as now, emotional realism. If all this risked seeming portentous, an extract from in interview with the gender-bending pop star Marilyn for the teen magazine *Just Seventeen*, on his daily cross-dressing routine, sought to locate the concepts of anima and animus on the known grounds of popular culture. To add further grist to the mill, the Berger quote ('Men look at women. Women watch themselves being looked at') was recycled, and the programme connected the production's gender preoccupations with contemporary eco-feminist and, in this instance, anti-nuclear agendas, with an excerpt from novelist Ian McEwan's introduction to his libretto for Michael Berkeley's eco-feminist, anti-nuclear oratorio *Or Shall We Die?*, which had been performed by the London Symphony Chorus two years previously ('one could characterize these two world-views, the Newtonian and that of the new physics [as] Shall there be womanly times, or shall we die?').

Presumably no irony was intended in the juxtaposition of the McEwan quotation with a full-page spread declaring the support of the production's corporate sponsor, Phillips Petroleum, and the programme also featured an appeal to an element of its audience that had by the mid-1980s become vital to the RSC's survival: 'For many companies sponsorship as a service to the community is its own reward; but as part of an overall marketing or public affairs programme, a properly planned sponsorship commitment to the RSC can also provide positive commercial benefits. The RSC has a larger, socially broader and geographically wider audience than any other arts organization, so your company's name will be seen by the greatest possible number of people.' This is followed by a list of patrons than runs from Amoco (UK) Limited to Texaco Ltd, few of whom would have much truck, I suspect, with 'womanly times'. No matter: as a total package, with its gallimaufry of cool graphic style, pop-cultural savvy, arthouse reference points, yesterday's scholarship, liberal-progressive identity politics, and a double invocation of cultural philanthropy and commercial nous, the programme for this *As You Like It* concisely articulated both the production's and the RSC's position in the 1980s theatrical marketplace.

Moment by moment, and scene by scene, the production was visually striking, and, in this respect at least, consistently conceived. The play began with wind effects and the distant rumble of drums, with Adam and Orlando in silhouette: the scene between Orlando and Oliver was played front cloth, the former (Hilton McCrae) in plebeian donkey jacket, the latter (Bruce Alexander) in city-trader suit and bowler hat; at the end of Oliver's dialogue with Charles, the wind swelling and a crash of thunder merged with a fanfare as the drapes parted to reveal Duke Frederick's court. The brash brass of the fanfare segued into the melancholy sweetness of minor-key flute and strings as Rosalind (Juliet Stevenson), another dark silhouette, glided onstage, crossed to the mirror centre, removed the white cloth draped over it and wrapped it round herself (it came off on 'I will forget the condition of my estate to rejoice in yours' (1.2.12–13)). Contemporary but with a vaguely Edwardian air, the court was formal, repressed and oppressive, sparsely populated by city types in evening dress sipping from champagne flutes; Rosalind and Celia wore debutante ballgowns. In the stage manager's notes held in the production files, these are referred to as their 'Hinge and Bracket' outfits, a reference to the long-running drag duo George Logan and Patrick Fyffe. Their act, as the eccentric dowagers Dr Evadne Hinge and Dame Hilda Bracket, consisted of high-camp renderings of parlour songs and selections from light opera, punctuated by waspish repartee and mild doubles entendres. The jokey construction of Rosalind/Stevenson and Celia/Shaw as surrogate male female impersonators in this phase of the play adds an intriguing new layer to its exploration of cross-dressing. Touchstone (Nicky Henson) was in tails and whiteface. Braziers were brought on and lit for the wrestling, and these remained in place in Arden for the exiled Duke and his followers to warm themselves; Charles was a poseur in a red silk dressing-gown who played mean and dirty, head-butting Orlando without warning before the fight started and only conceding defeat after a drawn-out, pantomime-style bout. Orlando arrived to wrestle in exceedingly skimpy leather briefs that revealed a good deal of buttock and that (at least during the performance recorded for the archive video) excited a fair amount of ribald juvenile laughter.

The banishment took place in the same cloth-draped space, and the transition from the end of this scene to the next – the move to the 'forest' – was effected by an act of theatrical sleight-of-hand that foregrounded the thematics of mirroring, doubling and metamorphosis. Repeating the gesture performed in Rosalind's opening mime, malign Duke Frederick (Joseph O'Conor) gathered a sheet around himself, walked through the suddenly glassless mirror frame (at once through the looking glass, down the rabbit hole and via Jung's 'little hidden door'), into Arden, and into his role as his benign alter ego, Duke Senior; at the same moment, the grandfather clock stopped its ponderous ticking, and its clock-face disappeared (there's no clock, of course, in the forest). The doubling (mirrored by the court lords, who likewise donned sheets to become foresters), Noble claimed, was the 'crucial decision' (Noble 337), from which the entire conception developed. With the floor and court furniture now fully covered and overlooked by a cyclorama moon, from which – at Rosalind, Celia and Touchstone's arrival in Arden – was pulled yards and yards of sheeting that gathered into a great tower of cloth centre stage, Arden was a schematic wintry nowhere, a 'landscape country of the mind', as Michael Ratcliffe, clocking the programme quotations from Jung, Frost, Eliot and McEwan, put it (*Observer*, 28 April): a space of transformation, identity games and role-play. During the first half, the sheeting remained in place, becoming a huge, spreading train for Rosalind's entry to the forest ('Well, *this* is the Forest of Arden'

(2.4.11)) that turned into a turbulent snowscape and the tree on which Orlando pinned his verses.

After the interval (taken at the end of 2.7), the sheeting had largely gone, revealing a mossy floor, furniture and a clock that had also turned green. At the front of the stage there was now a shallow pool of water into which, inevitably, Touchstone tumbled during the contretemps with William, and in which, more affectingly, Orlando found, in the liquid reflection of the Rosalind/Ganymede, who stood behind him gazing likewise into the water, hands on his shoulders, the cause to cry 'I can live no longer by thinking' (5.2.46). Phoebe (Lesley Manville) and Silvius (Roger Hyams) made their first entrance from beneath the silk, as did Oliver Martext (Griffith Jones); Rosalind wrapped herself in it on 'now I am in a holiday humour' – and then, breath-catchingly, allowed it to fall open on 'and like enough to consent' (4.1.60–1). In the last scene the sheets gathered up again to form 'the billowing roof of a tented pavilion for the final unravelling of the knot' (Hoyle, *Financial Times*), which parted for Hymen's entry (achieved here by a boomingly amplified voiceover) to disclose the moon once more, now stained pinkish-red, a sky-blue cyclorama, and the mirror from the first scenes. The play had come full circle, and in a move that reprised Duke Frederick/Senior's transition from the court to the forest, Jaques made *his* exit into a life of contemplation through the empty mirror frame. With a snap, its glass reappeared; the clock resumed its slow ticking. The dream was over.

As mentioned earlier, the sheeting was also the key component in Celia's own dream sequence. At the end of 4.1 she fell asleep centre stage; the lights dimmed, and, accompanied by pounding drums, Jacques entered and crossed diagonally, trailing a long, bloodstained cloth which dragged across Celia's face, causing her to start to her feet. To the sound of offstage hunting horns, she ran forward and sideways into a faintly menacing group of cloth-wielding forest lords; a shot was fired, cheers went up, and the sheeting momentarily washed crimson before turning white again. This episode was both difficult to read (I subjected the archive video to repeated viewings of this section, and I am still none the wiser) and, for at least one reviewer, representative of the production's stylistic and conceptual incoherence; as Hoyle put it, Noble had 'no overall vision beyond trying out a number of gimmicky ideas' (*FT*).[3] The production did have some admirers (the *Daily Telegraph*'s John Barber thought it 'an *As You Like It* for our generation ... an evening to delight the heart' (24 April), and Barney Bardsley of *Tribune* found 'seeds of greatness here' (3 May)), but in general the reviewers were divided between those who professed themselves mystified by the staging and those who found it all too obvious. It is probably not surprising that a Stratford production, opening on 23 April, that was described by Ratcliffe as 'as near to abstract Shakespeare as you are likely to find in any theatre this side of Brussels, Bochum or Cologne' (*Observer*), was not going to win friends easily, and terms such as 'fatiguingly perverse' (Kenneth Hurren, *Mail on Sunday*, 28 April) and 'perversely judged' (Jack Tinker, *Daily Mail*, 24 April) were the stock-in-trade of a right-wing press that had the still generously state-subsidized RSC very much in its sights. Meanwhile the Stratford *Herald*, dogged as ever in its determination to find an angle, articulated a more local – if inexplicable – sense of grievance, reporting that 'if the Forest of Arden in Shakespeare's *As You Like It* is, as commonly supposed, a state of mind, RSC director Adrian Noble needs either analysis or to move from his lodgings over the chip shop next to the bingo hall' (3 May).

It is easy not to grant too much time to complaints about an *As You Like It* lacking in woodland ('not a tree is in sight' fumed Hurren), but the charges of muddled thinking and stylistic inconsistency are more likely to stick. Michael Billington, a reviewer more inclined than most to afford an adventurous director the benefit of the doubt ('better a production with a concept than a bland retread'), conceded that the 'reading' was 'highly original' but thought it uncertainly executed: 'the conception behind this production is sound ... But, at the moment, it simply isn't being fleshed out by the two main performers' (*Guardian* 25 April). Characterizing the *mise en scène* as a scheme imposed upon the play and its actors by director and designer, other critics set the production more decisively against those who were given the task of delivering it. Thus, Tinker declared, it was 'not Juliet Stevenson's fault that her Rosalind is in a sexual limbo far from Shakespeare's making', while Henson's Touchstone 'cuts through these awesome miscalculations with some genuine muscular comedy' (*Daily Mail*) ; for Hoyle, 'Stevenson's warmth and common sense operate in a vacuum' (*FT*). Still, through the red mist of reviewers' anger with Noble, glimpses of the principal performances can be seen. 'Juliet Stevenson ... manages some romantic rapture', conceded Hurren, 'and Fiona Shaw ... a debby sophistication.' Tinker also praised Shaw for 'the sort of spunky glamour that has turned Sloane Rangers into memsahibs from generation to generation'. Billington offered more detail: Rosalind was 'an almost Chaplinesque figure in bowler, scarlet braces and baggy white pants', opposite an Orlando 'rather like an androgynous Scottish Mick Jagger', while Celia was 'beautifully played as a slightly woozy Mitfordesque deb who turns to mantras and meditation in the forest'. Ratcliffe admired McCrae's 'tousled' Orlando ('scruffy, humorous, brave and enormously likeable, if in need of a bath' (*Observer*)), but Tinker, who thought that he 'wrestles magnificently and speaks verse with a tin ear', did not. The performance that divided opinion the most was Rickman's Jaques. John Barber found him 'debonair and melancholy' (*Telegraph*), and Martin Hoyle, 'intelligent, sardonic – even faintly threatening', though he felt that 'the seven ages of man are milked, mimicked, mimed and generally pulled about for effect' (*FT*). Ratcliffe went further: 'Mr Rickman leaves the field of history standing for the outrageous contrivance of his 'Seven Ages of Man.'

The suspicion in some quarters that the production had been worked out in advance and then forced upon its actors is a standard reaction to the alleged evils of director's Shakespeare, and one that had found lucid articulation the year before *As You Like It* opened in actor Simon Callow's anti-directorial manifesto in his *Being an Actor*: 'the theatre has become colonized by a determined group of: the directors ... It is they who run the theatres, they who determine policy, they who put the stamp of their personality on the production itself, the end result of all our labours.' 'The important thing', Callow concludes, 'is to restore the writer ... and the actor to each other ... We don't need an interpreter – we speak the same language: or at least we used to' (Callow 217, 221). Mindful, perhaps, of such criticisms, Noble's conference talk characterizes the evolution of the production as a collaborative and developmental process, leading to a show whose essential shape and character were collectively determined and agreed upon: the first-person plural is conscientiously deployed throughout ('we made the first crucial decision'; 'we could immediately make comparisons between court and court' (Noble 337, 338)), and the narrative of rehearsal unfolds as a journey of unplanned discovery ('we started seeing oppositions, we started seeing mirrors at work within the play' (338)). Countering those who might accuse him of imposing a vision or pursuing an agenda, Noble ends: 'I have come to no conclusions because my business is not coming to conclusions.' 'My business', he disingenuously states, 'is putting people on in public places and telling stories' (342).

In most instances, so far as the RSC is concerned, there are few ways of knowing whether or not to take a director's account of the conception and development of a production at his word. For Noble's *As You Like It*, however, there is a range of evidence relating to the production process, both published and unpublished, that, without necessarily contradicting or conflicting with them, at once supports, challenges and complicates the director's pronouncements. First, the unpublished material: the production records of *As You Like It* are unusual, at least in my experience of the Stratford archive, in that they contain a very full and frank set of stage-management notes, initiated on the first day of rehearsal (6 February) and sustained through to the get-in on 6 April, when the show moved from the rehearsal room to the theatre. The stage manager, David M. Harvey, documents the making of the show in detail, tracing as he does so the progressive, accumulative and iterative nature of the work, the ideas that were proposed, tested and discarded as well as those which carried through into the show. Harvey is one of those whom Peter Holland has termed the 'lost workers' in the performance archive, and without doubt one of those whose normally invisible work generates, as Holland puts it, 'a sound that makes one stop to listen, to hope for further traces, to yearn to know the voice's owner' (Holland '*The Lost Workers*' 7). An early note (7 February) records that in 1.1 'Adam will probably be sitting on a bale or similar. Possibly some activity relating to apples but then again, not too naturalistic!' The following day, 'There will be a long thin lake on the forestage. This seems to raise the possibility of fishing ("traditional!"), this is all we know about the set for the second half (except it's getting on for spring).' Bales, apples and fishing rods were subsequently dismissed, and on 12 February Harvey notes that 'the second half will probably begin as the first half does with the forestage covered: This will slide apart to reveal the stream for 12a [3.2]. The subsequent scenes will then use a large piece of fabric that has covered the stage (ie like the cloth in the first half) which will then be suspended from the flys [*sic*] in different configurations to become what we will!' Harvey warns, ominously: 'this is all extremely nebulous at the moment'.

My suspicion that Harvey – at least in the early stages – was not entirely convinced by Noble and Crowley's non-realist scenic aesthetic (registered, perhaps, in those curiously emphatic exclamation marks) is strengthened by a note dated 25 February, reflecting on the difficult scene change between 3.2 and 3.3: 'This raises the tricky question of where the poems for Rosalind are attached without the subsequent scene changes affecting them.' 'Dare one suggest', he drily proposes, 'a tree?' Here and elsewhere, Harvey seems to cast himself as Sancho Panza to Noble's Don Quixote (or as Steward to his Timon), quietly and patiently undercutting the director's more extravagant and impractical ideas. 'Adrian has said it will be possible to swing on the silk', he records on 8 March; 'Could we confirm this please 'cos it sounds like a bad idea.' Two weeks later (27 March), 'the swing idea appears to have been elbowed. Now we are into the snake charmer image; that is, Ros (who has entered through the trap) playing pipes.' Yet, on 2 April, 'Adrian is still talking about swinging or pivoting on the trapeze but is convinced all this will be resolved on site.' Harvey drolly continues: 'I'm not sure he's entirely aware of the limitations.'

The first provisional props and furniture list (dated 24 February) has 'Twelve ten chairs/Grandfather clock without a face/Cheval mirror without the glass/6 black men's umbrellas/parasol/bale for Adam and Orlando to sit on'. The 'clock with no face' is, for Harvey, a problem: 'well, apparently', he irritably writes on 11 March, 'the clock will be going again in sc 21 [5.4] so it must have a face. Discussion please!' Discussion evidently took place, as the next day (12 March) Harvey notes: 'the grandfather clock starts with a face then becomes faceless when the mirror disappears. The reverse happens in sc 21.' The updated prop and furniture list (18 March) thus reads '10 chairs/grandfather clock with reversible face, one blank, one real/Cheval mirror with facility for glass in/out'. The deer-killing scene also changed between initial conception and eventual delivery. The earliest scene-by-scene props list has for scene 16, 'We've killed a deer' (4.2), the note: 'props – a deer (!)', a later (undated) version, 'props – a deer?' By 15 March, this has given way to 'Adrian would like three practical guns for the deer-killing scene. Also, a very blood stained sheet for Alec [Alexander Wilson, First Court/Forest Lord] to be wrapped in.' On 20 March, this becomes 'Killing the deer: 2 revolvers, one practical used by Alec Wilson.'

Harvey was not the only member of the stage management team to feel occasionally wrong-footed by seemingly impossible directorial demands. On 20 February he wrote, apropos the court furniture, 'Duplicates green required for 2nd half. Clock to have a blank face. Mirrors to be just a frame, no glass in it. Substitutes required in rehearsals as soon as possible!!!' Handwritten in the margin, signed 'S.M.', is the comment 'I'm pale with shock!' 'S. M.' is assistant stage manager Sara Myett, another of the 'lost workers' of this production, who is credited in the programme but thereafter disappears from the RSC records, perhaps irredeemably traumatized by the experience of Noble's production. Yet another can be traced through the last of the eight 'crucial reminders' on the show running list: 'Buy Alison [Alison Owen, deputy stage manager] a cup of tea.' The third reminder is of the type one would expect to be of more immediate interest to historians of the play in performance: 'When Juliet comes down from her D. Room check she has locket on.' I pause to consider the connection between Alison's tea and Rosalind's locket, less, I stress, to suggest an equivalence between them than for what they reveal (on this production, in 1985) both about the RST (and subsequently the Barbican Theatre) as workplaces, and about Stevenson's work as an actor. If Harvey's rehearsal notes document a ground-level perspective on a process that is contested, improvised and negotiated, the running list belongs to a space of urgently timebound mutual endeavour in which the tasks of the actor are facilitated through a collectively shared work of memory. It is as much Alison Owen's and David Harvey's responsibility to remember the locket that Rosalind must give to Orlando in 1.2 as it is Juliet Stevenson's; but this is no less important than the maintenance of the backstage regime of reciprocal courtesy, respect, obligation and small acts of kindness. The note also precisely illustrates the workings of what Evelyn Tribble defines as the cognitive ecology of the playhouse (here, late rather than early modern, but the point equally applies), whereby remembering is distributed throughout the workplace system, not stored in the head of the individual actor (Tribble 151–2).

With this in mind I turn from unpublished to published alternative perspectives on the production: the two essays written, respectively, by Fiona Shaw and Juliet Stevenson, and by Alan Rickman, on their experience of playing Celia, Rosalind and Jaques, for the second volume of the *Players of Shakespeare* series. This series,

4 Phoebe (Lesley Manville), Rosalind (Juliet Stevenson) and Celia (Fiona Shaw), Royal Shakespeare Company, 1985

part of the expanding field of practitioner discourse, has been subjected to searching scrutiny by Cary M. Mazer, who writes of how actors' narratives almost invariably deploy established tropes (including, frequently, the journey) to explicate the work of developing a Shakespearean role. The actor, Mazer writes, 'goes on a journey that arrives at the performance; and in performance the journey that the character makes across the breadth of the play takes the actor playing that character along on that journey, from which the actor learns even more about him- or herself' (Mazer 'Sense/Memory/Sense-Memory' 330). This is certainly the case with Shaw and Stevenson's jointly -authored essay. Their act of co-creation, uniquely in the series, both asserts the primacy of the Rosalind–Celia relationship and is a feminist gesture of sisterhood, a riposte to those whose 'relish of that friendship is based on the actresses' working in *spite* of each other – the kind of traditional "feminine behaviour" that is based on divisiveness rather than bonding' (Shaw and Stevenson 57). Like Alison's note, their joint authorship also implicitly articulates the relational, interactive nature of their (indeed all) acting work, as well as the distributive cognitive ecology that sustains it: Rosalind and Celia come into being *between* Stevenson, Shaw and their acting colleagues (see Figure 4).

The production, they state at the outset, was a 'voyage of discovery' which 'led us into a terrain more demanding, exhilarating, and enriching than either of us had previously known' (55). At the end, 'Like Rosalind and Celia, what we encountered was a journey' (71). The nature of that journey and of the terrain it traverses are, however, not at all clearly defined in their account. This is in part because they set themselves at odds both with Noble's conceptualization of Arden and with his (or the play's) reassertion of patriarchal values in its final scene, which, 'at the end of a play which so fully and radically explores the complexities of sexuality, maleness and femaleness, and sends gender boundaries flying, was endlessly difficult to play' (70). Noble and Crowley's design was, they report, endlessly debated; though supportive of the decision to 'reject the traditional conception of Arden as a kind of theatrical arcadia' (did such a 'traditional conception' *really* still exist? in 1985?), and willing to entertain the idea that this Arden was 'a metaphor', they pose the awkward – and possibly unanswerable – question: 'a metaphor for *what* exactly?' Disposing of the audience's imagined 'rustic expectations' meant that 'to make coherent the metaphor which replaces them became the production's most difficult challenge to itself. If it is a realm of the imagination, then of *whose* imagination?' Worse still, 'one cannot *act* with a metaphor, and the inhabitants of Arden must be allowed space and light' (63–4). Shaw and Stevenson note that the problems posed by the setting were to an extent alleviated when the production transferred to the Barbican in December and the white silks (and, perhaps, the metaphor) were made less obtrusive. It is worth recording that David Harvey notes on 20 November that Noble was toying with the idea of 'using a large mirror to represent the water', and that (mercifully) the proposal was ditched. But their main solution to these challenges was to develop emotional-realist character performances of Celia and Rosalind that, to use their own terminology, worked largely *in spite of* the production's ruling ideas rather than with them. The stag-killing sequence does not register at all in their account because it is utterly irrelevant to Shaw–Celia's journey; in their text, she falls for Oliver instantly because of her 'realisation of Rosalind's emotional absence': at the end of 4.1, 'Rosalind has abandoned all sensibility in relation to her cousin, and Celia is alone' (69).

The actors acknowledge that they are working against the grain of the script here and that, as with Rosalind's instantaneous passion for Orlando, 'falling in love at first sight presented us with a problem, as actresses, because it seems so often to require the abandoning of one's own experience to some Elizabethan stage convention' (60). Shaw and Stevenson nonetheless made these moments plausible and playable, in ways that are not in the least unusual for actors schooled in the methods of late twentieth-century emotional realist performance; more broadly, the choices that are made necessarily cohere with the larger intertwined trajectories of both parts. Shaw and Stevenson's essay is certainly a richly detailed, nuanced exposition of this approach in action: among numerous examples of imaginative readings of individual moments are their understanding of their first exchange ('there is a sense of urgency about their respective declarations which suggests that the situation for them both is gathering momentum over time, not easing with it' (58)); their recognition that 'for a play that seems primarily about *feelings*, it in fact allows the actors little space to indulge in these, for the drive forward springs constantly from the *thinking* which propels the action' (62); and their animation of Celia's vast stretches of silence in the fourth and fifth acts: '"Good sir, go with us" [4.3.175] – is her last line in the play, and the two women never speak to each other again … That Rosalind chooses to make her final entrance not alone, but with Celia, gave us a welcome opportunity to make contact with each other again, and afforded us a brief moment to resolve the journey the two women have travelled together.' The journey is not resolved, for 'it is Duke Senior who takes charge' (70). Nonetheless, the essay moves to a closure that is, in the way of such narratives, redemptive, recording how the actors 'found it a play of wondrous delights but formidable complexity', but considered themselves 'lucky that the production gave us, finally, the space in which to draw upon our own experience, our own humour, and our own lunacies, passions, and sensibilities – and, primarily, upon our own friendship' (71). It is the 'finally' that, probably unintentionally, resonates, indicating that the convergence of actors' and characters' journeys was eventual, hard-won and partial, achieved in spite of the production rather than because of it.

A different perspective on the direction and design is provided by Alan Rickman's essay in the same *Players of Shakespeare* volume. Rickman is emphatic that his account is his alone, '*my* version of the thoughts and decisions made between Adrian Noble, the other actors and myself' (Rickman 75). He opens with a Callow-style broadside, declaring that the play is 'a result of particular individuals playing the roles than of directorial schemes', stating that 'you can dress *As You Like It* in any clothes ... or slip and slide on white silk as we did', and affirming his 'love–hate relationship with white silk' (73). Recourse to the archive video suggests that the slipping and sliding is not merely figurative, and that the 'love–hate' relationship may have been more of the latter than the former. In a small but revealing moment, Rickman enters at a run, for the 'fool in the forest' aria (2.7.12–34), catches his shoe on the sheet that covers the stage – and skids, stumbles, and almost falls flat on his face before nimbly regaining his footing. I cannot know whether this near-trip was a one-off, serendipitously documented as part of the one performance that survives in the archive, whether it and incidents like it happened frequently, or even whether the stumble was intended, choreographed and executed at every performance (the promptbook reveals nothing), but to me it looks like an actor seriously at risk of falling over rather than an actor playing someone at risk of falling over. Impressively, Rickman instantaneously recovers his sang-froid and delivers a note-perfect rendition of the passage, but I cannot imagine that his work was facilitated by a set that was an obstacle to be negotiated rather than a world to inhabit, or a secure platform on which to stand. Still, Rickman is reasonably positive about the experience, writing that the production 'did ask us to lay ourselves on the line' and that he was encouraged to develop a Jaques 'who is perceptive but passionate, vulnerable but anarchic, and a man whose means of expressing these qualities was completely unpredictable' (75). He is with Noble on the production's 'devoted fans', among them 'school parties to whom Shakespeare had previously meant exams and boredom' (73). Yet, at the end, 'Jaques is just running on the spot': poignantly, 'you are left with an image of complete aloneness, mirrored, incidentally, by the fact that the actor walks into the wings and twiddles his thumbs while everyone else is dancing' (78). The isolation of Jaques as a character, and also perhaps Rickman as an actor, could not be better expressed.

Forever and a day

The RSC has staged eight productions of *As You Like It* since Noble's. None is completely devoid of interest, but, equally, none is sufficiently distinctive or historically significant to merit sustained inspection. John Caird's 1989 production had a setting that self-referentially rendered Duke Frederick's court as a mirror of the art-deco foyer of the Royal Shakespeare Theatre, and a gawky, daft-as-a-bottle-of-crisps Rosalind (Sophie Thompson), who divided opinion between those who thought her irresistible and those who found her very, very irritating. In 1992, director David Thacker and designer Johan Engels amplified the contrast between totalitarian court and idyllic Arden by styling the former as a 'lacquered mausoleum' (James Christopher, *Time Out*, 29 April 1992), and equipping the 'fully forested' latter with 'a glade that slopes over the stage edge down into a rustic pool' (Irving Wardle, *The Times*, 26 April 1992), in which, once again, Touchstone got a dunking. The production opened in the shadow of the hugely acclaimed all-male Cheek by Jowl production (see Chapter V); with relief, Charles Spencer (*Daily Telegraph*, 24 April) welcomed 'a traditional staging, sumptuously designed and costumed, with not a gimmick in sight', and (voicing the general view), in Samantha Bond, 'a delight as Rosalind'. This was perhaps not despite but because of the fact that, like almost every RSC actor in the role since Redgrave, Bond, with her 'clinging open-necked shirt and trousers cut as if to positively emphasise her femininity' (David Murray, *Financial Times*, 24 April), 'scarcely cuts a masculine dash at all and sounds forever girlish' (Nicholas de Jongh, *Evening Standard*, 23 April). This was the production that prompted Robert Smallwood to wonder whether he could find anything in it worth writing about, and to conclude that it 'provided a very pertinent example, worth contemplating, of a certain kind of skillful, highly professional Shakespeare production, satisfying audiences' expectations of a big "show", full of sound and fury, signifying ... not a great deal' ('Shakespeare at Stratford-upon-Avon, 1992' 349).

Four years later, Russell Jackson found Stephen Pimlott's production 'strangely muted', recording an 'aluminum-box' court that gave way to an Arden 'red in tooth in claw', epitomized by the 'genuine-looking carcass' that was 'dragged on for the blooding of a hunter' in 4.2, ultimately resolving itself in 'bland niceness'. The production was notable chiefly for the Stratford debut of three actors who would go on to become major stars. Victoria Hamilton's 'entrancing' Phoebe caught the attention of Nicholas de Jongh, who thought that she and Joseph Fiennes as 'a chronically love-sick Silvius' could have been cast in the leading roles (*Evening Standard*, 26 April 1996). Ian Shuttleworth and Robert Butler agreed: for the former, reviewing the Barbican transfer, they 'totally overshadowed' Cusack and Cunningham (*Financial Times*, 26 October); for the latter, at Stratford, Fiennes and Hamilton 'could just as well swap parts with the tousled Liam Cunningham and the earnest Niamh Cusack' (*Independent on Sunday*, 12 May). Their prayers were soon answered: Hamilton went on to play an acclaimed Rosalind at the Sheffield Crucible and Lyric Hammersmith in 2000,[4] and in 1998 Fiennes became Romeo and Orlando rolled into one as the lovelorn bard in the film *Shakespeare in Love*. As Touchstone, David Tennant was, simply, 'brilliant' for Jackson ('Shakespeare in Stratford-upon-Avon' 209), a sentiment that was widely shared. Scots-accented, sardonic and ferociously intelligent, kitted out as 'a red-suited, cap-and-bells court jester like an illustration from an old Complete Works' (Smallwood 'Shakespeare Performances in England' 206), he was 'a manic melancholic who would be quite at home on the alternative comedy circuit' (Spencer, *Daily Telegraph*, 24 April) and whose 'dialogue with Corin is one of the best pieces of Shakespearean clowning you're likely to see: actual Shakespeare jokes being actually funny' (Robert Hanks, *Evening Standard*, 28 October).

In 1997, the election of Tony Blair's first Labour government by a landslide coincided with a foundation of the Countryside Alliance, a campaigning organization dedicated, amongst other things, to the defence and promotion of 'field sports' (that is, fox-hunting and deer-stalking). By 2000, the group had become increasingly belligerent in its opposition to what it saw as the hostility of a left-liberal metropolitan elite to rural priorities and values; in addition to criticism of the government's handling of the ongoing crisis in the agriculture industry, there was considerable anger over its plans, announced in the 1997 election manifesto, to allow a free vote on a ban on fox-hunting. Observing that 'the play suddenly looked more topical than at almost any time since the 1590s', Michael Dobson records that the RSC's response to this new-found urgency in the form of Gregory Doran's 2000 production was 'a critical disaster' ('Shakespeare Performances in England 2000' 267, 271).[5] Designed by the textile artist Kaffe

Fassett, the production imagined the flight into Arden as a dream-journey into the fabulously colourful tapestry that Rosalind (Alexandra Gilbreath) was seen weaving in the black-and-white court of the first act, prompting Michael Billington to quip that Rosalind's exit-line at the end of 1.3 should take the fugitives 'to Liberty's and not to banishment' (*Guardian*, 25 March).

Gregory Thompson's 2003 production fared little better. It opened on 20 March under the cloud of artistic director Adrian Noble's precipitate departure from the RSC – just as his radical and deeply controversial structural reforms of the company began to implode – as part of a season that, launching Michael Boyd's tenure as Noble's successor, consisted of five productions in the RST (which Noble had earmarked for demolition), two in The Other Place, and five in The Swan, *As You Like It* being one of them. There was, at least, a new twist to the deer hunt. Celia (Naomi Frederick) became the deer, crumpling to the floor to be scooped up and carried aloft by the huntsmen. Frederick was this production's find: 'delightful ... touching, funny and full of vitality' (Charles Spencer, *Daily Telegraph*, 22 March), she would, according to Patrick Carnegy, have made a better Rosalind than the generally not-much-admired Nina Sosanya. Frederick duly went on to play an admired Rosalind at Shakespeare's Globe in 2009.

In 2005, Dominic Cooke directed the first almost-unanimously acclaimed production of *As You Like It* in a decade. Restarting an argument that was at least twenty years old, Charles Spencer arrived 'with some trepidation': 'I was taking my son Edward with me and didn't relish the idea of his first visit to Stratford being spoilt by some gimcrack production in which a director flaunts his ego at the expense of the play' (*Daily Telegraph*, 19 August). He need not have worried, as it was 'an utter delight'. Harking back to Negri's décor for the 1961 production, Cooke set the play (designed by Rae Smith) under the boughs of an enormous spreading tree (a chorus of 'Under the greenwood tree' opened the show), coated in snow for the court scenes, gradually thawing as the green world of Arden took hold, which then moved through springtime to summer. A real stag was back on the menu, supplying blood for the huntsmen to smear their faces in an Iron John initiation ritual; and, as in Noble's version, Duke Frederick (Jonathan Newth) and his men became Duke Senior and his entourage, here by swathing themselves in furs, which they shed as the sunshine broke through. Performances across the board were praised: Lia Williams as

Rosalind was 'large-hearted and rapturous, but, when needs be, subtler too' (Benedict Nightingale, *The Times*, 19 August), 'ardent, impulsive, reckless' (Michael Billington, *Guardian*, 19 August), capable of 'mischief, sexual electricity and nervy impetuosity ... and sudden moments of melting tenderness' (*Telegraph*). In a production in which 'every sexual boundary is probed' (Susan Irvine, *Sunday Telegraph*, 21 August), Williams's gender identity was beguilingly fluid, prompting the *Daily Mail*'s Quentin Letts to confess ('at the risk of being given life membership of the gay group Stonewall') that he found her 'actually a good deal prettier in her manly guise ... disconcertingly fancia-ble and coquettish in her boyish mode' (18 August). Although Letts's limp gag presumes that both he and his far-from-gay-friendly readership know that he at least is, *of course*, as straight as straight can be, it is a sign of how far sexual attitudes have shifted that he makes the joke at all; even in the world of the *Mail*, there is some recognition that heterosexuality is neither universal nor mandatory.

Michael Boyd's 2009 production inspired no such enthusiasm, being received for the most part as at best adequate: described as 'modest' and 'underwhelming' (Neil Norman, *Daily Express*, 29 April), it was 'short on easy charm' (Charles Spencer, *Daily Telegraph*, 30 April) and 'not quite the knockout you want it to be' (Dominic Maxwell, *The Times*, 34 April). The RSC had now moved into the temporary Courtyard theatre while the RST was being reconstructed, and the platform-stage setting was nondescript, consisting of bleached wood panelling for the court that opened up for the forest, revealing, to Carol Chillington Rutter's astonishment, 'the carcass of a deer hung by its hooves', called out of the place to which it had been retired 90 years earlier: 'Who in their right mind would restore that cliché?' ('Shakespeare Performances in England 2009' 346). Katy Stephens was Rosalind, strait-laced in a severe high-necked black frock for the court scenes, sporting a pencil moustache and little goatee for Arden, that lent her a faintly cavalier or piratical air. I happened to see the production three times, first at Stratford in 2009, then at the Roundhouse during the London transfer in spring 2011, and then again at Stratford in the summer, at the last-ever performance in the Courtyard. It grew on me and was not unmemorable, not least for Mariah Gale making Celia's silence in the wooing scenes completely compelling, and, less happily, for the decision to have Martext as a Northern Irish pastor who emerged from a trapdoor brandishing *a burning crucifix*. It was an agreeable enough rendering of the play, but not one to fall in love with; like Rutter, I thought that Forbes Masson's rampantly narcissistic Jaques, 'an over-weight Tom Jones fancying himself Lord Byron', was 'a monster' (*ibid.*, 346–7).

Finally, in 2013 came a production that pleased everyone – almost (Rutter gives good reasons for it being 'the longest, slowest, and least laughter-filled *As You Like It* of all time' ('Shakespeare Performances in England 2013' 412)). Directed by Maria Aberg, this had a pop sensibility to match Buzz Goodbody's, with music composed by folk-pop singer-songwriter Laura Marling and a Glastonbury Festival ambience that placed it, as Neil Norman put it (probably coincidentally), 'somewhere around 1973' (*Daily Express*, 26 April). In this laid-back world, Amiens (Chris Jared) channelled Nick Drake, Jaques (Oliver Ryan) was a superannuated acid casualty, and Duke Senior (Cliff Burnett) evoked 'David Bowie's Thin White Duke on a dress-down country weekend' (Fiona Mountford, *Evening Standard*, 2 April). A different, earlier Bowie persona was cited by Charles Spencer in relation to Pippa Nixon's Rosalind, 'one of the most entrancing', he declared, that 'I have ever seen': 'in her disguise as a boy, with a sharp haircut and a sock down her pants, she has more than a hint of the androgynous charisma of the young David Bowie, lithe, lean and fascinatingly enigmatic' (*Daily Telegraph*, 25 April). This is getting there, but still soft-pedalling. The Bowie who, during a Hammersmith Odeon concert (in, as it happens, 1973), simulated fellatio on his guitarist Mick Ronson's instrument was not 'enigmatic' but emphatically bisexual; and, indeed, Spencer continues: 'there is real chemistry between Nixon and [Alex] Waldmann [Orlando] ... When they kiss they really mean it – even though at this stage Orlando believes Rosalind to be a boy' ('even though'? why not 'because'?). Mountford found a 'pleasing complexity about the depth of sexual charge that Orlando feels for the "male" Ganymede' (*Evening Standard*), and Libby Purves thought Nixon 'magnetically, ambiguously attractive (I'd guess) to all sexualities' (*The Times*, 26 April). Here was an RSC production that, perhaps for the first time in the company's history, fully embraced the multifaceted queerness of the Rosalind–Ganymede–Orlando relationship, and whose relaxed tolerance and inclusivity were shared by reviewers and, one hopes, audiences. Here also, for Michael Billington, was a Rosalind 'who, for me, joins Vanessa Redgrave, Adrian Lester and the late Susan Fleetwood in the select pantheon of memorable Rosalinds' (*Guardian*, 26 April).

Although the broad terms of reference of successive RSC productions have remained stable, their context of production, reception and, importantly for my purposes, mediation and re-mediation, have over the same period undergone a transformation that has far-reaching implications for the ways in which they can be approached, engaged and remembered. This chapter, and those that follow, is an exercise in archival retrieval, deploying the long-established methods of the theatre historian to fashion a narrative from scraps and traces, which range from the relatively orderly documentation of performance (promptbooks, production records, stage management notes, photographs, show reports and the like; and in some cases video records) to no less valuable but more transient and indeterminate remains: newspaper reviews, interviews, practitioners' reminiscences, and sometimes even personal memories. I speak of performances that, though better-documented than many, have long vanished and that belong to a theatrical epoch rooted in, as Peggy Phelan has famously and influentially expressed it, disappearance, wherein 'performance's only life is in the present' (Phelan 146). Historically speaking, it is not only performance but performance's remains that have also disappeared (or at least retreated into places that are not always easy to access): without the organizing energies of the RSC archives at the Shakespeare Birthplace Trust, those at the National Theatre and the Victoria and Albert Museum Theatre and Performance Collection, and elsewhere, the reports of Billington, Wardle and Tinker, upon which historians so much rely, would have long gone the way of fish-and-chip paper.[6] For RSC productions prior to 1983, there are few video records (and those that do exist are adapted for the small screen); before 1960, as far as Shakespeare at Stratford-upon-Avon is concerned, there are none at all.[7] Even then, accessing and watching the archive videos is a draining and sometimes frustrating experience, involving a single fixed-camera perspective shot from considerable distance, which offers a view of a theatrically lit stage on which actors' faces are often tiny, unreadable and out of focus. And, more to the point for the purposes of this writing, they can only be viewed in situ; available to be paused, rewound and repeated, of course, but, as material for narrative, nonetheless as vulnerable to the vicissitudes of recall, of omission and misrepresentation, as any unrepeated, no-longer-present live performance.

Compare the situation of the researcher, the casual browser, or the interested theatregoer who wishes to examine the RSC's relationship with *As You Like It* during the second decade of the twenty-first century. A couple of mouse clicks take you to the company website's *As You Like It* page, where you find links to a plot synopsis, 'famous quotes', resources for teachers and – click – production history in pictures. Fourteen thumbnails summarize a history that, clicked in turn, commences in 1879 with the parade of the stuffed stag, proceeds via Margaret Leighton and Laurence Harvey (1952) and others to Vanessa Redgrave (uniquely, afforded two images: one as Ganymede and one in her white bridal gown), and from there through Eileen Atkins (with David Suchet, not credited), and Danielle Tilley (Phoebe) and Andrew Pointon (Silvius) in 2000, to Richard Katz as Touchstone in 2009. Production history is represented more substantially by links to Boyd's and Aberg's productions, yielding a further menu, which includes lists of cast and creatives, video, production photographs, trailer, and excerpts from reviews. Most enticingly of all, Boyd's production pages include the offer to watch the entire production online (£2.99 to rent, £6.99 to buy, £8.99 for HD). A search of YouTube finds that the company has posted two extracts: 5½ minutes each of Boyd's 2.1 and 3.2; alongside these is another result, 6 minutes of 3.2 from Aberg's production, encouraging the viewer to compare and contrast, and click, below the line, to comment. Katy Stephens 'looks really good in that mustache i would have mistaken her for a man if it wasn't for her voice' (says flamboyant69don); 'Bizarre', writes millernumber1, 'I thought for sure that Romola Garai was playing Rosalind, after playing Celia in Kenneth Branagh's film of the play – but apparently it's Katy Stephens.' Over on the Aberg version, the commentators have different concerns: nimium1955 reports being 'busy liking the acting, puzzled by the tempo – then realized that it worked well if the shared cigarette was not tobacco'; 'usually I prefer Shakespeare in its original 16th century setting', confesses Iloveshakespeare, 'but this one just works fantastically.' And: 'I have a recording of Vanessa Redgrave as Rosalind who is untouchable' (writes ok okok), 'but this lady comes a respectable second as the greatest Rosalind I've ever seen/heard' (the comment has prompted seven 'likes'). Aberg's version of 3.2 is flanked by three further clips: a short collage of footage from the production, the trailer, and a montage of interviews with the director, Nixon and Waldmann.

This is the archive with which historians of performance will increasingly have to engage in their work, as Barbara Hodgdon unforgettably puts it, of '[l]uring leftovers to life' (*Shakespeare, Performance and the Archive* 112): a vast, dispersed repository of traces of performance remediated, recirculated and restaged on a diversity of platforms, becoming itself *not* through disappearance but through potentially endless reiteration, commented upon by a far wider, more diverse, dispersed and violently opinionated critical community than the dozen or so souls that serve as the main eye-witnesses to the *As You Like It* productions of the pre-digital age. Materials that could once only have been accessed through the commitment of travel to, and time spent in, one of the places that Derrida calls 'a house, a domicile, an address' (Derrida 2) are available, in virtual form, instantaneously and anywhere. Newspaper reviews, once written, appear online and stay there, where they can be read not as cuttings but within the full discursive context in which they originated. One possible consequence of this still-new ontology of Shakespearean performance and its archive is that theatre history is in some ways easier to write: a trawl of the RSC's website (with some follow-up work on those of the major newspapers from which the reviews are taken), and a payment a fraction of the price of a theatre ticket to download the video, would yield more than enough to fabricate what would once have passed as a reliable account of Boyd's production.

In other ways, it makes the task even more challenging, less, perhaps, because it renders redundant some of the former responsibilities of the returnee from the archive – to reconstruct what has vanished, to make the unknown and unavailable known and available – than because it suggests that *As You Like It* performed can no longer be imagined (if it ever could be) solely as something that happens between persons who are co-present, in a particular space, and at a specific time. To afford the RSC's 2013 *As You Like It* its full weighting would mean not only inspecting those records that have served as the sources for the other productions scrutinized in this chapter, but also examining the wider conversations that it has initiated and participated in, the views and reactions of those among the communities of users whose views are minimally sampled here, the educational resources that it has generated, and the ancillary workshop activities that have accompanied it. This is a task beyond the scope of the current chapter, and, indeed of the current book; possibly it is no longer the task of a book at all.

Whatever forms *As You Like It* takes in Stratford in the future, and whatever means are devised of addressing them, that archive will continue to expand. Two things seem certain: first, that with or without forests, stags and dreams, the play will continue to find a home there; and, second, that Vanessa Redgrave will not be forgotten any time soon.

Notes

1. Thereafter Goodbody directed two more Shakespeares at The Other Place (*King Lear*, 1974, and *Hamlet*, 1975) before taking her own life; it would take a decade for another woman to direct Shakespeare at the RSC (Sheila Hancock's touring production of *A Midsummer Night's Dream*, 1984), and a further four years before a woman was invited to direct on the main stage (Di Trevis, *Much Ado about Nothing*, 1988).
2. The reference is to the commentator, television pundit, satirist and Christian polemicist Malcolm Muggeridge (1903–90), well known to Elsom's *Listener* readership for his jaundiced opinion-mongering, right-wing views and general distaste for the 'permissive society'.
3. Noble provides this rationale: 'it seems that the courtiers have gone from violence in the court, almost through a vegetarian phase, into an understanding and a harmony with their environment whereby they can kill a deer and be happy' (Noble 338).
4. Describing Hamilton as 'small, even birdlike', Michael Dobson liked her Rosalind very much, and recorded what sounds like a delightful moment: '"Were it not better,/Because that I am more the common tall..." had to become a joke, Hamilton standing on tiptoes and then jumping to reach the hand she held up at what ought to have been head height for the line to match the reality' ('Shakespeare Performances in England, 2000' 268).
5. This seems a bit strong: the reception was more mixed than this suggests. True, the *Evening Standard*'s Nicholas de Jongh described it as a 'risk-free' production that 'wins only faint praise' (24 March) and Billington and the *Daily Mail*'s Michael Coveney (31 March) both awarded it two (out of five) stars, but there were some very positive notices: 'exactly as we like it' was Benedict Nightingale's verdict in *The Times* (27 March); *The Stage* found that it 'builds to a joyous celebration of uninhibited love' (Gerald Berkowitz, 20 March), and the *Stratford Herald* called it 'a sheer delight' (Anne Tugwell, 30 March). In general, the local press was much more supportive than the nationals: the show was 'a feast of flawless flamboyance' (Vicki Gumbley, *Leamington Spa Courier*, 30 March), 'truly likeable' (John Murphy, *Berrow's Worcester Journal*, 31 March), 'just as I liked it' (Calista Duffield, *Warwick Courier*, 31 March), and a 'magical show with feelgood factor' (Enda Mullen, *Solihull News*, 31 March).
6. Alternatively, these would need to be laboriously tracked down through the British Library Newspaper Archive, which until relatively recently (November 2013) was located at the far end of the Northern Line in Colindale.

7   The BBC production of the 1961 *As You Like It* was followed, in 1965, by *The Wars of the Roses*; Nunn's 1972 *Antony and Cleopatra* was filmed and broadcast by ATV in 1974. Nunn's 1976 *Macbeth* reached the screen in 1979, and his 1977 *The Comedy of Errors* in 1978. It took years for another RSC Shakespeare to make it to television: Nunn's *Othello*, the final production at the original Other Place before it was demolished in 1989, which was broadcast on BBC Television the following year. Noble adapted his own production of *A Midsummer Night's Dream* for Film4 in 1996, and at the end of the decade Greg Doran's 1999 Swan production of *Macbeth*, with Antony Sher and Harriet Walter in the leads, was filmed by Channel 4. These were all versions reworked for film rather than recorded stage productions; in 1999 Doran's *The Winter's Tale* was filmed at the Barbican and released on DVD. Recent years have seen an increasing number of stage-to-screen adaptations: the Doran–Tennant *Hamlet*, broadcast on 26 December 2009 and released on DVD soon after, paved the way, and was followed by *Richard II* (2014), and then, in 2015, *Henry IV Parts 1 and 2*, *The Two Gentlemen of Verona*, *Love's Labour's Lost* and the play that Greg Doran affected to retitle *Love's Labour's Won*, *Much Ado about Nothing*. The RSC's DVD releases come on the back of its initiative of live screenings of performances to UK cinemas (followed by global replays).

CHAPTER IV

Between France and Germany

Rosalinde, ou Comme il vous plaira

In the second week of October 1934, the city of Paris saw the première of two productions of *As You Like It*. Both had been eagerly anticipated, though for very different reasons. One had been announced some months earlier: on 26 June, *Le Populaire* looked forward to the stage debut of the hugely popular screen star known as Annabella (Suzanne Charpentier) as Rosalind, in a production which promised big-name co-stars Aimé Clariond and Janine Crispin, a translation by acclaimed dramatist Jean Giraudoux, décor by Picasso, and direction by German émigré Victor Barnowsky, who had left Berlin when the Nazis came to power and whose distinction was to have directed Elisabeth Bergner as Rosalind at the Lessing Theatre in the 1920s (see Chapter VI). This production, which opened at the 1,900-seat, centrally located Théâtre des Champs-Élysées on 12 October, featured some real sheep, a musical score comprising excerpts from Mozart, décor by Balthus, eighteenth-century-style costumes, a translation not by Giraudoux but by the lyric poet Jules Supervielle, and a central performance from Annabella that charmed some but grated on others, not least *Le Temps* reviewer, Henry Bidou, who thought that she and her Orlando, Jean-Pierre Aumont, 'had not the slightest idea how to play comedy ' (15 October). *Sept*'s Gabriel Marcel, meanwhile, found that she had 'the gestures and the moves of a silly girl' (19 October). In common with most reviewers, Bidou and Marcel were more taken with the production of *As You Like It* that opened the day before Barnowksy's, in the much smaller (500-seat) Théâtre de l'Atelier (which translates as 'workshop' or 'studio'), located in Place Dancourt, at the point where sleazy Pigalle met bohemian Montmartre. 'Head for l'Atelier without delay,' urged Marcel, 'I promise you a delightful evening.' Renamed *Rosalinde* to avoid confusion with Barnowsky's version, this had the well-known Madeleine Lambert as Rosalind, Daniel Lecourtois as Orlando, and the celebrated mime Jean-Louis Barrault in a range of parts. But its real star was its director (who also played Jaques): Jacques Copeau.

The productions had been positioned from the outset by the press as rivals ('Is it a game?' asked Henry de Forge in *Le Monde* on 20 October, 'a challenge? a competition?'); in a city that was, at this time, more often than not a cultural, artistic, political, and sometimes literal, battleground. The postwar years in Paris were ones of extreme hardship, stark political divisions between the communist-aligned Left and fascist-inclined Right, and not-infrequent outbreaks of rioting and violence; the maimed and shell-shocked survivors of a war that had claimed the lives of one-and-a-half million French combatants found themselves on the streets alongside migrants from the devastated countryside as well as from across the whole of southern and eastern Europe, and the city was a magnet for every radical and anarchist group on the continent. Early in 1934, Paris had experienced one of the worst political crises of the interwar period, when the unexplained death of the government-connected fraudster Alexandre Stavisky provoked allegations of corruption, counter-accusations and high-profile resignations, and street demonstrations that led, on 6 February, to rioting that resulted in 16 deaths when the police turned their guns on the demonstrators. In such times, Shakespeare could not be above and beyond politics; in the most notorious instance, the Comédie-Française production of *Coriolanus*, which opened in December 1933, became the occasion for heated arguments in the auditorium for and against democracy, autocracy and mob rule. Paris in the 1930s was also the site of an extraordinary convergence of artistic and creative activity of every kind: in the performing arts alone, it was home to Jean Anouilh, Antoinin Artaud, Josephine Baker, George Balanchine, Jean-Louis Barrault, Gaston Baty, Maurice Chevalier, Jean Cocteau, Charles Dullin, Louis Jouvet, Georges Pitoëff, Igor Stravinsky, Tristan Tzara and Roger Vitrac; while Ernest Hemingway, James Joyce, Pablo Picasso and Gertrude Stein hovered in the wings. For the Dadaists and Surrealists, art in general and theatre in particular were, like politics, matters of shock tactics, confrontation, verbal and sometimes physical violence, and of taking sides; in the circumstances, the rivalry between the two productions of *As You Like It* was relatively polite. Nonetheless, most observers knew well enough where to place the 'small, thickset', monocle-sporting German producer (*Le Figaro*, 25 August 1934) in relation to the maker and teacher that many regarded as the saviour of French theatre: it was a matter of lavishness against simplicity, commercial against art theatre, French David against German Goliath.

Rosalinde marked the return to the Parisian stage of a figure who had been at the forefront of theatrical reform in the second decade of the twentieth century, who had directed two acclaimed Shakespeare productions, and whose teaching, training methods and practice would shape the future of twentieth-century physical acting. Born in 1879, Copeau began his theatrical career in his early twenties as a playwright and theatre critic, and from the outset he saw himself as an agent of reform. Appalled by the habits of bombastic declamation and empty gesticulation that defined early twentieth-century French acting, as well the complete lack of systematic or rigorous training, he did not mince words: 'the worst thing that was done in connection with the theatre,' he wrote, 'worse than the work of the theatrical people,' was 'that kind of leniency, that kind of facility with which the public and the critics accepted it ... I wrote in magazines for about ten years what I thought was the truth about the theatre, and I was bold enough to say that not one writer in the theatre was really a man of the theatre' (Rudlin 3). By 1913 Copeau had persuaded himself and others that he was such a man, and he assumed occupancy of a crumbling variety theatre, the Athénée St-Germain, which he found down a 'sordid alleyway' on the Left Bank, and renamed it the Théâtre du Vieux-Colombier (Rudlin 8). Here he established his signature style, rooted in the *plateau nu*, or bare platform: 'Our stage is such that it should be used without adding anything to it, no stairs, no moveable steps, no facile lighting effects, only the stage in all its truthfulness and implacability' (Copeau 85). Copeau saw Harley Granville Barker's *Twelfth Night* in London in 1913, and in 1914 the play (as *La Nuit des Rois*) became the Vieux-Colombier's breakthrough production. The staging, as described by one critic, '"drew" curved lines: it was fluid, free as if improvised. The comedians seemed to be inflated by air, or as if stuffed with straw – creatures of the imagination; they had neither the hair, habits nor swords of ordinary historical reality, and their acting had a peculiar, floating lightness'. Jean Villard-Giles, one of the actors, remembered how '[e]verything was there': 'music, colour, warmth, exquisite finesse, both in terms of tenderness and joy ... we were afforded some of those rare moments when mind and soul have one accord, and as if touched by a kind of grace we felt ourselves transported by one single flap of a wing towards the eternal peaks' (Rudlin 15). Copeau's project, as he defined it, was dramatic 'renovation'; but this was dramatic revelation. Viewing the production some eight years after it premièred, Granville Barker himself hailed 'the appalling discovery that French actors can speak Shakespeare better than English actors' (*Observer*, 1 January 1922).

La Nuit des Rois (a production that, for Henri Bourdeaux, 'begins with a sigh and finishes with a song' (Rudlin 18)) was followed by a less-well received *Le Conte d'Hiver* (*The Winter's Tale*) in 1919, which borrowed much of its look from the previous production. This time, the reviewers 'did not relish the idea of seeing a play performed on a bare stage with gray walls at the back clearly visible', and the response was lukewarm at best (Kurtz 65). By 1924, Copeau had had enough of Parisian theatre life; he announced the closure of the Vieux-Colombier and its Theatre School, and took himself and a select group of fellow artistes into voluntary rural exile – not to the forests of the Ardennes, still a war-damaged wasteland, but first to the Morteuil in Burgundy, and then to the tiny village of Pernand-Vergelesses, 315 km southeast of Paris. For the next decade Copeau researched and trained (whenever possible, in the open air) with a troupe of actors who toured France and Europe as 'Les Copiaus'; he gave lectures and solo readings to finance the work, and also experienced a deepening of his Catholic faith that strongly informed his later work.

In the early 1930s, Copeau resumed his directorial work in Paris, and early in 1934 he reached agreement with one of his old Vieux-Colombier colleagues, the actor and director Charles Dullin, to direct *As You Like It* at l'Atelier, which Dullin had established in 1932 as 'a sacred spot given over to experiment, to making and unmaking, where one seeks and sometimes finds, where one dreams and plans, where one cries with joy and laughs with tears at the smallest discovery'. Music and dance were integral to an Atelier production style that reached beyond realism into the realms of myth, fantasy and fairy tale, so that, for example, in Dullin's 1933 production of *Richard III*, 'a war dance had the extraordinary effect of revealing what was going on in the king's heart' (Kurtz 135). The appeal of l'Atelier to Copeau as a site for *As You Like It* was perhaps further enhanced by its charmed location. Visiting rehearsals to profile Copeau's company for *Sept*

(12 October), Léon Chancerel wrote of his encounter, at the far end of Rue d'Orsel, with the 'little village square' of Place Dancourt, in which the 'charming façade' of the theatre could be made out among trees 'already touched by an autumnal glow'; while *Marianne*'s Jeanine Delpech (10 October) found herself escaping from the 'screech' of Pigalle, via a stealthy entrance through a small side door, into 'a world apart'. Years later, the novelist Michel Mohrt recalled 'the fervent, the secret visions' of l'Atelier:

> the image of the theatre itself, hidden behind three trees that were no more real than those of a stage setting, at the back of the tiny Place Dancourt on the slopes of Montmartre – and the taste of the candied orange quarters impaled on little wooden sticks which I have come across nowhere else and which will always remain associated in my memory with the sublime divagations of the owner of the 'Atlas Hotel' and the smiling, doleful paradoxes of Jaques, in *As You Like It*. (Mohrt 106)

'A clandestine ceremony, a religious initiation, a precious *fête galante*,' writes Mohrt, 'an Atelier performance was each and all of them.'

In general, Copeau's production of *La Nuit des Rois* at the Vieux-Colombier has attracted attention as his most significant contribution to the history of Shakespearean performance, while his version of *As You Like It* has been largely overlooked by scholars. An exception is Jean Jacquot, who in 1964 published a lengthy examination of the production in the journal *Revue d'Histoire du Théâtre*, which drew upon the extensive archival resources of the Copeau collection in the Bibliothèque Nationale de France to argue that it was a 'revelation' on a par with that of *Twelfth Night* (Jacquot 119).[1] Robert Speaight, drawing on Jacquot's essay, also devotes three pages to the production in his history of Shakespearean performance, concluding that one could hear in it 'the music of humanity, still or sparkling, sad or merry' (Speaight *Shakespeare on the Stage* 193). As Jacquot was able to access resources that I have not, I have opted in the following pages to imitate my namesake and take my cue from Jacquot's impressively detailed and scrupulous account.

Jacquot begins with Delacre's translation, which, he thinks, leaves a lot to be desired. Whereas Théodore Lascaris's text for *La Nuit des Rois* had been a 'scenic translation', Delacre's was an 'adaptation' – and a drastic one at that (120). Referring to the programme note, which airily states that undue servility on the part of the translator is a form of betrayal and that theatre is a matter of neither linguistic subtlety nor erudition, Jacquot notes Delacre's concern with what he calls the *ordonnance* (arrangement or order) of the play, adherence to which, he asserts, affords the liberty to rephrase and simplify in order to avoid drastic cutting, and, more contentiously, to 'alleviate the text's *longeurs* by condensing it' (121). The result is a translation that preserves the outlines of the plot while offering a verbal text, composed of highly irregular free verse, which is occasionally given to some decidedly odd turns of phrase. To a certain extent Delacre was responding to what Jean-Michel Déprats has more recently identified as the challenge that Shakespeare poses to French translators, in 'the difference between the logic of the French sentence, which is based on linear development, and the prismatic nature of the Shakespearean one. The French sentence can only be understood when we reach its end' (Déprats 352). Consider the first four lines of Duke Senior's opening *tirade*, and Delacre's version:

> Now, my co-mates and brothers in exile,
> Hath not old custom made this life more sweet
> Than that of painted pomp? Are not these woods
> More free from peril than the envious court?
>
> (2.1.1–4)

> Eh bien! compagnons, frères en exile?
> L'habitude, aux antiques vertus,
> N'a-t-elle pas fait pour nous tous
> Une existence, en ce lieu, plus charmante
> Que celle où nous vîmes briller
> La pompe et l'artifice?
> Ces forêts ne sont-elles pas moins dangereuses
> Qu'une cour où règne l-envie?[2]
>
> (Jacquot 121–2)

This captures the sense, if not the metre, of the English, even if does so at twice the length and by unpacking and rationalizing Shakespeare's compacted imagery; the effect, perhaps, is to make the Duke even more long-winded and sententious than he is apt to sound in English. As Déprats suggests, if Shakespeare's 'dramatic force' is to be preserved, 'one is obliged to do at least some violence to the "genius" of the French language and its common usage' (Déprats 352). Elsewhere, Delacre is more ingenious with his transpositions. Jaques's 'I'll rail against all the first born of Egypt' (2.5.52–3) becomes 'J'irai demander à un hérisson de mes amis comment on se défait d'un importun d'importance, tout en restant parfaitement poli', the gist of which is that Jaques plans to seek advice of one of his hedgehog friends on how politely to get shot of a nuisance.

This is, to put it mildly, a free translation, and, Jacquot records, Copeau and Delacre did not always see eye to eye. Examining their often heated correspondence, he reads the relationship between director and translator as that of master and disciple, and offers examples of Copeau's revisions to Delacre's text to bring it back into line with Shakespeare's, including the treatment of Jaques's report of his encounter with Touchstone (or, French-style, Pierre Le Touche). 'And so from hour to hour, we rot and rot,/And thereby hangs a tale' (2.7.26–7), which Delacre has as 'Et caetera, Monsieur, et caetera/Jusqu'à la fin … jusqu'à la pourriture! …'/ En voilà une histoire!' (Et cetera, sir, et cetera/ Until the end … until we rot! …/And there's the story) is revised by Copeau to the more metrically congruent 'nous mûrrisons, nous mûrrisons – nous pourrissons, nous pourrissons – voilà toute l'histoire' ('we ripen, we ripen – we rot, we rot – that's the end of the story') (123). Delacre's translation was a talking point for the reviewers, some of whom seemed to consider it *too* Shakespearean. Jean Prudhomme in *Le Matin* wrote that Delacre had attempted to clarify and condense Shakespeare's text while preserving its pastoral quality, as well as its 'poetic tenderness' and 'comic eloquence' (13 October), but *La Semaine* à Paris (19 October) less favourably contrasted Delacre's 'more complex, more faithful, more Shakespearean' version with Supervielle's, which it found 'airy, light, and also easier on the ear'. The first of two reviews in *Le Temps* (12 October) referred to a 'faithful adaptation'; three days later, the same newspaper published a lengthier response by Henry Bidou, which included the observation that it 'obviously follows the text more closely' than Supervielle's and, as such, 'adds Shakespeare to Shakespeare, which is a little excessive.'

This seems at odds with Copeau's multi-modal conception of stage poetry as well as with a text with a running time of only 78 minutes (Slaughter 189). Delacre's extensive cuts and conflations included deep incisions to the expository opening scene and to the Touchstone–Audrey and Silvius–Phoebe episodes; in order to reduce the movement back and forth between court and forest, 2.2 and 3.1 were combined as a single scene. The finale of an already redacted play was truncated further by Copeau himself, who rejected most of Delacre's proposed additional dialogue for

Touchstone and Audrey, and who approached the final act in a spirit of improvisation, answering Delacre's objections to his cuts and rearrangements by admitting that he could not be certain about the shape it would take, but that he was 'working on it'. The solution, as Copeau saw it, had to be 'scenic', a matter of movement and rhythm rather than words (Jacquot 124). In the event, Copeau introduced a dance interlude to effect the transition from Rosalind's exit as Ganymede the end of 5.2 to the masque of Hymen in 5.4; it was, the *New York Times* reported, 'so ingenious an arrangement of Shakespeare's preposterous final scene as to make it almost tolerable' (11 November). This was one of a numerous dance sequences, choreographed by Bolshoi-trained Catherine Devillier and another Diaghilev associate, Lisa Sokoloff. The production's rhythm was also strongly determined by Georges Auric's musical score, which featured no fewer than 27 songs and instrumental pieces. It was a sign of the distance between Delacre and Copeau that the translator had proposed Thomas Morley's arrangement of 'It was a lover and his lass' and Thomas Arne's of 'Under the greenwood tree'. Auric, however, came to the production carrying the reputation of a member of Les Six, a group of popular musical avant-gardists formed and led by Jean Cocteau in the early 1920s; and, as Speaight comments, 'one did not look to "Les Six" for romanticism' (*Shakespeare on the Stage* 191). That said, Auric was by this time making his name as a composer of film scores, and his soundtrack for *Rosalinde* (described as 'pleasantly tart' by Pierre Audiat in *Paris-soir*, 12 October) wove skilfully between the diegetic and the extra-diegetic, from the guitar-accompanied songs of Amiens to the incidental orchestral music punctuated by the sound of distant hunting horns, creating atmosphere and linking scene to scene. Lacking an orchestra at l'Atelier, Auric, working at the forefront of the available technology, had most of his score recorded on gramophone discs: a profile in *Le Figaro* pictures the composer in rehearsal, requesting the stagehands to keep the noise down while he sits in armchair adjusting the sound levels, 'listening, correcting, strengthening it here, softening it there' (25 August). Asked if he was happy with the way things were going, he replied: 'I am confident.'

He had good cause. Jacquot states that Auric's score was one of the production's key means of effecting the smoothness of its scenic transitions to create an impression of rapid, near-simultaneous action, and in this respect it resonated with Copeau's desire to recapture at l'Atelier the energies of the bare open platform of the Vieux-Colombier (Jacquot 128). But whereas his final work at the Vieux-Colombier a decade previously had been characterized by its rather forbidding austerity, *Rosalinde* was opulent, seductive and rich in visual detail. A false proscenium was constructed, and the first court scenes were staged with Duke Frederick and Oliver's households on either side, suggested by drapes, the former decorated with a heraldic motif, the latter with the outlines of an orchard. These opened for the wrestling match, a brilliantly choreographed physical-theatre display which, according to *Paris-soir*, displayed Lecourtois's 'perfect torso' to good effect and solicited spontaneous audience applause (Bidou, *Le Temps*). Throughout, wrote Amédée Dunois in *Le Populaire*, the cast 'moves through this enchantment of lines and colours with the suppleness of athletes' (2 November). Later the curtains parted for the entry into the forest, here imagined as an escarpment of cubist blocks extending backwards and upwards. The costuming, subtly stylized, invoked a fantasy world, with the usurper's court dominated by angry reds and the exiled Duke's by cool blues; the production included inspired renderings of individual scenes. In a variation on frontcloth conventions, a huge parasol opened out upstage for Adam and Orlando's exchange in 3.3; at the end of the scene, this rolled away to reveal Duke Senior and his retinue at picnic tables for the repositioned 2.1 ('Eh bien! compagnons, frères in exile …'). Rosalind and Celia's departure for Arden was memorably atmospheric: after Duke Frederick stormed out, they sat sobbing as darkness fell and a lady-in-waiting descended a staircase, bearing a light which she placed on a table, then exited. The flame burned between them; and, after a time, Rosalind ceased weeping, smiled, rose to her feet: 'Ne vaudrait-il pas mieux que je me déguise en jeune homme?' ('Would it not be better if I were to disguise myself as a young man?'). Given Copeau's own spiritual journey, there is a special providence in the image of a light descending from above to inspire a personal transformation. As the women exited upwards via the staircase, Touchstone appeared below, mounted on a hobby-horse, to perform one of Auric's musical numbers, at the end of which they descended, costumed in a manner described by Jacquot as at once 'grotesque and charming', as Aliena and Ganymede (Lambert went into Arden sporting a risqué pair of high-cut shorts). Delacre had proposed here a standard comic song, but Copeau opted instead for something less specific and

JACQUES COPEAU

5 Jacques Copeau as Jaques, *Le Matin*, 13 October 1934

more haunting: an indistinctly worded, half-hummed air that seemed to offer the promise of freedom. At its end, Touchstone fell silent and joined them (Jacquot 129).

Touchstone (Arthur Devère, wrongly identified as Jean-Louis Barrault in a number of accounts) was another of the production's notable features. Costumed as a circus clown (perhaps more precisely, as the 12 October *Le Temps* reviewer recognized, as the legendary 'king of clowns', Grock), Pierre le Touche was indulged with a mime sequence in which he chased butterflies, and he aroused the dismay of a number of Anglophone commentators: the *New York Times* reported that 'the comic scenes ... appeared to have been inspired by the delusion that a Shakespearean clown and a circus clown mean and are the same thing. They were grotesquely labored.' Nearly half a century later, Richard David, reflecting unhappily on the cheeky-chappie Touchstone of Buzz Goodbody's RSC production (see Chapter III), remembered

Devère with what sounds like a shudder: 'I have seen worse: in Copeau's production ... he became a *circus* clown' (David 136; original emphasis). The clown was also equipped with a formidable arsenal of comic props: in addition to the hobby-horse, 'a pint of beer, a cheese sandwich ... a cocked hat, a sports hat ... a trumpet' and 'a fan' (Jacquot 127). He was not the only member of the cast to be allocated hand-held props: the *New York Times* noticed that both Copeau's Jaques and Lambert's Rosalind (as Ganymede) were given tobacco pipes, in the latter instance not altogether convincingly, as an index of masculinity. Madeleine Lambert was a persuasive enough, thoroughly conventional, Rosalind. She had the requisite 'mischievous spirit, playfulness and gracefulness' (*Le Matin*); was 'smart and saucy' (*Paris-soir*), 'generous with her smiles, her spirit, and her goodwill' (*Le Temps*, 12 October), and 'very likeable', according to the Paris edition of *Vogue* (November 1934). For *Le Monde* (20 October) Lambert and Lecourtois were 'the brilliant stars of a company of at least forty actors'.[3] Henry Bidou (*Le Temps*) was less impressed, describing Lambert as 'a pleasant enough boulevard actress ... and she looks it.' 'Smiling beneath her mop of fair hair,' Bidou sniffed, 'she looks less like a fugitive princess than a pretty woman playing at cross-dressing.'

Bidou was more interested in Copeau's portrayal of Jaques (see Figure 5), whose first entrance he described in detail:

> On the left, a pile of rocks some two metres high ... On the right, the old Duke, perched on a mound, held court, surrounded by his entourage, hunters and singers. Suddenly, there appeared between them a character from the world of bohemia, with a beret, brown jacket, and orange trousers. He looked thoughtful. The applause erupted. M. Copeau had returned to the stage. He was playing Jaques, the melancholy philosopher, companion to the Duke ... He played him as if he were the spirit of thought itself.

As Prudhomme put it in *Le Matin*, Copeau embodied a Jaques who 'sees everything in a black light', while Touchstone 'overflows with optimism': 'could there be a more striking image of the duality of the human condition?'

Rosalinde ran for 137 performances at l'Atelier, closing on 3 February 1935 with matinée and evening performances in which, the press release affirmed, Copeau would be seen in the role he had created (*Paris-soir*, 28 January). In the meantime, as far as the rivalry between his production and Barnowsky's was concerned,

Copeau undoubtedly had the last laugh. Although the press had maintained a façade of fair-mindedness towards the two productions, there had been from the beginning an undercurrent of resentment towards the perceived interloper: a couple of weeks before the twin premières, the 'Échos du Théâtre' gossip column in *Le Figaro* (24 September) complained about the imminent clash and darkly intimated that the president of the drama critics' association 'had been apprised of the situation'. Once the courtesies of the opening nights had been concluded, the muttering began in earnest. Back in 1921, Granville Barker had been struck by the distinctiveness of the 'very mixed' Vieux-Colombier audience, consisting of 'workmen, students, some foreigners, a taste of literary and learned Paris, a sprinkling of fashionable Paris'; 13 years on, the theatrical trade paper *Comoedia* noted that 'Parisians could not fail to notice the singular difference between the "house" attending *Rosalinde* at l'Atelier and that at the Champs-Élysées for Barnowski's [*sic*] *As You Like It*':

> The first consisted of regular professionals, and a lot of writers, artists, friends of the Vieux-Colombier or of Jacques Copeau. All, or nearly all, Parisian celebrities of the theatre and of the boulevard. It was quite the opposite for the foreign director. There was a large crowd of the curious and the specialist: theatre managers, film producers, celebrity film-makers, fashionable Parisians, actresses and cover stars, playwrights, etc.

Although 'the buzz of the great days of the *Ballets Russes* or Rubinstein' could be heard, this crowd, strutting its 'tails and furs', was evidently not one of which *Comoedia* approved: 'this persistent infatuation with everything that comes from abroad ... Where will it all end?' The play, the article concludes, 'demands the simple treatment'. It was perhaps with a sense of *schadenfreude*, then, that *Comoedia* was able to report just over a week later on the comprehensive box-office failure of Barnowski's production. The director ('metteur en scène allemand') appeared in the paper's pages again on 24 October, when it reported that the doors of the Théâtre des Champs-Élysées were now closed, performances cancelled, and cast (with the exception of Annabella) unpaid. *Paris-soir* (24 October) presented the situation somewhat differently, reporting that the stars had agreed to work for nothing so that the supporting cast could be paid. Two days later, in an opinion piece in *Comoedia* on exploitative practices and artists' wage levels in the cinema and theatre industries, Barnowsky was again singled out: the supporting cast at the Théâtre des Champs-Élysées, it was alleged, were earning a derisory 7 francs a day. A month later (22 November), the paper reported that it had learned, as it was going to press, that Barnowsky was the subject of an eviction notice, and that he planned to liquidate his assets in favour of his creditors; the report noted that he had already fled to London, complaining to his French friends that the conditions of his eviction were 'particularly distressing'. The next day (23 October), *Comoedia* praised the 'excellent intervention by the public authorities' in issuing a deportation order against the man it described as having 'amazed Paris by staging his version of Shakespeare's *As You Like It* concurrently and almost in competition with M. Jacques Copeau'. Paris was, allegedly, 'astonished' by Barnowsky's 'whimsical management' and 'inconsiderate treatment of the actors, Frenchmen employed by him whom he well and truly let down'. Barnowsky could not be served with the deportation notice in person, the article continued, because he had 'prudently put the English Channel between himself and his creditors' (cryptically, the article is signed 'Horatio'). Copeau and Barnowsky: two 'Dukes', both implicated in narratives of dispossession and exile, from which one only would emerge victorious.

Over at l'Atelier, as *Comoedia* (22 October) noted (in an article placed, presumably deliberately, next to the news of Barnowsky's sudden departure), preparations were in train for a gala reception for *Rosalinde* on 8 December, to be presided over by the poet Henri de Régnier and held at the Académie Française. Better still, in January 1935, in recognition of his contribution to French theatre and cultural life, Copeau was appointed an officer of the Légion d'Honneur, on which occasion the 'triumphant' *Rosalinde* was once again acknowledged (*Comoedia*, 15 January). For the French Shakespearean theatre more broadly, the success of *Rosalinde* was no less significant: as John Pemble observes, thanks to Copeau and others, 'the old "fable décente et régulière", in which Shakespeare was reconstituted for "French" taste and "French" sensibility, finally disappeared from the stage', unleashing '"Shakespeare mania" in which plays never seen before found themselves on French stages' (Pemble 165).

Come vi piace

Copeau's relationship with *As You Like It* did not end in 1935. In 1932, he began to engage with an area of theatre practice that would come to dominate the later stages of his life, when he directed a large-scale open-air production of the sixteenth-century Italian religious drama *Rappresentazione di Santa Uliva* in the cloisters of the Basilica di Santa Croce, as part of the Maggio Musicale Florentino. Coincidentally, this also involved a Shakespearean stand-off with a German director, on this occasion Max Reinhardt, whose spectacular open-air production of *A Midsummer Night's Dream* was performed in Florence's Boboli Gardens. Over a decade later, in a radio broadcast in 1946, Copeau reflected on the pairing:

> In a little less than two months, the result was two productions as opposed in character as could be. In the magic hands of Reinhardt, the *Midsummer Night's Dream* had become expanded and taken on an amplitude and a weight much greater than in Shakespeare. It was already an outline of the film that Reinhardt would later make in Hollywood. In comparison, in my poor little *Mystery of Saint Uliva*, there was no amplification, not the least eloquence ... And yet, against all expectations, that rather spare and awkward thing, pious and old-fashioned, did more than bear comparison with my German colleague's grand display. (Copeau 90–1)

'The evening of the première', Copeau declares, 'was a victory for France' (*ibid.*). Speaking as he was in the immediate aftermath of the war and German occupation, it is not at all surprising that Copeau should frame the shows in flagrantly nationalistic terms, nor that he should detect, in his rival's work, implicitly fascistic echoes of 'a deal of amplification, even systematisation' (91). Copeau was not unaware of the political sensitivities of making work under the gaze of Mussolini, tartly observing (unfairly, given Reinhardt's subsequent treatment by the Nazis) that Reinhardt's presence in Florence was evidence of how 'Hitler's Germany was already becoming dear to the hearts of Fascist Italy' (90); but he was comfortable enough with the situation to return in May 1938, during the tense period leading up to the Munich Agreement, to the Florentine music festival to direct *Come vi piace*, an expanded, re-translated, open-air version of his 1934 Paris production of *Rosalinde*, performed (in Italian) in the Boboli Gardens by an Italian cast.

The result was a production that, notwithstanding Copeau's words of censure, in some respects attempted to out-Reinhardt

Reinhardt. Created in the sixteenth century, the Boboli gardens comprise 111 acres of grass, walkways, grottos, water features and statuary, an elaborately managed, technologically sustained built environment originally designed to display the wealth and power of the Medicis, and Copeau's staging ingeniously played the site's highly stylized 'natural' features both against his own sets and against elements of 'real' flora and fauna. Employing medieval-style mansion conventions, he arranged the *mise en scène* in the area close to the gardens' monumental entrance: three structures, consisting of a two-storied pavilion containing a revolving stage to the audience's left, an 8-metre-high mound crossed by winding pathways in the middle, and, to the right, a low bridge that led to the gardens proper (Jacquot 131). The *New York Times* reviewer thought this a touch perverse: 'With all Boboli to choose from – a wealth of idyllic woodland sites,' he complained, 'there was keen regret at the selection of one of its least poetic spots: a cramped corner near the gate' (8 June). Nonetheless, both the means of delivery and the effects were on a much larger scale than had been possible at l'Atelier. Auric's gramophone discs were superseded by a full orchestra placed in the pavilion, and his score was replaced by one composed by Ildebrando Pizzetti, which provided a frequent filmic-style accompaniment to action and dialogue. The production revelled in wordless tableaux: light flickered in the pavilion as darkness fell, and the shadows of Rosalind (Rosanna Masi) and Celia could be seen as they prepared themselves for their escape; this was the prelude to their long walk into the distance, and into the depths of the gardens, and of the imagined forest. When Duke Frederick discovered their flight, he was accompanied by an entourage of courtiers (which included, Jacquot reports, a large black dog and a dwarf, bearing burning torches) and also by Hisperia, trailing in his wake 'like a broken doll' (Jacquot 133). Copeau had a large cast at his disposal: when Rosalind and Celia left the court for Arden, they were led by Corin to hide by the right of the pavilion; they stopped, watched and listened as the rustic inhabitants of Arden – including loggers, charcoal-burners, a shepherd tending his flock and a peasant family with a donkey in tow – crossed the performance space (Jacquot 134). Live animals were one of this production's notable features: in addition to the sheep and Duke Frederick's dog, the 'old religious man' (5.4.158) who effects his conversion (played by Copeau himself as a Franciscan friar in full habit) made an unscripted entrance for the finale 'followed by a lion, a tiger, and a bear' (Speaight, *Shakespeare on the Stage* 192; the echoes of as-yet-to-be-released *The Wizard of Oz* (1939) are entirely coincidental).

If this was a far cry from the *plateau nu*, it scarcely mattered; the verdict of the *New York Times* was that it was 'one of the finest spectacles witnessed in Italy in recent seasons', and that it once again proved Copeau 'a master of the stage':

> His keen insight into the poetic values of the play, his sensitive artistry, his ripe theatrical experience served to form a spectacle of opulent fantasy, of almost constant lyric élan, of fluid continuity of rhythm, of direct plastic clarity. True to his native aristocratic taste, the Gallic esthete excelled in fastidious groupings and movements, in happy interpretative finds, in infinite shadings of delicate half-tones (well supported by the suggestive period costumes of Lucien Coutaud) – in short, a minute elaboration of countless decorative details, achieved with a preciosity of stylization at times bordering on affectation.

The director and his production were, the report concludes, 'cordially acclaimed by a select cosmopolitan audience'. Copeau would have done well to enjoy the applause while it lasted, as *Come vi piace* was one of his last major productions and, with the exception of a muted *La Nuit des Rois* at the Comédie-Française in the occupied Paris of 1940, his last Shakespeare.

Wie es euch gefällt

West Berlin, September 1977. The distinguished music and theatre critic, senior editor of the *Süddeutsche Zeitung*, and Professor of Music at the University of Stuttgart, Joachim Kaiser, is on his way home after seeing Peter Stein's Berliner Schaubühne production of *Wie es euch gefällt* (*As You Like It*). When he checks in for his return flight at Tegel Airport, there is a minor incident: his bag sets off the security scanner alarms and he is taken aside for questioning. Opening the bag, however, the security staff are both surprised and disappointed: '"There are only Shakespeare books here", they marveled, "and we thought, it's dynamite".' Kaiser ruefully reflects: 'they were not far wrong' (*Süddeutsche Zeitung*, 22 September 1977). The funny story harbours a provocation: Shakespeare is nowhere near as innocuous as the powers-that-be would like to imagine.[4]

Kaiser offers this anecdote as a postscript to a lengthy review of a production which he pithily summarizes as a mixture of crudeness and brilliance, and which, he suggests, made the mainstream German Shakespearean theatre look 'sterile', 'bloodless' and complacently 'bourgeois' by comparison. The image of Shakespeare as high explosive, whether in the hands of West Germany's leading avant-garde director or in those of a respected university professor, indicates the cultural politics and context of Stein's production, as well as a glimpse of the circumstances in which it was received. A situation in which Kaiser's 'Shakespeare books' can be mistaken for terrorist weaponry sounds amusingly ironic, but it occurred in a time and place in which both airport security and the threat that it was designed to counter were considered far from laughing matters. Kaiser's visit to the divided Berlin of the Cold War era to see Stein's production involved a journey on what was already the most heavily policed and symbolically charged flight path in Europe. In the latter part of 1977, there was even more reason than usual for the German authorities to be vigilant and for passengers to feel nervous. During the final months of that year, they found themselves living through what came to be called 'the German Autumn', an anything-but-idyllic season of escalating terrorist violence almost exclusively perpetrated by the self-styled Rote Armee Fraktion (or Red Army Faction, also known as the Baader–Meinhof gang, after leading members Andreas Baader and Ulrike Meinhof), which had waged a prolonged campaign of bombings, shootings and kidnappings since the early 1970s. In its attempts to overthrow a capitalist system it regarded as inherently fascist, the RAF (the acronym references the British Royal Air Force, then extensively stationed across West Germany) targeted individuals identified as the state's representatives and instruments as well as the institutions of 'imperialism', bombing banks, police stations and American military bases, and shooting and kidnapping prominent public figures and business leaders. On 5 September, as *Wie es euch gefällt* entered its final stages of rehearsal, RAF members kidnapped the industrialist Hanns Martin Schleyer and demanded the immediate release from prison of four of the group's founders. On 13 October, three weeks into the production's run, the RAF responded to the West German government's refusal to negotiate by hijacking a Frankfurt-bound Lufthansa flight; five days later, federal border guards successfully stormed the aeroplane, but not before Schleyer had been shot dead by his captors. The same day, three of the four group members in prison committed suicide.

For the vast majority of West German onlookers, the events of the German Autumn confirmed what most had suspected from the beginning: that the RAF were not the revolutionary vanguard that they imagined themselves to be but a gang of delusional and pathologically violent criminals. But the Faction would not have survived as long as they did had they not initially enjoyed a measure of public sympathy, particularly from sections of the West German Left. This was due partly to the group's canny manipulation of its outlaw-chic image, and partly to its grasp of the avant-garde theatricalism of terror, but mostly to its capacity to articulate some of the more utopian aspects of the broader left agenda. Terrorism expert Konrad Kellen defines the RAF's ideology as 'millenarian', and defines their aim as nothing less than 'a total transformation of all existing conditions, a new form of human existence, an entirely new relationship of people to each other, and also of people to nature' (Kellen 49–50). Although many on the left were appalled by the RAF's violent tactics, the utopian dream of revolutionary change that underpinned them retained a considerable appeal, as did the group's sense that the postwar denazification of the Federal Republic of Germany had, at best, been only partially achieved.

One of the key places for the exploration of these hopes in 1970s West Germany was the theatre. As elsewhere in Europe and the United States, one consequence of the student activism of 1968 was a flourishing theatrical counter-culture that initially existed outside and in outright opposition to the state-supported mainstream, but was soon enough co-opted into it. It manifested itself in various forms of agit-prop, protest and political theatre, in avant-garde performance, and in performance art. The first West German experimental theatre festival was held in Frankfurt in 1966 and saw the première of Peter Handke's symptomatically titled 'anti-play' *Publikumsbeschimpfung* (*Offending the Audience*) and the birth of Rainer Werner Fassbinder's *antiteater*; in its wake, groups influenced both by the example of the Weimar years and by visits by leading American avant-garde companies (including, notably, the Living Theatre and the Bread and Puppet Theatre) made work for diverse audiences in a range of non-traditional settings. But the more lasting legacy of the radicalisation of the 1960s generation of theatre makers was that a number of them used the opportunity to take these arguments to the heart of the mainstream itself, and in the process to remake the classical canon as an artistic and political battleground, a site of symbolic rather than actual violence. This was the climate in which a theatre critic, music professor and senior editor of a national newspaper could set the 'sterile' and 'bloodless' theatre of the bourgeoisie in opposition to Shakespeare-as-dynamite; it was a climate that Peter Stein, as the most prominent figure to emerge from that generation, had done much to shape.

Wie es euch gefällt was Stein's first Shakespeare production in a career that began in Munich in 1967 with the German première of Edward Bond's *Gerettet* (*Saved*), as well as the first Shakespeare to be offered by the Schaubühne since *König Johann* (*King John*) in 1968. Stein became the theatre's artistic director in 1970, opening with Brecht's *Die Mutter* (*The Mother*); this was followed by major productions of Ibsen's *Peer Gynt* (1971), Labiche's *Das Sparschwein* (*The Piggy Bank*) in 1973 and Gorky's *Sommergäste* (*Summerfolk*) in 1974. None of these was a small-scale affair: reflecting Stein's admirable determination to utilize to the full the considerable resources placed at his disposal by the West German state, *Das Sparschwein*, for example, had a total budget of 229,000 deutschmarks (around £33,000 in 1973), equivalent at the time of writing to somewhere between a third and two-thirds of a million pounds. The budget for *Wie es euch gefällt* was twice as much again, in part because Stein's conception of the production was unable to be accommodated even within the far from modest confines of the Schaubühne. It was realized instead in the vast space of the disused Central Cinema Compagnie-Film GmBH (CCC) film studios in Spandau, located in the westernmost of Berlin's boroughs, 16 kilometres and a good hour by public transport from the company's home base. As Wilhelm Hortmann observes, Stein's excursus to the outskirts of West Berlin, and to the found space of the studios, was part of a pattern of migration among theatre practitioners in Germany during the period. Stein's main artistic rival, Peter Zadek, had made a similar move for his *Hamlet*, which opened just a week after Stein's *Wie es euch gefällt*: having staged *Der Kaufmann von Venedig* and *König Lear* (*The Merchant of Venice* and *King Lear*) at the Schauspielhaus Bochum (1973 and 1975) and an outrageously confrontational *Othello* at the Schauspielhaus Hamburg (1976), Zadek mounted *Hamlet* in a derelict factory on the outskirts of Bochum. Hortmann records that the business of 'leaving well-appointed theatres to perform in deserted factories or warehouses' was usually 'prompted by contempt for the "Stadttheater"' (Hortmann 273). In Zadek's case there was certainly a considerable degree of contempt on display for the traditions of German Shakespeare performance, and, it seemed, for its audience: 'once inside ... they were subjected to unwonted discomfort, if not treated as scarcely tolerated outsiders' (Habicht 297). With its fiercely iconoclastic, unromantic lead (Ulrich Wildgruber), bare-breasted Ophelia and Gertrude, harsh strip lighting, and 5½-hour duration, this staging 'used the open space', Dennis Kennedy concludes, 'to parody the play, the theatre, and its audience' (Kennedy 270). Stein's production was far less confrontational, though in its own way just as demanding.

Stein's occupation of the CCC Studios embodied a vision of the play's two worlds of court and forest. The spatial dynamic of *Wie es euch gefällt* had been anticipated in a large-scale Shakespeare project conducted by the Schaubühne ensemble at the CCC studio a year previously, which was in itself the result of half a decade of research. Under the tutelage of company dramaturgs Botho Strauss and Dieter Sturm, Stein's actors occupied their time between *Peer Gynt* and *Sommergäste* studying early modern culture, history and thought, as well as acquiring new skills by training in music, dancing and tumbling. As one of the actors, Elke Petri (who subsequently played Phoebe), recalled, the initial impetus for this came from an early decision that 'sometime we should do Shakespeare'; as time went on, and in the absence of a 'set plan', 'the more research and training we did, the more we realized the immensity of the task' (Lackner 81).

The product of this prodigious collective research process, opening in December 1976, was a mammoth two-part event, spread across two evenings, titled (in English) *Shakespeare's Memory*. Part living-history exhibition, part installation, part animated lecture, and part performance medley, this was an interactive, participatory, environmental event which combined large-scale spectacle, tableaux, and huge set-pieces ('The Cage of Fools', a pageant-wagon packed with actors dressed as Shakespearean clowns who invade the arena; a planetarium; a life-size fragment of a ship's hull), excerpts of Shakespearean and non-Shakespearean text, demonstrations of hand gestures, swordplay, juggling and circus skills, and appearances by historical figures (the youthful and aged Queen Elizabeth, Sir Walter Raleigh, George Peele).

Throughout, the actors engaged with and addressed spectators directly, who were encouraged to wander around the performance area, taking in bits and pieces of the show's multiple and concurrent components. The second evening culminated in a Shakespearean showcase in which the actors convened on a composite structure – assembled from platforms and wagons – simultaneously to perform multiple interwoven extracts, 'mostly monologs [sic] or those between two persons' (Lackner 87).

Shakespeare's Memory established the research base, the environmental template, and, importantly, the durational framework for *Wie es euch gefällt*, which opened on 20 September 1977. The 1976 show lasted (reports vary) anything between 7½ and 9 hours in total over two evenings; *Wie es euch gefällt* ran for 4½ hours (three times as long as Copeau's *Rosalinde*, and nearly twice the length of most the productions addressed in this book). Even more challengingly, whereas the promenade format of *Shakespeare's Memory* had allowed its audiences plenty of opportunities to take a break and to stretch their legs, *Wie es euch gefällt* was played without an interval, ending long past midnight. The play began with the audience (no more than 300, a fraction of the usual Schaubühne house) ushered in to experience what Benjamin Heinrichs (*Die Zeit*, 7 October) described as the 'torture' of standing for 40 minutes in a vast, high-ceilinged chamber with ice-blue, featureless walls, representing the court, austere, inhuman and sterile, a realm from which all traces of the natural world had been eradicated. Ranged around the walls were platforms upon which, at the start of the play, the actors, lit from below, stood isolated, looming over the standing spectators like waxworks or museum exhibits, frozen in tableaux, the only sound or movement coming from Rosalind (Jutta Lampe) silently weeping. They were costumed exactly, sumptuously and stiflingly in period, in dark, heavy fabrics fringed with lace, studded with pearls and flecked with silver and gold, men and women alike encased in neck-restricting high collars. The sense of a repressive, timebound, backward-looking world was metatheatrically enhanced – for some, disconcertingly – by what appeared to be a display of deliberately old-fashioned acting ('statuesque', according to Habicht [298]): as Patterson put it, the performances had 'something of that irritatingly stilted manner which is characteristic of so many German municipal theatres' (136). When Orlando, in the muscular shape of the blonde, shaggy-haired Michael König, entered in a dark shirt open to the waist, he came as a rock-god emissary from another world (production photographs suggest Led Zeppelin's Robert Plant, circa 1976 (Herrmann 199–208)). Stripped to a heavy thong, he efficiently floored Charles (professional wrestler Günter Nordhoff, 'a human monster that would do credit to a horror movie' (*Die Zeit*)), in a grimly silent, choreographed display that was as deliberately devoid of spontaneity as court protocol demanded. Stein reordered the first act of the play as a filmic-style montage, layering and juxtaposing and compressing, with actors giving a fragment of a scene, then freezing as the action shifted to the other side of the hall. It had the effect, as David Zaine Marowitz saw it, of 'breaking up Shakespeare's interminable information monologues, and also of interweaving the various plots and character fates so that their dilemmas are witnessed in confrontation rather than in reflection' (*Plays and Players*, October 1977). Touchstone (Werner Rehm) delivered his gags face-to-face before bystanders and had a macabre sense of humour that was manifested in such gags as popping a dead mouse out of his mouth during the first exchange with Celia and Rosalind.

The cue for the shift to Arden was the recorded sound of barking dogs (perhaps not unlike those that accompanied East German border guards patrolling the wall's 'death strip'), forcing audience members to leave the hall through a narrow door and pass along a tunnel. If the court scenes obliquely evoked a lived and imagined West Berlin, surrounded by insurmountable walls and cut off from nature, the tunnel burrowed down towards one of a more deep-seated element of the city's imaginary. In a place iconically defined by the Brandenburg Gate and Checkpoint Charlie, where two West Berlin U-Bahn lines passed from north to south through closed and guarded subway stations stranded in East Berlin, and where the main border crossing between East and West was located in the subterranean depths of Friedrichstrasse station, tunnels, corridors, passageways and gateways played a central role in the organisation of a divided civic space and of the forms of consciousness it shaped. Stein orchestrated the walk from the court to Arden as a journey through history, most obviously, that explored in *Shakespeare's Memory*, from which various artefacts were retrieved and displayed. As spectators made their way, single file, through the dark, winding tunnel hung with creepers and dripping with water, they negotiated a 'narrow, thorny, and labyrinthine path obstructed with (artificial) briars and puddles, through gusts of wind and patches of blinding light', and were faced with 'such surprises as a wild bear and a sleeping hermaphrodite' (Habicht 299), 'water-courses, workmen's huts, plaster figures in idyllic poses, displays of shells and natural habitats' (*Plays and Players*), 'a (dead?) black ape' crouching 'in a barred cave' (*Die Zeit*), 'strange-looking skeletons, hermits, cages' and 'trumpeting wild animals' (Hellmuth Karasak, *Der Spiegel*, 26 September). With the sound of the dogs fading into the distance, the sound of hunting-horns grew louder. Emerging from the tunnel, audience members were greeted with the immense space of the CCC's main studio and with Karl-Ernst Herrmann's stunning, meticulously detailed forest. As 'a total environment for the text, a full-bloom wrap-around cinemascope world picture' (Marowitz), this placed the audience seating amidst a vision of Arden that included real trees, an abundance of foliage, a pond, a cornfield, a butterfly display, and forest dwellers' huts; catwalks and multi-levelled platforms extended the action around, between and behind the seated ranks of spectators who, once they took their places, remained in them until well after midnight. As an environment, it was constantly active: Audrey (Libgart Schwartz) could be seen churning butter in the distance, hunters fired shotguns, and Jaques (Peter Fitz), 'wearing sometimes a magician's robe, sometimes the garb of a witch' (Habicht 299), and sometimes a tartan shawl that gave him a Scots aspect, prowled the perimeter when not in his scenes. The inhabitants of this world were not restricted to the dramatis personae of Shakespeare's play: Robinson Crusoe could be seen (calling for 'Freitag'), as could Robin Hood and his merry men, a fur-clad wild man who muttered and roared menacingly behind the audience, and a witch-like old woman.

The total effect, achieved though means of a scenic profligacy that mixed the hyperreal with the non-real (the huge Elizabethan-style model globe suspended over the performance space), was of inexhaustible (and for some reviewers, exhausting) visual richness, and of a vision of a green utopia that, Stein knew, was an impossible dream. Aspects of the scene, for some reviewers, bordered perilously on kitsch: Heinrichs (*Die Zeit*) described it as a 'child's dream', ranging from 'Valhalla to Disneyland', a view mirrored in *Der Spiegel*'s vision of a 'half nature reserve ... half Disneyland'. Peter Iden (*Frankfurter Rundschau*, 22 September) reported an actor whispering 'the truth is in the forest' in his ear as he took his seat, but this 'truth' was, in the end, far from

6 Rosalind (Jutta Lampe), Touchstone (Werner Rehm) and Celia (Tina Engel), Schaubühne Berlin, 1977

reassuring. The director's far from romanticized view of pastoral was set out in the 128-page programme ('I'll read it at leisure one of these days', Jürgen Deisner wryly commented in the *Darmstädter Echo*, 24 September). In addition to lengthy extracts from Northrop Frye's *A Natural Perspective* (Frye 3–143), Agnes Latham's introduction to the Arden second series edition, and Jan Kott's 'Shakespeare's Bitter Arcadia', the programme presented an album of stark monochrome woodland images, most of which challenge as much as they embrace the imagery of pastoral, and more of which are rooted in the German and American landscape than the English one. The first image, 'Sonntagsspaziergang [Sunday stroll] am Waldsee' (also captioned 'The forest is full of wonders'), credited to Georg Meister and dated 1958, pictures an elderly couple and a young girl, backs to the camera, standing on the shore of a lake, gazing at a vista of tall pines and distant mountains in relation to which they appear tiny and insignificant; the final one is of the Celtic stone circle at Castlerigg, north Cumbria, set on a bleak open heath and utterly devoid of human life. In between there are images of forest labour (loggers, pictured in 1977 and 1890); hunters; American pioneer heroes (Jim Butler and Matthew Lewis); a solitary bare-chested youth reading beneath a tree; two girl scouts, dated 1912, studiously sharing a picnic; Californian Redwoods; and the exposed, tentacular roots of a felled giant sequoia.

Rosalind, Celia and Touchstone arrived in Arden, having abandoned their court costumes, in contemporary dress: heavy coats, mufflers and headscarves, the garb of refugees (see Figure 6), of those that had made a dangerous and forbidden frontier crossing (with a hint, Sybille Wirsing noticed in the *Frankfurter Allgemeine* (22 September), of 'Hansel and Gretel'). They dragged with them a cart piled with suitcases: objects that, as Andrew J. Webber points out, contain the weight of twentieth-century German history: whether carried by migrant, refugee or captive, in flight, across borders or en route to the camps, the *Koffer* is a repository of memory 'used to represent longings of different kinds and qualities' that is 'caught between a sense of loss ... and a sense of potential return and recuperation' (Webber 19). The world they had fled to was at first a wintry one, where Duke Senior offered his opening speech to his followers ('Nun, meine Brüder und Gefährten im Exil ...'), while shivering under a tarpaulin, and this was a landscape of hardship and hard work; as the evening wore on, summer returned, and Rosalind was free to surrender her winter wrappings for a baggy shirt, floppy hat and loose cotton trousers, while Celia opted for an Edwardian-style sailor suit, accessorized with a butterfly-net; Orlando sported a natty cream suit and broad-brimmed hat. Like the costumes, the production's verbal idiom also traversed the centuries: once in the forest, the ponderous Stage German of the court scenes gave way to a compound (or mish-mash, according to some reviewers) of the venerable Schlegel–Tieck early nineteenth-century verse translation, Johann Joachim Eschenburg's eighteenth-century prose version, and a partially modernized, vernacular discourse devised by Stein's dramaturgs Ellen Hammer and Dieter Sturm. Take, for example, Rosalind and Orlando's exchange in 4.1: 'What would you say to me now, an I were your very, very Rosalind?' 'I would kiss before I spoke ...' (ll. 63–6). In Schlegel–Tieck it runs, more or less word for word, thus:

> ROSALINDE. Was würdet Ihr zu mir sagen, wenn ich Eure rechte, rechte, Rosalinde wäre?
> ORLANDO. Ich würde küssen, ehe ich spräche.
> ROSALINDE. Nein, Ihr tätet besser, erst zu sprechen, und wenn Ihr dann stocktet, weil Ihr nichts mehr wüsstest, nähmt Ihr Gelegenheit zu küssen.
>
> (Schücking 543)

In Hammer and Sturm's version, this is streamlined as:

> ROSALINDE. Was würdest Du jetzt jetzt zu mir sagen, wenn ich Deine wahre, leibhaftige Rosalind wäre?
> ORLANDO. Ich würde Dich küssen.
> ROSALINDE. Falsch, Du solltest erst etwas sagen, und wenn Dir dann der Gesprächsstoff ausgeht, ist das die beste Gelegenheit für einen Kuss.
>
> (Rischbieter 15)

Or: 'What would you say to me now, if I were your true, real-life Rosalind?' 'I would kiss you.' 'Wrong, you should say something first, and if you run out of conversational material, that's the best opportunity for a kiss.' The second part of Rosalind's reply ('Very good orators ... to kiss' (ll. 69–71)) was cut. Here, Hammer and Sturm's translation of heightened prose is more colloquial, more informal and direct ('I would kiss you', rather than 'I would kiss before I spoke'), and more intimate (the formal second-person *Ihr* becomes the informal *Du*). Elsewhere they preserved some of the text's formality while loosening blank-verse form. Duke Senior's opening address (in Schlegel-Tieck, 'Nun, meine Brüder und des Banns Genossen/Macht nicht Gewohnheit süsser dieses Leben/Als das gemalten Pomps?' (Schücking 509)), in Hammer and Sturm's version, becomes 'Nun, meine Brüder und Gefährten im Exil. Ist dieses ursprüngliche Leben nicht viel süsser als das Leben in aufgeschminktem Pomp?' (Rischbieter 14); 'Now, my brothers and companions in exile. Is not this unspoiled [natural, primitive] life much sweeter than the life of painted [decorated] pomp?' The production's linguistic palette was not restricted to German: Orlando made his entry into Arden singing in Italian, and Jaques, starting 'Die ganze Welt ist Bühne', decided that the translation was not up to scratch and, 'bizarrely gesticulating', delivered the speech in English (Günther Grack, *Neue Zürcher Zeitung*, 27 September). This was Jaques's party piece, and one of a number of metatheatrical touches; another was the placement of the first Silvius–Phoebe scene on a makeshift platform stage built over the pond: existing in their world of high artifice, the pair were players within a play within a play.

Jutta Lampe's performance as Rosalind (spelt, as a number of reviewers noticed, English-style rather than the German 'Rosalinde') was rooted in a quasi-Brechtian approach that prioritized playing the situation over character psychology, and was generally well received. Reviewers admired Lampe's versatility, her multidimensional range: whether she was affecting courtly airs, playing her 'cheeky-ironic double-act in men's clothing' or 'girlishly confessing to falling in love', the *Augsburger Allgemeine*'s Liselotte Müller (22 September) recorded, her charisma was irresistible. Jürgen Deisner (*Darmstädter Echo*) liked her 'laddish charm' as Ganymede, the 'hearty, throaty voice' that commanded 'undivided attention'; Jürgen Beckelman (*Bremen Weser-Kurier*, 29 September) similarly applauded her 'saucy, mischievous charm' and felt that she radiated a 'bittersweet beauty'. Ingeborg Keller (*Sozialdemokratische Wochenzeitung*, 6 October) wrote that as a 'passionate young woman in love in boyish clothes', she struck the right balance between 'delicacy and boldness' and was convincing 'in every nuance'. Lampe's playfulness did not preclude emotional intensity. For Peter Iden, her performance made the 'long evening worthwhile': the love which started as 'a playful whim to pass the time' becomes 'an overwhelming passion which she can hardly bear', and she gave this 'desperate' passion 'the most determined expression' (*Frankfurter Rundschau*).

Others were less impressed. For some she was at odds with the romantic image of Rosalind: Friedrich Luft, for example, thought she was 'sometimes touching', had at times an 'amusing gruffness', but failed to convey Rosalind's 'youthful fervour, her spirited and tender leading role in this magical play' (*Die Welt*, 22 September). *Die Zeit*'s Heinrichs was disappointed on different grounds: 'there was always something inaccessible, inexplicable about this actress and now she is totally, and solely, enchanting, the darling of her audience'. Heinrichs found this symptomatic of the production as a whole, which he regarded as monumentally self-indulgent and anodyne. Kaiser (*Süddeutsche Zeitung*), though respectful of Lampe's performance, suggested that she had trouble making an impression in the production itself, a living, profuse, total spectacle that perhaps overwhelmed its human participants. There is some justice in this observation: Stein's use of continuous simultaneous action across and around the space made it difficult if not impossible for spectators to focus exclusively on the lovers, and the playing of situation through image not only externalized the central relationships but simplified, scaled up and sometimes abstracted them. A striking example of this was seen in the staging of the deer-killing (4.2). As at Stratford in 1973 and many times since (see Chapter III), this was a symbolically charged sequence: a deer was skinned on stage while Celia *and* Rosalind fell asleep together; one of the hunters wrapped himself in the deerskin, the others placed horns on their heads, and they began to execute a primal dance. Meanwhile Orlando made himself up as a woman, 'play[ing] at being Narcissus with a makeshift mirror' (*Plays and Players*), caressed his chest and then grappled with the deerskinned hunter; Rosalind and Celia, locked together, rolled across the floor. Patterson records that Stein 'refuses to "explain" this episode', quoting him to the effect that '[i]t formed a part of a dreamlike mime sequence which possessed musical and visual meaning rather than any narrow interpretable significance' (Patterson 145).

Stein reserved some of his biggest effects for the end. At the beginning of 5.4, at the very moment the comedy appeared to be heading for its resolution, the idyll was brutally shattered as a huge door in the back wall flew open and Duke Frederick and his invasion force crashed into the forest. Cutting their way downstage through the bracken, they seemed to surrender to the forest's charms, one by one collapsing to the floor or into the pond, discarding their armour. But if the forest had prevailed in the struggle for peace, the victory was only temporary and equivocal. The entry of Hymen (Gerd David) brought on one of the monster pageant-wagons from *Shakespeare's Memory* and initiated a full-circle return to the beginning: upstage, the door stayed open 'so that the audience saw again that cold blue light beckoning in the distance', and the restored Duke, his followers and the united lovers dispensed with their timeless-contemporary clothing, and identities, to reassume the fabulously ornate and oppressive Elizabethan costumes of the first act. As they piled into the wagon, imploring in chorus for Jaques to come with them, it rolled ponderously towards the door and the court; 'But the wagon wouldn't fit through the door, stopped with a bump and knocked off the actors, who stumbled back on foot to the world of politics and intrigue' (Kennedy 265). Phoebe, utterly inconsolable at the loss of Ganymede, sobbed distraughtly at the side, Corin resumed his work clearing up after the city-dwellers had gone, and Jaques stayed behind, 'a solitary, grumbling Englishman with a muffler, umbrella and little black bag' (*Plays and Players*).

Habicht records that when Orlando crashed into Duke Senior's picnic he was 'behaving as a terrorist' (Habicht 299). The observation incidentally brings Stein's production squarely into line with the bombings, shootings, hijackings and kidnappings of the German Autumn: even in this Arden, the green world of which the country's young millenarian radicals dreamed, bloodshed (and Shakespearean dynamite) was always just below the surface, ready to erupt. It was, then, perhaps entirely coincidental, but absolutely apposite, that Stein chose to dispense with Rosalind's epilogue and instead had Frederick, lying beside the beech tree, reciting (in German) the French poet Francis Ponge's 'Le cycle des saisons' ('The cycle of the seasons'):

> Weary of turning in on themselves during the winter, the trees suddenly take it into their heads that they have been duped. They can no longer endure it: they pour forth their words, a wave, a vomiting of green. They would like to explode into branchfuls of words ... But in fact everything has been arranged in advance ... 'You cannot escape from trees by tree-like means.' A renewed weariness, a renewed spiritual inward-turning. 'Let all this turn yellow and fall. Let the period of silence approach, the stripping bare, the AUTUMN.'[5]

For Patterson (whose translation this is), the poem 'summarized [Stein's] view of Arden: the freedom of nature is an illusion'

(149). Perhaps it also indirectly comments on the green fantasy that underpinned Germany's autumnal season of violence: let the period of silence approach.

Notes

1 These include the script, extensive correspondence between Copeau, Delacre and others, design sketches and ground plans, and notes on Auric's musical score. As well as Jacquot's essay, I have made use of the extensive resources available on the BNF's historic newspaper website Gallica (http://gallica.bnf.fr). All translations are my own.
2 Literally, 'Well, companions, brothers in exile; custom, the ancient virtues, has it not made our life in this place lovelier than the one where we saw pomp and artifice? Are not these forests less dangerous than a court where envy rules?'
3 The reporter appears to have miscounted. A complete cast list, published in *Comoedia*, 22 January 1935, gives the number of performers as 30. In addition to the major personnel listed in the Appendix, the article lists the following: Ed Beauchamp, Charles; Gilles Margaritis, Denis/William; de Baudy, Le Beau; Jean Saran, First Lord; Jean-Louis Barrault, First Lord/First Spectator/First Dancing Shepherd/Hymen; Daniel Gilbert/Serge de Sawely, Second Lord/Second Spectator; Pierre Valde, Third Spectator/First Forester; Bobby Blanc, First Page/Second Dancing Shepherd/the Doe; Gino Paul, Second Page; Pierre Herbé, Singing Page/Duke Frederick's Second Guard; Paulette Leibon, Page Musician; Paul Higonenc, Second Forester; J. Motley, Duke Frederick's First Guard; Marthe Herlin, Hisperia; Hélène Gerber, Female Spectator. François Vibert, who evidently took over at some point during the run, is listed as Jaques.
4 My account of Stein's production draws upon copies of press reviews supplied by the Shakespeare-Forschungsbibliothek München, which also provided a copy of the programme. Extracts from the production text are included in Rischbieter. All translations are my own.
5 'Las de s'être contractés tout l'hiver les abres tout à coup se flattent d'être dupes. Ils ne peuvent plus y tenir: ils lâchent leurs paroles, un flot, un vomissement de vert. Ils tâchent d'aboutir à une feillaison complète de paroles ... Mais, en réalité, cela s'ordonne! ... 'L'on ne sort pas des arbres par des moyens d'arbres.' Une nouvelle lassitude, et un nouveau retournement moral. 'Laissons tout ça jaunir, et tomber. Vienne le taciturne état, le dépouillement, l'AUTOMNE' (Ponge 48–9).

CHAPTER V

At all points like a man

A bloke in a frock

The National Theatre's 1967 all-male production of *As You Like It* opened on 3 October, with Ronald Pickup leading as Rosalind, Charles Kay as Celia, Richard Kay (no relation) as Phoebe, and Anthony Hopkins as Audrey. Among those in attendance at the first night was the veteran drag artist and popular entertainer Danny La Rue, then in the second decade of a long and lucrative career as a female impersonator that began, he later claimed, in childhood amateur dramatics, when, as reported in his *Daily Telegraph* obituary, 'My Juliet was very convincing' (1 June 2009). Being 'convincing', however, was not in the least the aim of La Rue's act: whether belting out impersonations of, amongst others, Marlene Dietrich, Zsa Zsa Gabor and Bette Davis from the stage of his revue club in Hanover Square, or wowing pantomime audiences with his Widow Twankey or Fairy Godmother, La Rue insisted that he was 'a variety performer': 'I never want people to forget that I'm a bloke in a frock' (*Telegraph*). With his pneumatic bosoms, feathers, furs and sequins, colossal wigs and a vocal and gestural repertoire that constructed an image of femininity as 'faintly grotesque, with glitter and elegance' (Dennis Barker, *Guardian*, 2 June 2009), there was not much risk of that; and had La Rue taken the opportunity to leaf through his programme, he would have found himself included in a portfolio of cross-dressers through the ages, alongside Edward Kynaston (the last male actor of women's parts on the Restoration stage), the celebrated Peking Opera artist Mei Lanfang, the Chorus of Splinters (a transvestite concert troupe that toured the trenches during the First World War), Alec Guinness in *Kind Hearts and Coronets*, Jack Lemmon and Tony Curtis in *Some Like It Hot*, a schoolboy Laurence Olivier as Kate in *The Taming of the Shrew*, and images of burlesque, music hall, cabaret and pantomime. If this represented the production's attempts to situate itself on the grounds of popular drag entertainment, it appears not to have impressed La Rue himself (who had sent the cast a first-night telegram, 'COME ON IN THE WATER IS FINE'), as overheard in the Old Vic's crush bar during the interval: 'Well, it's very interesting, of course, but I don't see the point of it' (*Observer*, 8 October 1967).

He was not alone. Ronald Bryden, the *Observer* reviewer who reported La Rue's remark, considered that it was the 'best verdict' on a production that 'proves nothing – it's hard to see what it could hope to – about Shakespeare's play'. The *Guardian*'s Philip Hope-Wallace, while more favourably disposed, 'did not feel that any theory had been irrefutably proven' (4 October), and Jeremy Kingston in *Punch* (11 October) considered that while '[a]n extra ambiguity is added to Rosalind/Ganymede's wooing of Orlando and the mock marriage … [W]hether this constitutes a valuable discovery is difficult to determine.' On the other hand, there were those who thought that the casting was completely vindicated by the production's results. W. A. Darlington confessed that ever since it had been announced, he had been 'trying to think out what point this experiment would serve, without success', but concluded that 'it has come off brilliantly' (*Daily Telegraph*, 4 October); Harold Hobson, similarly, wrote that he had been 'opposed from the beginning … As soon as the idea was first mooted, it was self-evident to me that the experiment would be a failure.' 'Well,' he concedes, 'I was wrong. This *As You Like It* is not a failure, but an outstanding success' (*Sunday Times*, 8 October). As we shall see, those who considered the show a success differed amongst themselves as to how and why it did so; what is worth noting is that all of the reviews, positive, negative, or neutral, shared the view that, as an 'experiment', this was a production with a point to prove or a thesis to test.

I shall return to this issue below, but first, I should explain that it was an experiment with a protracted and fraught back-story, and that the complex circumstances of its genesis partly contributed to a perceived sense of multiple, possibly contradictory agendas and mixed messages. According to Pickup, the idea first surfaced in 1966: while he was watching a rehearsal at the Old Vic, John Dexter – then one of Olivier's associate directors – 'leaned over and said: "Get a pair of fucking legs. You're going to play Rosalind in a year's time"' (quoted in Matt Trueman, *Guardian*, 13 July 2015). Dexter had been reading Jan Kott's essay 'Shakespeare's Bitter Arcadia' (in *Shakespeare Our Contemporary*) and was much taken by his line on *As You Like It*, prompted by Kott's chance encounter with 'a young couple kissing, both in jeans, both with long hair', so that he 'could not decide which was the man, which the woman' (Rosenthal *National Theatre Story* 128). Kott's interpretation was informed by 'the theatrical aesthetics of Genet': '[i]n the love scenes of the Forest of Arden ... the theatrical form and the theme completely correspond with and inter-penetrate each other; on condition, that is, that female parts are played, as they were on the Elizabethan stage, by boys' (Kott 218–19).

The production was announced for the following spring in *The Times* on 24 August 1966, when it was stated that Kott would be acting 'as advisor to the production'; at that stage, John Stride (who later took over from Hopkins as Audrey) was slated for Orlando and Dacre Punt was to design. By December the production had been postponed to the autumn of 1967, with its scheduled slot taken by Tom Stoppard's *Rosencrantz and Guildenstern are Dead*. In the meantime, Dexter and Kenneth Tynan had tried to persuade Paul McCartney (then in full *Sgt. Pepper* mode) to compose the music for the production; having initially expressed an interest, the cheeky Beatle gave it the thumbs-down: 'I don't like the play, or Shakespeare, enough to do something good ... I've ... probably fucked up your plans. I'm sorry' (quoted in Rosenthal *National Theatre Story* 128).[1] By the end of January, Dexter, dissatisfied with the proposed casting, had withdrawn from the production; two months later, on 23 March, *The Times* reported that a replacement director was yet to be announced (in fact, Olivier had engaged Clifford Williams immediately following Dexter's departure). On 7 August, *The Times* confirmed the final line-up for the National production: in addition to Williams, Ralph Koltai was identified as designer and Jeremy Brett as Orlando, and the report cited 'a note in the theatre's news folder': 'in Shakespeare's own day *As You Like It* was presented with a male cast in costumes of the current time'.

Two weeks before the production opened, Jan Kott was profiled in *The Times*. He had been 'watching rehearsals with enthusiasm and approval', the work convincing him that 'actors who do not speak in falsetto or mime a woman's gestures and walk can solve the problem of ... a play about love regardless of sex'; the acting 'is very honest and very natural' (18 September). Kott's notion of genderless love was one that Williams appeared to endorse. Dexter, according to Rosenthal, had envisaged an explicitly queerer production than the one that Williams directed: a gay man, Dexter was 'convinced that Rosalind was bisexual' (*National Theatre Story* 131); by coincidence, his return to the London stage in the autumn of 1967 was marked by his West End production of Simon Gray's *Wise Child*, which centred on Alec Guinness in drag – and involved in games of dominance and submission with his pretty-boy companion, Jerry. As Alan Sinfield writes, the 'queer nuances' were unmistakable: 'nearly everyone knew what was being talked about' (Sinfield 275). Williams would in 1970 direct Tynan's satirical nude revue *Oh Calcutta!*, a show which, taking advantage of the abolition of the Lord Chamberlain's Office's powers of theatre censorship in 1968, sought to engage in sketch format with as many aspects of sex as an evening's entertainment could accommodate – with the complete exception of homosexuality.

In 1967, Williams appeared to be in more chaste mood. Having inherited a production concept whose scope for queer reading was, as far as the mainstream traditions of Shakespearean performance were concerned, unprecedented, he went out of his way to minimize its more radical implications. Quoted at length in the programme, Kott is also, bizarrely, the subject of a disclaimer in Williams's 'Production Note': 'The examination of the infinite beauty of Man in love – which lies at the very heart of *As You Like It* – takes place in an atmosphere of spiritual purity which transcends sensuality in the search for poetic sexuality. It is for this reason that I employ a male cast; so that we shall not – entranced by the surface reality – miss the interior truth.'

Williams is indicating, I think, that casting women in the female roles naturally and inevitably eroticizes them, but that male actors are equally and obviously *not* liable to desiring scrutiny; the assumption is that women are by definition distractingly sexual in ways that men simply are not. How much Williams believed all this is anyone's guess, but in an interview given some years later he was franker about what was at stake. Having admitted that 'we read Kott's essay, and decided that it was absolutely daft', Williams reveals that 'Kott, who is unusually sexually aware, came to rehearsals. He said that his thought had been to use boys about 14 years old. He spoke of Shakespeare and pederasty, and said there is in the text a quote from Christopher Marlowe who had a bigger thing about small boys than Shakespeare' (the reference is to Phoebe's invocation of the 'Dead shepherd' and citation of *Hero and Leander*, 'Who ever loved that loved not at first sight?' (3.5.80–1)). As if the shade of the 'unusually sexually aware' professor (meaning what, exactly?) musing on paedophilia were not enough, there was also the palpable worry that the show was skating on thin ice: 'For the opening night as the Old Vic, we were apprehensive. We suspected it might offend members of the audience, many of whom are elderly and from the middle class.' The safeguard was that, 'from the start, we were determined that there should be no female impersonation, no mincing, no attempt to speak in a falsetto, no feminine gesture. In drag, it would have been hideous, a very boring travesty, if you watched a chap trying to get his voice higher all night' (quoted in Paine Knickerbocker, *San Francisco Sunday Examiner and Chronicle*, 21 July 1974).

Williams was probably right to have been concerned that some members of the audience might take offence at the production, but less convincing as to the likely source of that offence. The immediate risk, as he identifies it, is that of bad drag performance; but the real, unspoken worry concerns the possibility of same-sex desire. By running them together, he seems to hope that fixing the former somehow neutralizes the threat of the latter. Williams was responding to what Marjorie Garber has described as 'the hegemonic cultural imaginary ... saying to itself: if there is a difference (between gay and straight) we want to be able to *see* it, and if we see a difference (a man in woman's clothes), we want to be able to *interpret* it ... [T]he conflation is fuelled by a desire to *tell the difference*, to guard against a difference that might otherwise put the identity of one's own position in question' (Garber 130).

In the same interview, Williams reveals that at one point he had thought of staging the play as a performance by inmates of a Japanese prisoner-of-war camp, thereby providing a rationale (or an alibi) for the all-male casting, and allowing one kind of camp to displace another. In the event, the range of gender performances offered by the production, spread across the multiple personae of Hopkins/Stride/Audrey, Kay/Celia, Kay/Phoebe, and Pickup/Rosalind/Ganymede, was framed within a *mise en scène* that, *pace* Kott, styled the production's Shakespeare as contemporary by pitching it somewhere between Carnaby Street and the shiny plastic milieu of 1960s science fiction. This was a world in which, but for the odd fetishistic flash of leather, little was not ersatz or synthetic:

Koltai's chicly minimalist settings were based on plain, geometrically angled surfaces, 'a transparent plexiglass wall' upstage, 'a few geometrical forms, half pyramids and half conic cubes' on the stage floor (Baumgärtel 250), over which transparent tubes hung from 'a snowflake ceiling ... and not a tree in sight' (David Nathan, *Sun*, 4 October); this was 'some lunar culture that is yet to dawn' (Herbert Kretzmer, *Daily Express*, 4 October), inhabited by 'courtly astronauts in gleaming PVC, Lurex and snowy nylon fun-furs' (Bryden, *Observer*). Amidst all this glacial beauty, Frank Wylie's Duke Frederick, 'got up to resemble the villainous Gabriel in [Joseph] Losey's [1966 film] *Modesty Blaise*', was a flashily sinister combination of gangster, nightclub owner, rock-band manager and drug dealer, who led 'a band of sexless fascists dressed in chilly plastic uniforms who fittingly perform their rituals in what looks like a modern store window' (Philip French, *New Statesman*, 13 October 1967). As Jaques, Robert Stephens, 'like some last of the Bloomsburians in a faded white alpaca suit' (*Guardian*), sported a transparent PVC mac and brolly; and Touchstone (Derek Jacobi) wore very contemporary motley: striped tailcoat with epaulettes, calf-length boot on his right foot and co-respondent shoe on his left. The Swinging London groove was enhanced by the live music: a combo of drums, bass, electric guitar, accordion and saxophone underscored and punctuated the action with snatches of hot jazz (for the court scenes), folk-rock blended with echoes of Elgar's *Enigma Variations* (for the transition to Arden), 'futuristic' instrumental pop on the lines of the Tornadoes' 1962 hit 'Telstar', and, for 'It Was a Lover and His Lass', skiffle – a mixing of musical styles that suggests that the hybrid *Sgt. Pepper* McCartney spirit was in play after all.[2] The lighting contributed to the aura of glamorous unreality: 'At one point, the stage is bathed in golden winter glow, at others in silver, red or – for the nuptial celebration at the end – an almost psychedelic profusion of colour' (Frank Marcus, *Plays and Players*, 1967). For Marcus, this 'inorganic' Arden was the right environment for characters who were 'a-sexual', with the result that 'the experiment in female impersonation, far from being the most noteworthy facet of the production, became quite unimportant – indeed, almost irrelevant – to it'.

The *Daily Mail* agreed: in his naughtily titled review ('Taking a dream trip with the bard'), Peter Lewis adopted an even more overtly psychedelic line, considering the overall effect 'so strange, so visually and aurally hypnotic' that 'the fact that all the girls are really men takes its place as merely one of the elements in a dream-like total experience, which you accept along with the rest' (4 October). As a result, love, in this production, was 'sexless, or rather sexually ambiguous', a position also adopted by Kretzmer in the *Daily Express* ('an affair of unusual panache and purity'), and by Hobson in the *Sunday Times*: 'Mr Pickup's performance ... divorces love from sex': 'So do the performances in the other transvestite parts. The result is that when one comes to the marvellous quartet on the ache and unfulfilled desire of love near the end of the play there is a purity, a "magical release from material dominion", as Mr Williams himself says, that has probably not been achieved in any professional performance for the last 300 years.' These reviewers, at least, found the proposition that the all-male casting rendered the performance sexless perfectly credible. Not all agreed: Milton Shulman (*Evening Standard*) thought that 'one can catch nuances of a homosexual attraction between Orlando and Ganymede' but that Pickup's performance was severely constrained 'to justify the thesis that absolute love

7 Audrey (Anthony Hopkins) and Touchstone (Derek Jacobi) in rehearsal, the National Theatre, 1967

is absolutely neuter', and that Charles Kay as Celia 'is allowed to teeter into high queerdom'. But for the most part the possibility of queer desire, even in the context of a production that opened two months after the 1967 Sexual Offences Act partially decriminalized sex between men in the UK, was not so much rejected as not even countenanced.

Williams's insistence that there had been 'no female impersonation' in the process of making the show is at odds with what the reviewers reported, and what can be seen and heard in the production records. In one respect the production was absolutely in line with mainstream drag conventions. A major element of the appeal of drag performance of the Danny La Rue variety is its display of conspicuous, indeed brazenly profligate, expenditure on jewellery, wigs, frocks and sundry accoutrements; similarly, with respect to the frontline mechanism of female impersonation, the costuming, the National spared no expense in its construction of femininity as extravagant sartorial masquerade. The records include a costume inventory that, Henslowe-style, itemizes and prices every single element of the production wardrobe; and Rosalind and Celia's costumes combined account for one-fifth (£661) of a budget approaching £3,000 (around £50,000 in today's terms). Rosalind had four outfits: white wool dress and belt, white shoes and scarf for her first scene (£60, also including, as a reminder of the genital reality beneath the fiction of femininity, '1 jock strap'), gold lurex negligée, chain and locket and bracelet for 1.3 (£70), white PVC trouser suit, two blue shirts, orange silk scarf, black boots and (a nod to Vanessa) white corduroy cap for Arden (£75), and, for the finale, white shoes and socks, white elbow-length gloves, and white silk dress 'with silver/PVC appliqué' (£60). Celia also had four: white shoes and wool dress, accessorized with turquoise scarf (£60, including jock strap), silver lurex negligée (£60), silver lurex minidress, scarf, thigh-length silver boots and 'blue fab-fur coat with hood' for the forest (£65), and a final-scene costume identical to Rosalind's (£60). Audrey and Phoebe, by comparison, were cheap dates: the former had white sandals, PVC fringed dress and string of wooden beads (and jock strap) at £75, the latter, shoeless, a silver lurex dress, bangle and 'grey jock strap' at £70. The predominance of synthetic over natural materials is of its time but also, in terms of the production's ruling ideas, speaks for itself: as the primary signifier of gender identity, these costumes, like those of the play's men, were as close to the naturalistically real as it was possible to get, and at the same time absolutely and ostentatiously fabricated.

The simplicity of Audrey and Phoebe's costuming in some ways matched the relative straightforwardness of their actors' performances, both of which, however, trouble Williams's claims. For most reviewers, Anthony Hopkins's Audrey was the easiest to locate on the spectrum of female impersonation, and it was the one that most obviously treated the exercise as a joke. As anyone who has spent time with rugby players can confirm, the urge to strap on fake breasts and climb into stockings and suspenders at the slightest social opportunity is shared by many of the most self-professedly hyper-masculine, non-queer men; Philip Hope-Wallace linked Hopkins's performance with well-established entertainment traditions in the British armed forces, 'the kind of camp concert resorted to in a battle ship' (*Guardian*), and Ronald Bryden labeled it 'basic ENSA knockabout' (*Observer*). For a number of reviewers, Hopkins's Audrey had a mock-Wagnerian dimension: along with a number of colleagues, Irving Wardle referred to her a 'Brünnhilde', who, he continued, 'sits expressionlessly through Touchstone's advances, and then grasps him in a bear-hug' (*The Times*). Wardle thought that this, 'the funniest of all the performances', had 'grown out of embarrassment'. Perhaps he had in mind an article in the *Sunday Times* (1 October), which reported that Hopkins had arrived at the first rehearsal 'wondering whether he would play Audrey as a female impersonation or as a woman. Full of anxiety.' On 2 September, burdened with 'a complex he could not overcome', he was threatening to walk out: 'There's a huge wall ... I don't think I can make the sexual leap.' At the next rehearsal, however, Hopkins 'wears a rough shift and it dictates the way he walks. He then adds a wig of long hair and the natural gestures to keep it out of his eyes help to ease the problem.' In the rehearsal photographs, Hopkins is the only one of the four cross-dressers in wig and skirt; as it turned out, this comically Method commitment produced the performance most removed from naturalism (see Figure 7). The audio recording (made on 14 May 1968, with John Stride now in the role; Hopkins left the show on 16 November) places the audience response to Audrey precisely: before she has uttered a line, there is a big laugh, a smattering of applause, and, tellingly, some ironic wolf-whistling.

While Audrey's status as a character readily lends her to pantomime-style send-up, Celia seems less obviously amenable to guying; yet in Charles Kay's performance she emerged as almost as much of a male parody of femininity. Primped up in short skirt, bobbed wig and thick-framed spectacles, Kay's Celia, as a number of reviewers remarked, strongly resembled the *Daily Mirror* agony aunt and media personality Marjorie Proops; for Wardle, this 'mini-skirted governess' was 'an exercise in suppressed camp', while Bryden saw 'straight if muted camping: a comic performance based on recognizable masculine imitation of female mannerisms' (as noted above, this was for Shulman 'high queerdom'). But while Audrey and Celia could be safely relegated to a zone of comic transvestism where they posed no sexual threat, this was not the case with Richard Kay's Phoebe. He was the one actor in the production to convincingly pass not only as female, but also as desirably so. Kay, Darlington observed, was 'so feminine in voice and gesture that he might have been a woman' (*Telegraph*), 'a nightclub female impersonation', in Bryden's view, 'a languorous, lipsticked sexpot with curiously hard muscles' (*Observer*). John Higgins (*Financial Times*, 4 October) described Kay as 'succulent, tartish'; Pickup later remembered that Kay was 'truly womanlike … You'd see people checking their programmes when he came on' (*Guardian*, 13 July 2015). For at least one reviewer, his desirability crossed a line: Kay, wrote Martin Esslin, was 'disturbingly pretty, large but with lovely legs and a fine face. It's really disturbing if one also becomes aware, at the same time, that this pretty girl is a man' (*New York Times*, 15 October). A look at the production photographs confirms the source of Esslin's unease: in his slinky minidress, cut to display a great length of smoothly shaved leg, Kay is unambiguously positioned as the object of the desiring gaze. As, too, is Silvius (John McEnery), whose open-to-the-waist tunic and cropped breeches focus attention on his muscular calves, abdomen and chest. This corner of Arden, at least, was far from 'sexless'.

According to the majority critical view, the same could not be said of Pickup's Rosalind. Esslin, who found himself disturbed by the erotic stirrings provoked by Phoebe, was bothered in a different way by Pickup, whom he characterized as resembling 'a vicious caricature of Vanessa Redgrave', and as 'totally devoid of sexuality, ambiguous or otherwise'. Wardle concurred: Pickup was 'completely non-erotic'. Pickup 'speaks beautifully, moves well', wrote Higgins, 'but has to spend too much of his time thinking about femininity to stir the pulse … the verses pinned to the tree and even the mock marriage fail to produce any sexual feelings'. Opinions differed as to whether Pickup was attempting female impersonation at all. For Bryden, his Rosalind was 'pure Noh: a woman's role, played with no pretences by a man'; Darlington felt that he 'was no more expecting us to take him for a woman than Dorothy Tutin [RSC, 1967], in her scenes as Ganymede ... expected us to take her for a man'. At the same time, this reviewer noticed, there were lapses into camp: 'Occasionally, when he overdid the mincing walk which goes with long skirts we had an impulse to giggle.' Others recorded subtler touches of gender play: his Ganymede was 'uncanny in its observation of how, for example, women believe men throw back their arms and laugh' (Kingston, *Punch*), and he 'always manages through mere hints of movement to suggest that he was a girl pretending to be a boy' (David Nathan, *Sun*, 4 October). Wardle found that Rosalind 'begins demurely with a few well observed female gestures, and takes on character only during the Ganymede scenes'. The sense that Rosalind, rather than Pickup, was not entirely at ease in her female role was also detected by Shulman: 'a weedy, gauche creature', Rosalind appeared 'uncertain of what to do with her hands or when to cross her legs' in the court scenes, but 'naturally comes into her/his own when she wears male clothes as Ganymede' (*Evening Standard*). For the most part, Pickup's performance was quietly praised, in particular for the delicacy and tact with which he and Jeremy Brett played their central scenes. There was, Wardle wrote, 'real excitement in seeing Rosalind and Jeremy Brett's very masculine Orlando being taken unawares by serious emotion in the midst of their game'. Bryden provides the detail: 'In his scenes with Orlando, Pickup plays simply an emotion, with no attempt to characterize. His eyes fasten, blazing, on the object of his love, with a passion to which sex and identity itself seem irrelevant. For a moment Orlando recoils, blinking uneasily, then surrenders to its current, a force impossible to resist or suspect as light ... For a moment, transparent as Koltai's Perspex props, the theatre floods with pure, lucid love' (*Observer*).

Philip Hope-Wallace saw it differently: 'the margin of gain in those crucial exchanges ... seemed dubious. If not embarrassing, they were somehow less effective than one has seen them' (*Guardian*). Listening to the audio recording, I am inclined to side with Wardle and Bryden: judged on voice alone, Pickup's performance is varied, rich, passionate and vulnerable. And it is delivered without the slightest attempt vocally to impersonate a woman: unlike Charles Kay, whose mannered, arch diction employs every trick in the drag queen's book, and unlike Richard Kay, audibly pouting through every line, Pickup employs his natural register throughout, as both Rosalind and Ganymede. The effect is simple, clear and, for its time, quietly radical: what I hear in the scenes between Rosalind and Orlando is the sound of two men falling in love. It is not for me to challenge the testimony of the reviewers (they were there; I was not), but I cannot see this as sexless, platonic or ambiguous, nor as so wrapped up in multiple levels of role-play that the nature of this desire cannot be identified or recognized. There is a risk of oversimplifying what, I suggest, some of the reviewers were over-thinking, but in this Arden there was an equal risk of not seeing the wood for the trees. Perhaps the sex-free line was the only way that a non-heterosexual reading of the play and of its central relationship could be imagined in a culture in which homosexuality was unthinkable other than in terms of camp, scandal or monstrosity.[3]

As You Like It was the hit of the 1967 season, and the original-cast production stayed in the repertoire until 1969, a total of 96 performances that included a brief UK and European tour that took the show to Sunderland, Liverpool, Stockholm, Copenhagen, Belgrade and Venice. Evidence suggests the production was more warmly regarded by its audiences than by its critics, and that it was better received as its run progressed. Reporting on the first night for the *New York Times* (6 October), Dana Adams Schmidt noticed the 'long-haired boys and short-haired girls among the enthusiastic viewers' – a rather different, and perhaps more socially and sexually diverse, constituency than that anxiously anticipated by Williams – and that '[a]lthough audience reactions suggested the cast had struck the right tone of nimbly balanced mockery and cynicism, most of London's critics were not impressed'. A number of reviewers commented on the slow pace of the show on press night (at 3 hours and 11 minutes, this was by some degree the longest of the run); by the fifth performance, according to the show report, the 'new cuts' brought the show down to just under 3 hours; towards the end of the run, it was regularly running at around 2 hours and 50 minutes.[4] Other measures suggest that the production really settled into its stride some months into the run. As standard, the show reports document the number of curtain calls, with any additional to the three noted as 'set'. The first 35 performances all record calls as 'set'; at the thirty-sixth performance (25 April 1968), there was an additional ovation, and this was repeated for the next five; audiences at this stage in the production's life were demonstrably enjoying it more than their predecessors, and it is possible that their willingness to let the actors know this had an energizing effect. When the show embarked on its European tour things really took off. The first performance in Stockholm, on 28 September (the show's fifty-second), earned no fewer than four additional ovations, as did the second; the third and fourth, in Copenhagen, earned three; the National Theatre in Belgrade prompted four ovations at the first performance, three at the second, and six at the third (6 October). Back at the Old Vic for the seventy-fifth performance on 12 November, there was one additional call, as there were for all but five of the remaining 21 performances of the run; the final show, on 16 July 1969, ended with two.

Perhaps the sound of this applause rather than the responses of the reviewer persuaded the National's management to keep the production in its repertoire for nearly two years; perhaps, also, the memory of that sound tempted someone to keep it going longer than it should have. In 1974, Williams revived his production, with identical sets and costumes and a new cast, for a tour of the United States and Canada, with Gregory Floy taking the place of Pickup as Rosalind. In San Francisco, where the show opened on 17 July, the notices were largely favourable: the *San Francisco Chronicle*'s Paine Knickerbocker found it 'utterly beguiling', with Floy's Rosalind, 'an exciting and attractive woman' with – somewhat contradictorily – 'only the slightest hints of femininity'. Stanley Eichelbaum of the *San Francisco Examiner* also had a 'singularly enjoyable' experience, and predicted that '[n]obody ... will find the drag portrayals objectionable, notably because they're so chastely and intelligently done' (18 July). When the production made its way eastwards from the gay capital of America to New York in November, the reception was very different. Douglas Watt of the New York *Daily News* (4 December) called it 'a bore', declared that 'despite all disclaimers, this is necessarily Shakespeare as camp' and judged that '[t]he mod costumes ... are unfortunately just a bit out of date but fit the background'. The sense that this was a production whose moment had passed was also expressed by the *New York Post*'s Martin Gottfried, who reported that it was 'the talk of London six years ago, and it looks it' (4 December).

For this reviewer, the production's sexual dynamics were crude, confused and objectionable: 'the homosexual implications cannot be ignored even when they never make sense'; the male lovers were 'infantile studs', Floy was 'mincing his way through Audrey Hepburn', and '[a]s for those women played by men, there seems no way to make them anything but gay'.

More damagingly, Clive Barnes in the *New York Times* (4 December) characterized the revival as a second-rate retread of the original that misleadingly traded on its National Theatre status, pointing out that 'only one actor, playing a minor role' had ever appeared there. Barnes, who had admired Pickup's performance, thought that Floy portrayed Rosalind 'as a rather pretty girl played by a man. The voice flutes, the face is coquettish, even the wearing of the clothes is oddly naughty and not at all ambiguous.' 'Perhaps', he concluded, 'the National Theater should remember that it is not in the franchise business like Kentucky Fried Chicken.' He followed this with an article in *The Times* (14 December) which reiterated the point that this 'sub-standard version' was 'not at all good for the reputation of the National Theatre, or for that matter British acting', and drew the killer comparison: 'The Royal Shakespeare Company orders things differently. At least it does in America.' Williams was sufficiently provoked to respond in a letter to *The Times* (27 December), in which he attempted to rebut Barnes's charge that the revival was not a 'genuine' National Theatre product, insisted that 'glowing reviews' had been received across the United States, and concluded that 'Clive Barnes did not like the production. When he saw it some years ago at the Old Vic he did. Which proves that either the production, unfortunately, has changed for the worse – or Clive Barnes has.' Maybe Williams felt a score had been settled, but it seems a sadly petty final word on a production of this play that – despite the intentions of its director – pushed at sexual boundaries in ways that would be unmatched for nearly a quarter of a century. I prefer Pickup's own perspective on the show, as reported in the previously cited *Guardian* piece nearly fifty years on: 'becoming Ganymede was the most natural thing in the world. It felt like a release, like a creature being set free in the forest … [O]ur Arden had a different kind of wildness to it; a freedom, a real joy … In our ambisexual Arden, anything went. It was a kind of utopia – but it didn't seem revolutionary. We were just actors having a ball.'

Alias Touchstone

If there is one thing that actors and critics can agree on, it is that Touchstone – at least in theory – is not funny. Recalling his dismay when he was cast in the part in Steven Pimlott's 1996 RSC production (he had auditioned for Orlando), David Tennant writes of how he 'could see that Touchstone was supposed to be funny in terms of the structure of the play, the tone of his scenes, and the fact that everyone keeps going on about how hilarious he is ... yet I could find nothing in the part to make me smile'. As it turned out, Tennant made a notable success of the part (see Chapter III), largely by making a decision to 'stop striving for the logical through-line and to play each moment as it comes' (Tennant 32, 40), but this was against his own expectations and those of the reviewers: 'Tennant's archly Scottish Touchstone', wrote Jack Tinker, 'is a sprightly comic re-invention of this often tiresome fool' (*Daily Mail*, 3 May 1996). George Bernard Shaw, reviewing George Alexander's St James's Theatre production in 1896, notoriously proffered the much-quoted view that 'an Eskimo would demand his money back if a modern author offered him such fare' (Shaw 25; quite why the Inuit is picked on in this way is impossible to fathom), and from that point onward reviewers have routinely prefaced their comments on Touchstone by observing that the clown is terminally unamusing. Yet what has become equally routine, as in Tennant's case, is the pleasurable surprise that the same critics go on to express when they discover that this or that actor has succeeded in making the part work after all. Derek Jacobi's performance in the Old Vic production was no exception to this rule. Shulman wrote that Jacobi 'has managed the incredible feat of making this clown actually very funny' (*Evening Standard*), and *Plays and Players* found that Touchstone was 'for once, genuinely funny'; the *Financial Times* was relieved not to be presented with a 'lumbering clown'. The last two reviewers respectively likened Jacobi's persona to 'a cockney taxi driver' and 'a camp East End number'. His performance was identified by several critics as the campest in the production, and a number also traced its source in the vocal and gestural mannerisms of the popular comedian Frankie Howerd, whose air of perpetually wounded gentility, mastery of innuendo and of the mock-outraged double-take, and simultaneously conspiratorial and combative relationship with his audience, served as Jacobi's main template (the audio recording also reveals hints of camp raconteur Kenneth Williams). Jacobi's Touchstone was thus in part impersonation as well as characterization, a hybrid of stage personae that made his text workable by rendering it as 'material' to be manipulated rather than fully inhabited.

This approach was taken considerably further in Peter Needham's performance in Cheek by Jowl's landmark all-male production of the play in 1991. Like Kenneth Branagh in the Renaissance Theatre Company production three years previously, Needham rooted Touchstone in mid-twentieth-century traditions of popular entertainment by making the clown a variety turn, 'a perky Archie Rice keen to regenerate his love-life' (Benedict Nightingale, *The Times*, 5 December), a 'jobbing variety hack' (Ian Shuttleworth, *City Limits*, 12 December), 'a cheeky cockney chappy straight out of music hall' (Charles Spencer, *Daily Telegraph*, 6 December). Sporting loud check too-short trousers, yellow waistcoat and flat cap, the white-haired Needham (in his early sixties when the production opened) conjured the memory of post-1950s British light entertainment (as memorably channelled through Olivier's rendering of Osborne's seedy, doomed Archie Rice in the 1957 Royal Court production of *The Entertainer*). More specifically, as only three reviewers noticed – or thought worth mentioning – Needham's Touchstone was precisely modelled on the veteran popular stage and screen entertainer Bruce Forsyth; as the archive video reveals, the portrayal does not merely evoke or allude to Forsyth's persona, but is a note-for-note near-perfect copy of it.[5] Born in 1928, Forsyth cut his teeth in variety, pantomime and circus, offering a mix of song-and-dance, comedy and strong-man act; he first came to wider public notice in 1958 when he became frontman for the long-running television variety show *Sunday Night at the London Palladium*. In 1971, he made his career-defining move to host *The Generation Game*, a role he was to perform, on and off, until 1994. With an act that combined avuncularity, slightly aggressive jocularity and occasional flashes of spite, and that frequently drew attention to the ropiness of his material, Forsyth provided Needham with the template for an entertainer who, Irving Wardle noted, 'scores his points from the fact that Touchstone never gets a laugh' (*The Times*, 29 January 1995). Deploying the classic variety-comedian 'Don't blame me, I didn't write this stuff' shtick, Needham found a metacomic solution to the problem of Shakespeare's comedy: what's funny is that it isn't funny, and we all know this. It also licensed Needham with considerable scope for extra-textual ad-libbing: when the 'pancakes' riff fell flat, he interjected a quick 'Please yourselves' (one of Frankie Howerd's catchphrases, as it happens), 'Jane Smile' (2.4.43) prompted lascivious memories ('Jane Smile ... yeah, Jane Smile'), Corin's admission that he does not 'shear the fleeces that I graze' (2.4.71) provoked an aside to Adrian Lester's Rosalind: 'I don't think he's your sort', and 'if you like upon report/The soil' (2.4.89–90) the outburst, 'O my gawd!' (this phrase also accompanied 'good meat into an unclean dish' (3.3.31)). At 5.3.7, Touchstone expanded his greeting to the pages ('By my troth, well met') with 'O yeah, all right, help yourselves'; he brought Audrey (Richard Cant[6]) on in the final scene with 'Come on, Audrey, we're going to be late if we're not careful', and the 'seven degrees of the lie' was played, with Audrey as his 'lovely assistant', as a version of the climactic *Generation Game* routine, in which 'Brucie' cajoled the winning contestant to list from memory the consumer-good prizes that had just trundled past her eyes on a conveyor belt. The gags and interpolations risked sounding cheap and obvious, but the frame-breaking and fourth-wall breaches were an entirely logical manifestation of this Touchstone's half-in, half-out positioning in the production's world.

The sense of a curiously doubled clown performance, of Needham playing Forsyth playing Touchstone (or of Needham playing Touchstone playing Forsyth) was in accord with the prevailing theme of a production in which the fundamentally performative nature of identity – and in particular of sexual and gender identities – was centrally at issue. Cheek by Jowl's *As You Like It* has been much discussed, in terms both of the radicalism of its sexual politics and of the theatrical daring with which these were articulated and addressed. Reflecting on the production two decades after it was made, director Declan Donnellan recalled its historic and political context: 'the British government was trying to pass a bill that described the gay experience as a "pretended family relationship"' [the reference is to the notoriously vindictive Clause 28 of the Local Government Act of 1988, which, in addition, prohibited the publication of 'material with the intention of promoting homosexuality'], '[designer] Nick Ormerod and I were working on a new play at the National called *Angels in America*, which Tony Kushner described as a "gay fantasia on national themes" and which described the impact of Aids, but its chief concern, like *As You Like It*, was the complexity of human love. It is now quite difficult to remember the uncertainty and fear of those days.' *As You Like It* was the tenth-anniversary production of a company that took its name from an ethos of close and immediate contact between actors, audience and text, and that had earned both critical acclaim and popular success; and the production was initially perceived as something of a risk, 'a strange experiment', as Donnellan put it (*Guardian*, 14 November 2014).[7] The director's remarks indicate that although the show 'had no direct agenda', there was no way, in the climate of its time, that an all-male production of the comedy could not be political. Its politics, though, embraced a cultural field that included, but was not restricted to, sexuality: as Donnellan observed at the time, 'I think we've lived in a decade of Thatcherism where a human failing for confusing illusion and reality "in a bad way" has come to a peak. The insane getting and spending ... We've chosen works which have been obsessed about the relationship between illusion and reality because I think the distinction between those two is something that was specifically lacking in the 1980s' (*Plays International*). The political gesture is less polemical than aesthetic or thematic. Twenty years on, Donnellan's position remained studiedly non-polemical: the show 'seemed to open imaginations and pose subtle but important questions. Above all, I think, it gave permission for ambivalence' (*Guardian*).

Bearing in mind both the landmark status of the production and the complexity of the relationship between intention and performance effects, however, and the widely divergent ways in which these have been interpreted by its immediate reviewers and by subsequent commentators, the sexual politics of the production need to be unpacked with care. In retrospect, it may seem surprising that in the first instance Donnellan was careful to state that 'our production is not a gay production': even though 'it's hard to see Jaques [Joe Dixon] as anything but a gay character, and Celia [Tom Hollander] has an enormous crush on Rosalind', the play 'in the end ... is basically about the celebration of the principle of marriage' (quoted in Sarah Hemming, *Independent*, 20 November 1991). The remarks date from the period immediately prior to the show's opening; at this stage, Donnellan appears, if anything, more interested in the theatrical possibilities of an all-male cast than in the homoerotic ones, referring to 'the honesty and humour with which Shakespeare portrays the complexity of sexuality ... you don't end up with androgyny: it's not as if sexuality cancels itself out in the middle – the players are somehow all men and all women at the same time'. Donnellan's view does not in itself provide the key to the production, and it cannot account for or anticipate the more single-minded reactions (as far as Laurence Brown of *Capital Gay* (2 February 1995) was concerned, 'This reading is largely a queer one'), but it resonates with some of the more considered responses to the cross-dressing.

A handful of reviewers can be said to have engaged in what James C. Bulman characterizes 'avoidance behavior', in the sense that they refused 'to grapple with the homophobic social attitudes and government policies which ... formed the context through which the production should be viewed' (Bulman 'Queering the Audience' 568). Bulman quotes John Peter (*Sunday Times*, 8 December 1991) asserting that the production proves that the play 'is not about sexuality – hetero-, homo-, bi- or trans- – but about love, which both transcends sexuality and includes it', as well as Katie Laris in *Theatre Journal*: 'The same-sex casting ... makes explicit the point that gender is ultimately unimportant in human relationships' (Laris 300). Others, however, found it less straightforward: Jane Edwardes, recognizing that 'it becomes clear how strange and brave it is that Orlando should agree to practise his wooing on a man', registered 'a definite *frisson* as one's sense of gender becomes increasingly confused' (*Time Out*, 11 December). A sense of disorientation was evident elsewhere: reviewing the 1994–95 revival, Bill Hagerty stated that those who regarded Rosalind's 'gender-bending pursuit' of Orlando as 'head-spinningly complicated' had better stay away, 'for it can only flummox them even further" (*Today*, 26 January 1995); Neil Smith (*What's On*, 1 January), meanwhile, saw 'an open challenge to the audience to jettison all preconceived conceptions'. Charles Spencer was refreshingly honest about the source of his unease: in a 'strange, challenging evening', Lester's 'disturbing sexual ambiguity', he confessed, 'left this hetero viewer feeling decidedly uncomfortable' (*Daily Telegraph*, 6 December 1991). More broadly, a significant number of reviewers acknowledged and indeed applauded the implications of what Kenneth Hurren, adopting a bravely contrarian position in relation to his own newspaper, described in the *Mail on Sunday* (8 December 1991) as 'a timely intrusion into the gathering cacophony of homophobia that threatens to overwhelm us all'. Benedict Nightingale judged that '[t]he effect was no more, no less, than to give the play a strong homoerotic feel, especially in the first half', and that the 'closing moral' of the show was that Orlando (Patrick Toomey) 'has had doubts and self-doubts all along, but now he accepts the scope and contradictions of his sexuality' (*The Times*, 5 December). The *Independent*'s Paul Taylor (6 December) likewise saw between Lester and Toomey 'a beautifully comic erotic tension and sexual ambiguity that's heightened because both players are men' and, comparing the production to Cheek by Jowl's mixed-sex *Twelfth Night* (1986), reported that 'the homosexual element in the hero's attraction was not suddenly swept aside in the statutory fifth-act pairing-off of straights'.

The *Evening Standard*'s out-gay Nicholas de Jongh was less persuaded by 'a brave attempt to play significant gender games with Shakespeare' that lacked 'sufficient magic insight or sexual courage in its breaking of barriers', not least because Toomey and Lester 'recoil from the homo-erotic implications of the production – wrongly so' (5 December). Fleet Street's only other openly identifying gay critic at the time, Jack Tinker, who was one of the few reviewers to actively dislike the production, saw it differently, finding it less homoerotic than too camp by half: 'among other twee-for-two touches, Celia tenderly kisses and nibbles Rosalind's legs, and Jaques, a closet gay, embraces the same "girl" in her male disguise. I quietly squirmed' (*Daily Mail*, 5 December). When the revived production came to the West End in 1995, Tinker completely revised his view: now it was 'stunning', with 'no drag queen indulgence' and 'no overtly gay totem' (*Daily Mail*, 3 February). Nightingale also noted the leg-play ('One of the two men-women clearly likes the other lifting her skirt and stroking her leg'), and mused that '[w]hen Celia tells her father that they have slept together, "coupled and inseparable", we wonder if he hasn't more than one reason for ridding his court of Rosalind'. At the same time, Nightingale detected in Rosalind and Celia's sexually charged first scene more than a hint of stereotyping, with Hollander 'in blue dress and pearls', affecting 'the slightly camp, mincing voice only seldom to be found among gay men, let alone women', and Lester responding to a remark about Orlando 'with a long "ooh", as if to say "get you, ducky"' (Edwardes also thought Hollander 'as trapped as any transvestite in a male concept of femininity').

Spencer, 'uncomfortable' with Lester's Rosalind, was particularly exercised by these scenes: 'Are we meant to accept them as bona fide women? Or are we meant to take them as transvestite homosexuals whose disguise has remained miraculously unrumbled in this masculine Edwardian environment?' This may sound deliberately obtuse, but Spencer's uncertainty as to how to read the disguising is a response of sorts to the production's metatheatricality. The idea that the production was centrally concerned with gender identity as performance was clearly signalled in a prologue sequence at the top of the show in which the first three lines of 'All the world's a stage' were given with the 14-strong company, identically dressed in plain white shirts and black trousers, assembled on a bare stage. At 'And all the men and [pause] *women* merely players' (2.7.140), Lester, Hollander (Simon Coates in 1995), Cant and Sam Graham (Wayne Cater in 1994) stepped stage left as the rest of the cast moved stage right, a division that both indicated the mutability of gender and established the terms of the game. For Donnellan, the central point was to invite the audience 'to tread a tightrope of willed belief, a quintessentially theatrical act of faith'. Inverting Brechtian logic, the director stated that '[e]xposing the nuts and bolts of theatre actually makes you more involved in the play. Instead of a clever essay on gender confusion the device opened up the play's emotional heart' (quoted in the *Independent*, 4 January 1995).

The seeming paradox resonates both with the actors' comments and with the contradictory quality of many of the reviewers' responses. Posing the question of why, on tour, the show had been a hit with 'Russian Mafiosi and Romanian schoolgirls' (two more divergently gendered groupings can scarcely be imagined), 'what, exactly, is he doing right?', the interviewer, Dominic Cavendish, reveals that '[n]either [Donnellan], nor his actors, seem quite able to put their finger on it'. Indeed, the sense that something about the way that show worked eluded definition or explanation is linked, associatively, with the uncanny: 'It was very strange in rehearsal,' Donnellan recalls, 'because they wore practice skirts and when they stopped to go off and have a coffee or light a fag it was as though there had been women in the room.' For Lester, getting it right came about through reverse engineering: 'Initially, I was trying to be a woman and the more I tried, the more the audience noticed the gap. It was the moment I got into trousers and forgot about trying to be female that the audience started to believe I was.'

This was borne out in a number of the reviews, which found Lester's Rosalind at its most camp, winsome, and least engaging in the first scenes (my viewing of the archive video inclines me to agree). Costumed in a long red silk dress and matching headband (Celia wore blue; the scheme was reversed in the revival), pearl earrings and necklace, and saddled with owlish spectacles and schoolgirl satchel, Lester played Rosalind as ill-at-ease both in a hyper-macho court populated by overgrown rugger-bugger public schoolboys in dinner jackets, and in her own body: Lester as Rosalind had a slight stoop, as though attempting to conceal her six-foot-two height (*Plays and Players'* Gwyn Morgan reported from rehearsal that 'Lester looked in a mirror and decided that he, like Rosalind, was too tall to be a socially acceptable woman' (February 1992)). As mentioned, Rosalind and Celia's deeply intimate relationship was regarded with deep suspicion by Duke Frederick (David Hobbs, who doubled as a slightly crazed Duke Senior chased, shirtless, onstage by his forest lords for his first scene), and this was perhaps the real impetus for their propulsion into Arden. Here, Lester as Ganymede came into his own, assuming loose brown herringbone-pattern trousers, white collarless shirt, green bandana and a straw hat, and a gestural repertoire that enabled him to move seamlessly between genders. Confronting Orlando (3.2.275) like 'the lady leaping out of the cake to a musical flourish – wantonly inviting, yet all of a flutter' (Hodgdon 'Sexual disguise' 193), Rosalind-Ganymede was 'trying valiantly to act like a boy in the presence of the man to whom she longs to expose herself ... yet sensible that she can trick him into making love to her by pretending to be his Rosalind as part of the "cure"' (Bulman 'Queering' 569); 'performing gender became a game, as when Orlando playfully punched Ganymede's arm and Rosalind awkwardly returned the male gesture, though the actor could easily have punched him back' (Holland *English Shakespeares* 91). Such doubling, teasing and layering, I suggest, rather than, say, misogyny or homophobic denial, prompted reviewers to account for Lester's Rosalind–Ganymede in apparently logic-defying and oxymoronic terms. Michael Billington, invoking the Kabuki conventions that Donnellan acknowledged as an influence, suggested that 'the gender switch in some strange way reveals the quintessence of womanhood' (*Guardian*, 21 January 1995). Writing of stage transvestism, Laurence Senelick proposes that its true power lies in its capacity to transport its viewers to a place far beyond mimicry and mimesis: 'it does not symbolize some pre-existing reality so much as it establishes a new reality ... if the stage is a mirror, it is a funhouse mirror, magnifying, distorting, and ultimately sending out an image in which the shock of recognition is promoted by an alienation effect' (Senelick 7). Seen in this light, Billington's phrase 'in some strange way' is key. The reviewers' challenges were exacerbated by the casting of Lester, a black male actor, in what to date had in the UK been an exclusively white woman's role.[8] Lester's Rosalind was a key moment in the history of colour-blind casting, the first time since Ben Kingsley had played Hamlet at the RSC in 1975 (in Buzz Goodbody's Other Place production) that a male actor of colour was cast in a traditionally white leading role by a national company. As Sujata Iyengar has demonstrated, Lester's skin colour had a now-you-see-it, now-you-don't status in the reviews that in both crude and complex ways inflected their accounts of Rosalind's gender, whereby his 'blackness and his maleness were simultaneously the greatest obstacles to be overcome in order for him to "become" Rosalind' (Iyengar 56). The cross-dressed black man, Garber proposes, is perceived as a conundrum: 'constructed by majority culture as *both* sexually threatening *and* feminized, as both super-potent and impotent', black masculinity is already paradoxical; black transvestism exacerbates the contradiction, in that '[t]he crossing of racial boundaries stirs fears of the possibility of crossing the boundaries of gender' (Garber 271, 274). Even for those who bought into it, the imposing (perhaps threatening) spectacle of black masculinity seemed even to trouble the legibility, and credibility, of Rosalind–Ganymede. 'The odds against a strapping 6ft black male actor being able to create not just a convincing but a captivating Rosalind', wrote Taylor in the *Independent*, 'are, you might have thought, fairly formidable'; 'Tall, black and male, Adrian Lester *nevertheless* makes an extraordinarily feminine Rosalind' (Spencer, *Telegraph*; emphasis added). Tinker (*Daily Mail*), on the other hand, was not at all convinced: 'as if it were not confusion enough that Rosalind is a man playing a girl playing a man, she is played by a strapping black actor'. Even worse, 'Orlando, adding colour-blindness to myopia, doesn't notice that either, though no one else is of this complexion.' Tinker evidently did not notice Joe Dixon, doubling Jaques with Charles; nor did Wardle, who described Lester as 'the only black actor in the company'. When the production was revived, the cast included two other black actors, Rhashan Stone (Amiens, William and Hymen) and Sean Francis (Le Beau, Jaques de Boys), so that, Iyengar points out, Lester's skin colour no longer registered. Three reviewers in 1991 made specific comparison between Lester and Josette Simon, the first black British female actor to secure leading roles at the RSC: 'In physical terms', de Jongh (*Evening Standard*) observed, 'he looks uncannily like the RSC's graceful Josette Simon'; David Nathan mentioned his 'close relationship to Josette Simon' (*Jewish Chronicle*, 13 December); and Taylor also noted a 'spooky resemblance'.[9] As Iyengar puts it, 'it seems bizarre to compare the two actors in this way' as the actors, apart from both being black, look nothing like each other, but the effect is recuperative: 'the race of Lester and Simon *undoes* the gender trouble evoked by Lester's male Rosalind: Lester is compelling as Rosalind because he reminds reviewers of another tall, black actor, but one who happens to be female' (58). Perhaps; but I would suggest gender and race trouble did not thereby disappear. Indeed, as these critics' deployment of the terminology of the uncanny suggests, they were interlinked constituents of the production's exhilarating but also unsettling oddness.

The gender games involved the spectator also: most provocatively, in 4.1, when Rosalind, at the end of her dialogue with Jaques (who, played as a predatory Wildean queen, saw in Ganymede another of the many young men in the forest who caught his wandering fancy), seized his hand, and placed it on his/her breast. Performing a gesture that would with a female actor incontrovertibly confirm gender as biological truth, Lester conjured a female body that was pure theatrical fiction. As Jaques pulled back, dumbfounded by his discovery of the breast that the audience knew wasn't there, Lester raised a 'don't tell' finger to his lips: as Cary Mazer observes, by revealing 'a secret Jaques now shares with the audience', the moment 'both foregrounds the performativity of gender and erases it', suggesting that 'the biological markers of the actor's gender identity are both essential and inescapable and at the same time invisible and occasionally irrelevant' (Mazer 'Rosalind's Breast' 98–101). Two further, related, shocks lay in store. The gentler, though no less stunning, of these came during the epilogue. On 'If I were a woman' (5.4.204–5), Lester removed a single earring and his bandana, and dropping a semitone or so, spoke in his own natural register for the first time in the show. For Donnellan, this was one of his 'favourite moments': 'you realize that a whole group of people on stage have come to believe in a lie temporarily ... and now ... that's the end of the illusion' (*Plays International*, December 1991). Its import was open-ended. For Bulman, the shift maintained 'the indeterminacy of sexual identity' ('Queering' 573), whereas Holland heard a line that is 'gibberish when spoken by a woman' delivered with 'simple charm' (*English Shakespeares* 94). There was a harder twist to the final-scene discovery. Rosalind returned in 5.3, veiled and adorned in a golden bridal gown, clutching a bouquet, as fully female – whatever that meant – as in the first scenes. Lifting the veil, Orlando recoiled in alarm and pulled away as she collapsed in tears; after a pause, he appeared to relent, took Rosalind in his arms, and they kissed. More, perhaps, than anything else in the production, this was a moment open to multiple readings. Holland interpreted Orlando as first 'shocked at the trick and shamed at his failure to have recognized her', then 'back in control, fully accepting Rosalind, unashamed and more in love than ever'. As such, it epitomized the production's emotional truth, 'an answer for the character in a realism of lived experience' (94). Alternatively, as Bulman suggests, it might have shown 'a man confronting the fact that the object of his desire had along been male, here simply cross-dressed in woman's attire' (573). Carol Chillington Rutter saw something else again: Orlando, 'furious at the disastrously miscalculated joke' of Ganymede in skirts, only realized that this was 'really' Rosalind on Duke Senior's line 'If there be truth in sight, you are my daughter' (5.4.107). As he reached out his arms, seeing her for what she was, his eyes registered 'a complete wipe of his gender memory' ('Maverick Shakespeare' 351).

The staging allowed no singular answer, as Rutter notes: 'extraordinarily, at the end of *this* production, everybody saw something different' (*ibid.*). Taken together, these three moments point to the combination of breathtaking directness in some respects and tantalizing indeterminacy in others that sustained the production worldwide and that prompted Billington to define it as 'one of the great Shakespeare productions of our time' (*Guardian*). Although Lester's extraordinary performance was at the heart of the production's appeal, its greatness stemmed from much more than that. Contemporary without being tied to the early 1990s, the show was staged with maximum clarity and simplicity, with the idea of Arden suggested by a lighting shift (a filter effect of foliage) and few lengths of green silk that descended, to a brassy flourish, on 'Hang there, my verse, in witness of my love' (3.2.1; the archive video reveals that the earlier 'Well, this is the forest of Arden' (2.4.11), spoken on a bare stage, earns a good-natured audience laugh). This was an ensemble, multi-doubled piece of story-telling, rooted in the small-scale touring aesthetic that Donnellan and Ormerod had taken a decade to hone. The opening tableau of the entire company on stage was reiterated at the start of the second half, which had the group in silent attendance as Orlando wrote his verses (the interval was placed after 2.7, which ended with the image of Jaques listening to Amiens singing). At the end of the show, the company launched into a joyously energetic, partner-swapping dance. In this emphatically non-naturalistic setting, every characterization and relationship demonstrated meticulous attention to emotional realist detail as well as comic possibility. As noted, the production gave Jaques's melancholy a context and a rationale by making him a cruising semi-outsider, 'with his cashmere overcoat, bow-tie and effete, supercilious manner: a would-be sugar-daddy to both Ganymede and Patrick Toomey's pale, intent Orlando' (Nightingale, *The Times*, 5 December 1991); in 4.1, he made a play for Ganymede but not before offering a cigarette on 'I prithee, pretty youth ...' (4.1.1) to the exiting Sylvius. The staging of the deer-killing in the following scene introduced one of the production's few truly dark notes: here, Jaques became 'the victim of a vicious gay-bashing' at the hands of a group of bare-chested forest bullies (Bulman 'Queering' 572). Nonetheless, not wanting Jaques 'to skulk back into the forest empty handed again' (*Guardian*), Donnellan requalified Shakespeare's qualified happy ending by pairing him up in the final dance with Hymen (Conrad Nelson in 1991; Rhashan Stone in 1994, who doubled with Amiens, the object of Jaques's wistful gaze at the end of the first half). Although it was probably not what Donnellan intended, Jaques, as the one character explicitly played as gay and identified as such by reviewers, served to an extent as the production's lightning-rod, as a means of locating queer desire in a contained place. Not everyone approved: Holland thought that Dixon 'had difficulty avoiding being mannered, partly the consequence of the repressed sexuality suggesting too neatly a rationale for his tense misanthropy' (*English Shakespeares* 94), while Billington complained that his inclusion in the final couplings 'misses the point that in Shakespearean comedy one character is always excluded by choice or design from the prevailing sexual harmony' (*Guardian*).

There was a place in the production for lesbian desire too. I have already touched upon the intimate nature of Rosalind and Celia's first scenes (let me here also note one great moment in 1.3: Celia's smugly self-satisfied 'No longer Celia, but Aliena' (l.

124) prompted from Rosalind an unsuccessfully suppressed snort of laughter); as Celia, both Tom Hollander and Simon Coates used her lengthy silences during the courtship scenes to convey jealous anger at Rosalind's betrayal of their relationship. In both versions, Celia was certainly camper, closer to conventional drag, than Lester's Rosalind. Hollander, 'making disapproving *moues* from the sidelines' (Kirsty Milne, *Sunday Telegraph*, 8 December 1991, was 'a master (perhaps that should be mistress) of the camp put-down' (Spencer, *Telegraph*), a' stocky, saucy young trout, the perfect product of the ruling classes, who knows how to break the rules, but also knows when enough is enough' (Clare Bayley, *What's On*, 11 December). Coates, 'looking like an older member of our royal family in twin-set and pearls' (Jane Edwardes, *Time Out*, 18 January 1995), was a quietly reproachful, melancholy presence during the wooing, 'very often sitting at the front of the stage, schoolgirl's diary forgotten, like Anderson's grieving mermaid' (Jeremy Kingston, *The Times*, 27 January). Billington had 'never seen the Rosalind-Celia relationship better handled' (*Guardian*); but for Kate Kellaway (*Observer*, 29 January), who, uniquely, confessed that she 'loathed' the show, Lester and Coates succumbed to a 'camp style', that was 'death to the play': 'Coates's Celia looks like a prim middle-aged transvestite in glowering red silk ... [T]he astringent wit of Celia's lines is lost in favour of the amusements of drag.' The possibility that these 'amusements' might have appealed to at least some spectators rather more than was intended is suggested by the comment of one of the New York critics, reviewing the production on tour, who disapprovingly noted 'the knowing giggles of an audience all too ready to read more into the cross-dressing than Shakespeare ever imagined ... [A] lot of the laughs seemed to have less to do with the text than with the double-entendres sought out by the audience' (Vincent Canby, *New York Times*, 16 October 1994).

Positioned towards the camper end of the female impersonation spectrum, Celia perhaps served to heighten by contrast the realism of Lester's Rosalind. Richard Cant as Audrey and Sam Graham (Wayne Cater in 1994) as Phoebe went still further into stereotype. Inverting well-established casting and playing conventions, Donnellan had 'Audrey, a bold prancing blonde, set in contrast to Sam Graham's seriously unattractive Phoebe, both hotter for passion than Mr Lester's Rosalind' (de Jongh, *Evening Standard*). Cant (possibly the only actor in the play's professional stage history to have doubled Adam and Audrey), 'bulging out of a clinging mini-dress' (Spencer, *Telegraph*) and sporting a blatantly fake long wig, was a 'promiscuous girlie goatherd' (Louise Doughty, *Mail on Sunday*, 29 January 1995), 'a yodelling blonde who teams up with Touchstone as a female clown' (Wardle, *Independent on Sunday*, 29 January). Phoebe, likewise, was played all-out for laughs: Graham's performance was largely overlooked by reviewers, but de Jongh noticed Cater's 'glorious Phoebe, in grunge wig and hideously floral clothes', casting 'sly, lustful glances at Lester, jettisoning Gavin Abbott's Silvius' (*Evening Standard*); Wardle recorded that the role 'changes from a haughty nymph to a waddling Welsh sexpot, eyes glowing avidly under her tea-cosy fringe' (*Independent on Sunday*); and Billington saw 'a squat, curl-tossing figure vaguely resembling Les Dawson as Mother Goose' (*Guardian*). With Audrey and Phoebe, the production was firmly (and, all agreed, successfully) on the terrain of bloke-in-a-frock British sex comedy, where both male and female desire are rampant and ridiculous, and where the pangs of unrequited passion are the source of ribald laughter. It was a sign of the production's range that it was able to accommodate both this and Lester's Rosalind.

Even so, there were some who still needed convincing. In this respect, the last word belongs to Donnellan, who amusingly concludes his retrospective *Guardian* piece by reporting on the occasion when, on tour, the baggage truck carrying the set, props and costumes broke down on the Romanian border. The actors did what they could with the resources available, and 'the first night audience ... stood and cheered, and at the next morning's press conference the critics enthused':

> 'Amazing! – and later today your truck will arrive?' 'Yes!' the actors replied, swelling with their inventiveness. The Romanians continued: 'Also you will have the set tonight?' 'Yes, yes!' 'Also the costumes tonight?' ... 'Yes, yes, yes!' '... And also the actresses?'

Notes

1 Rosenthal records that Dexter also approached the so-called (actually woefully misnamed) 'British Bob Dylan' Donovan to compose for his production, who 'immediately recorded an arrangement of Sonnet 18 ... and a sprightly, jazzed-up 'Under the Greenwood Tree', Hammond organ and snare drum to the fore' (Rosenthal *National Theatre Story* 129). Donovan's contribution was not used, though the latter track was included on his 1967 album *Gift from a Flower to a Garden*.

2 The score was composed by Marc Wilkinson and the musicians were Harry Krein (accordion), Laurie Morgan (drums), Ron Prentice (guitar), Stan Robinson (saxophone) and Cedric West (bass guitar). The quintet seems to have been a source of difficulties and disruption throughout the run, with show reports (authored by stage manager John Rothenberg) repeatedly recording deputizing to cover absences, late arrivals and general indiscipline. After the forty-second performance (2 July 1968), it was noted that 'if we have deps in future who haven't seen the show it would be a good idea if they had a band call beforehand', and after the eighty-fourth (7 March 1969) that 'Mr Morgan (drummer) late for 1st 4 cues owing to traffic jam. Mr Prentice 'busked' for Mr Morgan + the other cues were sans drum.' It was presumably with mingled relief and sarcasm that Rothenberg recorded 'No deputy musicians!', and 'Once again no deputy musicians!' for the matinée and evening shows that followed on 8 March.

3 Peter Holland writes: 'I was young (16) and certainly don't remember seeing it as Brett and Pickup as two men falling in love but that doesn't mean it wasn't there. It was more of its flirtation with a gay culture that I hadn't seen so explicitly on stage before then, at least in its allowing some relationships not to be solely recuperated into the dominant view of homosexuality = camp' (email to the author, 3 February 2016).

4 The 'new cuts' are impossible to identify from the promptbook. Rosalind and Orlando's 'time' duet (3.2.296–320) is marked as a cut, in a different ink from that of the rest, but it is given in full in the British Library recording. Elsewhere a total of 137 lines are cut.

5 Held in the National Video Archive of Performance in the Victoria and Albert Museum Theatre and Performance Archives, this was recorded at the Albery Theatre, London, on 11 January 1995. The majority of the production's performances took place on tour in 1991 and 1994, and the Forsyth connection may well have been entirely unrecognized outside the British theatre context.

6 The casting of Cant introduced another element of British television intertextuality that would again have been internationally invisible, was remarked upon by only one reviewer, but was, at least for me, pleasingly resonant. Louise Doughty (*Mail on Sunday*, 29 January 1995): 'For several moments I racked my brains to work out why the bloke playing a promiscuous girlie goatherd looked so familiar ... It was when he yodelled that I got it. Richard Cant has the same goofy grin as his father, *Playaway* presenter Brian, and puts it to side-split funny use.' For the benefit of younger and non-British readers, Brian Cant was one of the most popular television children's entertainers of the 1970s, presenting first the long-running pre-school series *Play School* (1964–85), and its (only) slightly more grown-up offshoot *Playaway* (1971–84). Cant's charm, good humour and versatility as a clown, song-and-dance man and storyteller, which contained a gloriously subversive streak of pure silliness, provided a beguiling front for the 'pretend families' of British children's television. Part of the appeal, I suspect, lay in the possibility that there were many of us who wished that our own dads might have been a bit more like Brian Cant – though if your dad were Bran Cant, you might take a different view.

7 The production opened at the Redgrave Theatre in Farnham on 11 July

1991, toured to New York and South America in late July and August, then returned for a UK and Ireland tour from September to November. On 4 December it began a run of 32 performances at the Lyric Hammersmith; from January to March 1992 it travelled to Tokyo, Dublin, Stratford-upon-Avon, Breda, Rotterdam, Wellington, Adelaide and Madrid. The 1994 revival began its tour in Norwich on 13 September 1994, and then went, in succession, to Manchester, New York, Princeton, Moscow, St Petersburg, Barcelona, Dusseldorf, Pilsen, Carlova, Bucharest, Sofia, New York, Tel Aviv, Jerusalem and Paris, totalling 66 performances (the last 16 of which took place at Peter Brook's Théâtre des Bouffes du Nord). This was followed by a final run of 23 performances at the Albery Theatre, from 23 January.

8 The first female black actor to play Rosalind in Britain was Tanya Moodie at the Bristol Old Vic in 1997; she was followed by Ivy Omere for the English Shakespeare Company in Michael Bogdanov's 1998 production. The part has since been taken by Stephanie Street for Natural Perspectives Company in 2002, Nina Sosanya for the RSC in 2003 (see Chapter III), Tracy Ifeachor for Dash Arts in 2009, and Cush Jumbo at the Royal Exchange, Manchester in 2011.

9 Josette Simon joined the RSC in 1982 and played Rosaline and Nerissa in 1984, and Isabella in 1987, returning to play Titania and Hipplolyta in 1999. In 1995, she played Katharina at the Leicester Haymarket.

CHAPTER VI

Woeful pageants

Heavily Rosalind

The world première of Paul Czinner's *As You Like It* at the Carlton cinema in London's Haymarket on Thursday 3 September 1936 was, by the standards of the time, quite an occasion. Announced, a touch excessively, as 'London's greatest opening night' (*The Times*, 1 September), the film premièred before an audience that included the director, its co-stars his wife Elisabeth Bergner (Rosalind) and Laurence Olivier (Orlando), the composer of its score, William Walton, and an array of British film and theatre celebrities, including Robert Donat, Gracie Fields, Noel Coward and the author of the treatment, J. M. Barrie, as well as a lone American movie star, Edward G. Robinson. Was there an element of national pride in play, a sense of the significance of the event of the first British-made Shakespeare feature film (even if this was directed and led by a Hungarian–Ukrainian director–actor partnership)? Possibly, given that it had been reported at the start of the year that the MGM mogul Irving Thalberg planned to build upon the anticipated success of George Cukor's *Romeo and Juliet* with a follow-up *As You Like It*, which he described as 'one of the best cinema possibilities' (*Observer*, 26 January 1936). If so, this element was misplaced, even irrelevant. As it turned out, Thalberg dropped dead on the day of *Romeo and Juliet*'s première (20 August), the film was not well received on either side of the Atlantic, and it lost the studio so much money that Hollywood avoided Shakespeare, now seen as box-office poison, for decades. Nonetheless, Cukor's film, which premièred in London in October, did sufficiently well to rank fourteenth among the highest grossing films released the UK in 1936; *As You Like It* did not make the top one hundred.

In his study of British cinemagoing habits of the 1930s, John Sedgwick has calculated that for the flagship first-release cinemas, 'a weekly audience in excess of 40,000 would generally be sufficient to warrant a further week's exhibition' (Sedgwick 64). *As You Like It* was screened three times daily from 3 September to 13 October in a cinema seating 1,159; even at capacity, it would have run at a substantial loss. The film managed a second London release at the end of November, at the smaller (610-seat) Regent Street Polytechnic cinema, where it was screened continuously in a double bill, first with the rather more commercially successful romantic drama *East Meets West* (which Graham Greene, then the *Spectator*'s film critic, had warned audiences to 'avoid like the plague' (Greene 101)), second with the travel documentary *Pirate Coast* (billed as 'an Eastern cavalcade'), and finally, over Christmas, with the 1926 silent short *Mr Cinderella* ('the old fairy tale up-to-date'), before closing on 2 January 1937. Thereafter the film for a long time almost completely disappeared from view, briefly resurfacing in May 1964 as part of a National Film Theatre season of international Shakespeare films, screening on German television in 1965, and eventually securing VHS and DVD release in 1987 and 1999, respectively. Thanks to the internet, where Czinner's film is freely available in its entirety, it has in the past half-decade probably been seen by more viewers than in its entire previous history: uploaded to YouTube on 11 August 2011, it had by the end of 2016 attracted in excess of 200,000 views. The comments below the line are overwhelmingly positive, and the 'likes' outnumbered the 'dislikes' by twenty to one.[1]

Czinner's *As You Like It* has not been kindly treated by history. Its lack of availability in home-viewing format partly accounts for its absence from the critical literature on Shakespeare and film that first emerged in the late 1970s: Jack J. Jorgens's *Shakespeare on Film* (1977) affords it two brief mentions (one as an instance of 'reductive' cutting, the other referring to the 'comic' dissolve 'from the ludicrous, moustachioed, melodramatic villain, Oliver, to the wiggling posterior of a swan' (Jorgens 'Realizing' 36)). Thirty years later, in a British Film Institute guide to Shakespeare on film, Daniel Rosenthal declares that Czinner's version 'did the play grave disservice', citing Bergner's 'monotonous and eventually tiresome jollity', Leon Quartermaine's 'pompous' Jaques, and Olivier's 'slightly deranged' Orlando (Rosenthal *100 Shakespeare Films* 5). In the interim, Samuel Crowl wrote in 1992 that the involvement of *Peter Pan* creator Barrie superimposes the gender ambiguities of the boy who never grew up upon Shakespeare's 'more complex and daring' text, the effect being 'to minimize the intellectual vibrancy of Shakespeare's comedy and to maximize opportunities to treat it with sentimental clichés which flirt with cute rather than clever' (Crowl 68–9). Kenneth Rothwell affords it a place in his survey of a century of Shakespearean cinema by conceding that so far as Bergner and Olivier are concerned, no one 'in the realm of filmed Shakespeare ... has yet succeeded in being more likeable', while asserting that only the former's 'sprightly' Rosalind 'saves the picture from utter ruin' (Rothwell 52, 49). In the 300-plus pages of his *Shakespeare and the Visual Cultures of Modernity* (2008), Anthony R. Guneratne refers to Czinner's *As You Like It* twice only, via a one-word epithet: 'static' (56, 275).

Rosenthal cites Graham Greene's *Spectator* review to characterize the film as preoccupied more with 'livestock than philosophy' and to conclude that 'there is little in Czinner's version that one could not have found in a 1930s theatre, and several of the performances, notably Quartermaine's, belong there, rather than on screen' (Rosenthal *100 Shakespeare Films* 7). Rothwell goes further: repeatedly labelling the film 'stagy' and stating that it 'remains firmly rooted in London's West End theatre', he targets Quartermaine in particular, waspishly referring to his credit as 'dialogue supervisor' as proof of 'the old adage that "those who can, do; those who can't, teach"'.[2] He thus finds that '"All the world's a stage" ... looks and sounds too theatrical while trying not to be theatrical' (50–1). Rothwell is merely roasting one of the oldest chestnuts in Shakespearean film criticism (the obsession with eradicating the contaminating traces of 'theatricality' from the medium, in the hope, as Rothwell polemically puts it, of escaping 'the prison house of the proscenium stage', to make 'a film that did not look as if it had been photographed with a camera nailed to the floor in the sixth-row orchestra' (7–8)). The attack on Czinner's *As You Like It* for being insufficiently cinematic allegedly finds confirmation in the reactions of contemporary reviewers: the critic of the *New York Herald Tribune* is cited as ('typically') judging it 'a photographed version of a stringently cut stage production' (Rothwell 50).

The difficulty with such criticisms is not that they are without substance, but that they make little effort to understand the film historically; nor do they acknowledge that its staginess is the result not of accident or ineptitude but of a conscious strategy of theatrical and cultural commemoration. Approaching the film more sympathetically in this vein, Russell Jackson has demonstrated that its genesis lay in Czinner's determination to preserve what was widely regarded as 'one of the acknowledged "great performances" of the second decade of the twentieth century, Elisabeth Bergner's Rosalind' (Jackson 'Remembering' 239). Renowned for a dangerously double-edged sexual magnetism that combined skittishness, vulnerability and voracity, Bergner brought to Rosalind some of the polymorphous qualities of Wedekind's Lulu and Shaw's St Joan, and the German theatre critic Herbert Ihering caught the flavour of this when he saw her in the role at the Lessing Theater, Berlin, in 1923: 'Bergner spun one into another shame and jubilation, boyishness and girlishness ... one experienced the double transformation: from the girl into the boy and from the boy into the girl he was playing. An exhilarating experience' (quoted in Jackson 'Remembering' 245).

If this is what Czinner and Bergner sought to capture on film, the results were mixed. The Rosalind of the first act emphasizes vulnerability and restraint. Bergner first appears seated forlornly on a bench, in a long white medieval/fairytale-princess gown and sporting a tall conical hat, her elfin face framed by a close-fitting wimple, while Celia (Sophie Stewart), swinging a butterfly net, cavorts cheerily behind a pond crowded with swans. Set against the assertively, coldly luxurious background of the sweeping stairways, terraces, water features, arches and pillars of Duke Frederick's palace, the pair present a vision of femininity contained and constrained; during the wrestling scene, they seem almost nun-like in their white robes, distinct from the rest of the court ladies and in opposition to the completely black-clad Duke (Felix Aylmer), who with his dark feathers has the aura of a malign peacock. In her first exchanges with Olivier, Bergner is demure, deferential to Celia, even timid; during the wrestling, Rosalind and Celia avert their eyes when Orlando is subjected to a particularly vicious fall. In keeping both with the film's idea of female decorum at this point and with Rosalind's relative powerlessness, the wrestling bout, in which Olivier performs a series of bizarrely implausible lifts and throws on an opponent at least twice his size, is seen not from the women's perspective but from that of Touchstone (Mackenzie Ward). His meeting and dialogue with Rosalind and Celia in 1.2 (ll. 38–118) having been completely cut, Touchstone, costumed in signature cap-and-bells motley, is introduced through his mimed reactions to the fight, which develop from simple mirroring into a one-man re-enactment that has him attempting to wrestle himself and then complacently awarding himself the win. If Touchstone comically over-identifies with the spectacle of inflicted violence, the women, as in the classic horror movie scenario, first cannot bear to look, then are drawn back in, but, for now, remain on the sidelines (Celia's 'I would I were invisible' (l. 181) is very much to the point).

The turning point comes in the next scene. The Duke having pronounced the sentence of banishment, which takes place in a vast apartment with a mirror-surfaced floor in which Rosalind and Celia again appear small, powerless and insignificant, Celia's introduction of 'my uncle in the Forest of Arden' (1.3.103) prompts Rosalind to place her hand conspiratorially over her cousin's mouth – at which moment there is a dissolve to the forest itself, and a jump forward to 2.1, and to Duke Senior (Henry Ainley) and his men seated around a campfire, led by Amiens in a chorus of 'What shall he have that killed the deer' (transposed from 4.1). The environment is patently a studio set, and this is one element of the film that has attracted criticism, even derision. Some contemporary reviewers were impressed, others were not. *The Times* conceded that the forest was 'photographed with an extremely ingenious use of lighting', but thought it 'often looks like a wild garden temporarily assembled at Olympia' (4 October 1936); Raymond Mortimer in the *New Statesman and Nation*, who likened the 'vulgar' ducal palace interiors to the art-deco 'foyer and corridors of a Super Cinema De Luxe', found the forest 'prosaic, stuffy and sadly lacking the beauties of art or nature' (12 September). The *Observer*'s C. A. Lejeune was more willing to be seduced: 'There is nothing about it that is quite real or tangible; Meerson's cloud-castle settings, Walton's cold-clear music, are suggestions of a state of mind' (6 September). The *Illustrated London News* reviewer, Michael Orme (who thought *As You Like It* one of two 'great' films of the week, the other being *The Great Ziegfeld*), went further: 'There is ... in the sun-dappled glades of the Forest of Arden, an elusive loveliness that transforms their solidity into a delicately patterned tapestry' (19 September 1936). By embedding the first glimpse of Arden within the women's plans for escape, Czinner perhaps aimed to suggest this fantasy aspect, the transitions back and forth creating a temporal ambiguity around the exiled Duke's musings: perhaps this is happening now, perhaps it has already happened, perhaps it is always happening.

Following Ainley's set-piece rendering of 'Now, my co-mates ...' and a verse of 'Blow, blow, thou winter wind', the camera tracks back through the trees, and there is a dissolve to Celia's chamber, to 2.3, where the two women, having experienced a passage of time and a costume change, are released from their court-lady frocks into simpler, understated dresses and plain bonnets. When it comes, 'Were it not better ... That I did suit me all points like a man' (1.3.110–12; 'more than common tall' is cut) is a moment of transformation, the first time in the film that Rosalind speaks with determination and purpose, and it makes Celia gasp with shock. This is the version of Rosalind that audiences were waiting to see; and, at half an hour into a 97-minute film, it marks the transition from the first to the second act. This section of the film ends with a brief sequence, underscored by the sound of jester's bells, in which the heavily cloaked Touchstone (who is yet to utter a word), Celia and Rosalind steal past the Duke's swans under cover of darkness: 'Now go we in content/To liberty and not to banishment' (1.3.133–4).

The next time Rosalind appears, she is in Arden, in a version of the Ganymede outfit that Bergner had worn on stage since 1923: a tunic cut to just above the knee, white shirt with loose sleeves and squared-off collar, dark tights and calf-length boots, bobbed hair beneath a neat cap adorned with a single feather. In this not particularly boyish get-up, less doublet and hose than gymslip and tights, she encounters Olivier's Orlando: 'Hail, forester, do you hear?' (her version of 3.2.275, 'Do you hear, forester?') is delivered in an affectedly gruff, mock-butch register that provides the scene's keynote: from this point onwards, as a number of commentators have observed, Bergner and Olivier (who are infrequently in shot together) seem to be in separate dimensions, perhaps even at cross-purposes; as Jackson puts it, 'Olivier has to act opposite something called "Bergner's Rosalind" rather than an interpretation that might be altered or developed by whatever he does' ('Remembering' 247). For their exchange in 3.2, Bergner carries a paper baton fashioned from one of Orlando's rolled-up poems, which she waves, points, waggles for emphasis, jabs and, on 'hangs oaths upon hawthorns' (3.2.332), mockingly unscrolls; the effect is that Ganymede appears both domineering and weird, and Olivier's contribution is mostly restricted to reaction shots that signal bafflement tinged with mild alarm. In their next scene, Bergner carries a leafy switch which she wields, dominatrix-fashion, like a riding crop, while at times vocally pitching her Ganymede-as-Rosalind somewhere near a squeak. As in the previous scene, Bergner is restless, fidgety, forcing the camera and a palpably uneasy Olivier to track her movements. When he exits, he looks and sounds decidedly irritated rather than entranced. The scene has one good gag, during the mock-wedding: bossily instructed to 'say the words' of the ceremony, Sophie Stewart mischievously delivers 'Will you, Orlando, have to wife this Rosalind?' (4.1.113; Celia's line is fed to her in full by Bergner) as over-enunciated, thick-accented mimicry of the film's star; for a moment, at least, the film makes a joke at its own (and its lead's) expense.

The film's other, more considered, moment of playful self-consciousness occurs at the end. A truncated finale cuts straight from the last lines of 5.2 to the sight of swains and sheep streaming through the gates of Duke Senior's new habitat (a walled space that has nothing to do with the overgrown ruins where he had previously dwelt) to dance to the tune of 'Tell me where is fancy bred?', imported from *The Merchant of Venice*. The film jettisons all but 33 lines of 5.3, and the camera pulls back through the gates to reveal Rosalind, in her wedding gown. In a cinematic version of a front-cloth epilogue, Bergner speaks straight to camera for the first time; on 'my way is to conjure you' (5.4.199), a rapid cross-fade transforms her momentarily into Ganymede, and on 'as please you' (l. 201), she reverts back into the bridal dress. The lines dealing with kissing and beards being cut, the film ends, on 'the play may please' (l. 204), with a curtsey and a fade to black.

Bergner's performance, and Czinner's film, are temptingly easy to patronize, but to do so on the grounds that they are excessively 'theatrical', as the scholars quoted at the beginning of this section do, presupposes a standard of naturalness that is historically insupportable. The *New York Times* reviewer cited by Rothwell is not representative of the general view, which on the whole was supportive of the film and appreciative of Bergner's performance. For the *Manchester Guardian* (4 September), the film was 'the first attempt to set Shakespeare on the screen naturally, and with dignity', and she was 'a Rosalind who is tender and roguish by turns and more lively than any we have seen': 'She will wheedle the words, throw them from her like darts, or draw out the lines as if they were threads with which she is braiding her thoughts.' In the *Daily Telegraph* (7 September), Campbell Dixon conceded that Bergner was 'not a great Shakespearean actress' but 'essentially modern' and not to everyone's taste ('Some found her Rosalind alarming'), but praised her 'razor-keen intelligence, her flair for humanising stagy situations with little bits of business, her gift of pathos', as well as 'her impish sense of humour, her personality that many of us find irresistible and others merely irritating!' The *News Chronicle* (4 September) also admired the 'blend of gaiety and wistfulness that is a feature of her characteristic charm'. Accusations of 'staginess' were mostly voiced in the American press: alongside the *New York Times*, *Variety*'s reviewer (November 1936) referred to the 'mighty phony make-believe forest scene' and declared that 'Stripped of production lavishness, the play is reduced to a filmization of old-fashioned drama.' Nonetheless, this reviewer found space to praise Quartermaine's Jaques, damned by Rothwell and Rosenthal, as 'darn near perfect', and in this respect was in accord with the majority view. *Picture Show* (17 October) had 'nothing but the highest praise' for the performance; the *New Statesman and Nation* thought it (with Olivier) 'triumphantly good', and the *Illustrated London News* singled out Quartermaine's 'masterly perfection of diction and phrasing', though none went as far as the *Observer*: 'When Quartermaine begins his fatal speech on the Seven Ages, you can feel every nerve in the audience quivering ... his successful achievement of that speech is probably the most heroic feat ever accomplished in the history of the movies.' This is hyperbolic, no doubt, but it touches upon what was for this viewer at least the key to the film's simple, innocent charm: 'you suddenly realise that it is rather a lovely speech, that it is rather a lovely play, that you are going to enjoy yourself very much. And then, at first with a grudging surprise, and presently with a complete and frank abandonment, you do.' Seventy years on, the thousands who have given Bergner's Rosalind a new lease of life online would appear to agree.

A date with the Bard's birds

According to Cedric Messina, the initiator of the BBC/Time-Life Television Shakespeare and producer of its first and second series, *As You Like It* has the distinction of being the play that served as inspiration for the entire enterprise. In 1975 Messina was location shooting at Glamis Castle for a Play of the Month production of James Barrie's *The Little Minister*; he decided that it was 'the perfect setting for Shakespeare'. Before long, this idea had become an ambitious scheme to film all but one (*The Two Noble Kinsmen*) of the 37 plays. The repercussions of Messina's literal-minded approach have been extensively discussed, and from the outset popular and academic commentators on the series drew attention to its deficiencies, but it carried sufficient authority at the time to secure the substantial backing of American corporate funders to enable the series to go ahead. One of the key factors underwriting the project's financial sustainability, in both the short and longer terms, was that it was conceived at a crucial moment in broadcasting history – the birth of the home videotape industry – ensuring a market for personal and educational use for years after the first airings. One consequence was that the imperative to 'stand the test of time' intensified the already considerable conservative bias of the series.

For the first six productions Messina recruited a team of directors who were for the most part industry veterans with undistinguished or nonexistent track records in Shakespeare (which Messina apparently regarded as an advantage). *As You Like It*, broadcast on 17 December 1978, was assigned to Basil Coleman, who on paper had better credentials than most. With a background in opera and theatre, he had previously directed *The Tempest* and *Love's Labour's Lost* for the BBC's Play of the Month series in 1968 and 1975, respectively. Throughout the series, casting was based on a combination of leading Shakespearean stage actors and familiar television faces. For *As You Like It* this meant Helen Mirren (who during filming was also playing Queen Margaret in the *Henry VI* plays for the RSC at the Aldwych) as Rosalind, RSC stalwart Tony Church as Duke Senior (the fourth time he had been cast in the role) and Richard Pasco reprising the Jaques that he had given in Buzz Goodbody's 1973 RSC production (see Chapter III). It also meant James Bolam (then best known as the sardonic Geordie waster Terry Collier in the 1960s BBC sitcom *The Likely Lads* and its 1970s sequel *Whatever Happened to the Likely Lads?*) as Touchstone., and Angharad Rees, female lead in the nineteenth-century-set bodice-ripper *Poldark* (screened from 1975 to 1977), as Celia.

As one of the only two productions in the series to be shot on location (the other being *Henry VIII*, directed by Kevin Billington, which was generally better received), the BBC *As You Like It* has been criticized for its scenic literalism; speculating that Messina, 'like others before him', was 'succumbing to rural enchantments',

Marshall claimed that 'the effort to naturalise Arden within the confines of the small screen alienated viewers', and that 'despite the fresh scenery', the realist treatment 'overwhelmed the theatricality of pastoral' (79–80). Jorgens stated that 'seldom have natural settings been used to less effect', and that throughout 'a kind of warfare took place between images of cultivated or uncultivated nature in court and forest and a play which is essentially a fairy tale in verse' ('The BBC-TV Shakespeare Series' 412).[3] The suspicion that text, setting and medium are fundamentally at odds also surfaces in James C. Bulman's account of the production's 'perils of pastoral', which concludes that 'the location that appealed to Messina as "wonderful" seemed far too earthbound, too specific for the elusive joys of the Forest of Arden' ('*As You Like It*' 174).

Although it is certainly the case that this version locates the play's action in a real green-world setting that might have delighted Oscar Asche, the director's comments on his choice of locations indicate that these were chosen with care, and that Coleman did not envisage the forest as a mass of undifferentiated, decorative greenery. He originally wanted to film the play over the period of a year to capture the seasonal shift from winter to spring, but the realities of a two-week shoot in June dictated otherwise; his plan had been to shoot the banished court scenes 'in carefully selected pine woods ... in late winter, early spring, when there were no leaves at all', but when he came back to film he found the forest choked with three-foot-high ferns: 'they have such an extraordinary and unusual quality that I like to feel they have added something, even though they may have defeated my attempt to get a winter feeling'. The wooing scenes were shot 'in a very beautiful oak wood where bluebells were still flowering and the young bracken hadn't opened out and was still making these wonderful V shapes', and 'we used beech woods for the final scenes where everybody is brought together' (Fenwick 22). The various natural and semi-natural environments employed in the production do considerably more than act as realist *mise en scène*. The brothers' first encounter takes place in a high-walled garden well-stocked with shrubs and topiary, laboriously tended by Orlando (Brian Stirner) and a monkish-looking Adam (Arthur Hewlett), as Oliver (Clive Francis) practises fencing with an anonymous lackey; the sense of nature tamed, circumscribed and confined is heightened further in Rosalind and Celia's first scene, which is placed in the highly styled setting of Glamis's Italian garden, whose severe straight lines, stone pathways, box-cut hedges and immaculate lawn 'convey the formality of the court' (Fenwick 22–3). In this micro-managed (and, it is implied, sterile) environment, Rosalind and Celia are identically clad in long cream gowns and bulky, oddly antlike headdresses, edged with gold braiding, that render them, from a distance, indistinguishable, and, closer up, virtual mirror-images. Costumed thus in 1.3, Rosalind and Celia almost merge with the grey stone walls of one of the production's few interior settings; staged in the castle's crypt, which, with its 'wonderful barrel-shaped stone ceiling', Coleman felt matched the 'very harsh' mood of the first act (Fenwick 22), the banishment is also an act of release: anxious and restrained throughout the first act (during the first encounter with Orlando, she seems about to burst into tears), Mirren briefly comes to life when hatching the cross-dressing plot.

'To liberty and not to banishment' (1.3.134) cues the move to Arden via a dissolve that sees stone brickwork melt into the running water of the brook in which Duke Senior rinses his face. This is a relatively open space, a sparse woodland of pines and ferns, and it is in similar woodland that Celia, Touchstone and Rosalind as Ganymede are first discovered. The sense that the travellers are somehow smaller and less significant than the world they have entered is suggested by a low-angle shot that places them between a foreground packed with ferns and a background of pine trunks that tower upwards and out of sight. 'Well, this is the forest of Arden' (2.4.11) is spoken, forlornly, as Mirren gazes at a distant huddle of sheep. Celia, as Aliena, now wears a simple dress, shawl and a broad-brimmed hat that is a near-exact copy of the one she sports as *Poldark*'s Demelza; Mirren as Ganymede has a flower-pot-style cap, a long cloak, and a curly perm that affords her a passing resemblance to the 1970s popular entertainer Paul Nicholas. Touchstone retains the nondescript clothes that he wore at the court, though, since Bolam appears to be channelling all of Terry Collier's truculence and none of his mordant wit; and, given that neither Celia nor Rosalind shows any sign of finding him amusing or even agreeable company, it is hard to fathom why they have brought him along.

The 'love scenes', Coleman felt, 'needed a certain seclusion without being too shut in', and he found 'a marvellous chestnut tree of great age and beauty, with branches so heavy they bowed down to the earth and then grew upwards again. Under these huge sculpted arches of wood we staged the love scenes' (Fenwick 23). In 3.2, the wooing takes place amidst the pines and ferns, but in 3.4 Mirren is discovered under the boughs of said tree, which is also the site of 4.1, where the semi-enclosure certainly enhances the sense of intimacy (Celia is mostly out of shot, and thus out of mind, for the first part of the scene). The tangled, gnarled and twisted 'arches of wood' also provide a strong visual contrast to the stark verticals of the woodlands elsewhere: here is a sense of nature run wild ('an untouched quality', Coleman thought, that 'was very effective' (Fenwick 22)) that well suits Mirren's spirited playing of Rosalind playing Ganymede playing Rosalind – one of the few times in the production that she appears to be enjoying herself.

Nonetheless, as in all of Orlando and Rosalind's meetings, there is zero sexual ambiguity in this scene, not least because throughout Mirren makes no attempt to play either man or boy. Overall, moreover, as Marshall observes, 'there is no chemistry between Rosalind and Orlando, or Rosalind and Celia, or any other couple' (80). Flawed as it is, this *As You Like It* rewards scrutiny less on the basis of its limited contribution to the performance history of the play than for what it, and the season which it was part of, reveals about the place of Shakespeare on television at its moment of transmission. Much published commentary on television Shakespeare has, understandably enough, originated within Shakespeare studies rather than television or media studies, and one of the consequences of this has been a tendency to treat it in terms of the television *text*, rather than the *event*, a process which has been encouraged, in the case of the BBC Television Shakespeare, by its issue and reissue in VHS, DVD, and most recently, online formats. From a television studies perspective, however, a key principle in the analysis of output is not the discreet programme but the practice of watching, which was influentially conceptualized by Raymond Williams in 1974 in terms of 'flow', whereby 'the real programme that is offered is a *sequence* or set of alternative sequences of these and other similar events, which are then available in a single dimension and in a single operation' (Williams *Television* 87). Simply put, the meaning of an individual programme inheres not just in itself but in its relation to what lies on either side of it. As far as an evening's viewing in 1978 is concerned, at the point where the video technology that enables postponed viewing or re-viewing was just beginning to be established, this was the moment when switching channels still meant, for most viewers, physically getting out of one's chair to do so.

Fifteen years earlier, the BBC version of the Redgrave–RSC *As You Like It* (see Chapter II) was broadcast at 8.20 p.m. on a Friday evening, broke after an hour for the news, and then continued until 10.45 p.m. It thus cut right across the BBC's usual Friday-night schedule, which consisted of long-running medical soap *Dr Kildare* from 7.30 to 8.20, *Comedy Playhouse* from 8.20 to 8.45 p.m., *Indoor Athletics* from 8.45 until 9.15 p.m., the news, and a one-hour television play from 9.25 p.m. Meanwhile, on ITV, viewers were offered another American import, *Bonanza*, from 8.00 to 9.00 p.m., the news, and, from 9.15 to 10.15 p.m., *Television Playhouse*. At this time, the BBC was still a one-channel station; following the bifurcation of its output in 1964 with the launch of BBC Two, its Shakespeare productions continued to be shown mainly on BBC One, as part of the Sunday-night *Play of the Month* series. In 1978, the BBC Shakespeare season was scheduled for BBC Two on Sunday nights at 8.00 p.m., each programme running from between 2½ to 2¾ hours, with a short break around 9.00 p.m. for the news. In television drama terms, this was on the lengthy side: 1 to 1½ hours remained the norm for a television play, and even the Play of the Month productions (versions of classic stage plays or adaptations of novels) ran to a maximum of 2 hours.[4] The series thus revived the practice of Shakespeare programming that commanded an entire evening's viewing (*Richard III*, on Sunday 22 January 1983, ran to nearly 4 hours, from 7.15 p.m.); the last time this had happened was with the BBC's screening of the RSC *The Wars of the Roses* in 1965, which ran for three consecutive Thursdays in April from 8.00 until 11.00 p.m.

In 1978, Sunday nights on BBC Two usually consisted of an eclectic and variable mix of arts programmes, classical music, nature documentaries and film, while BBC One's December scheduling for Sunday evenings centred on period-drama series (*A Horseman Riding By*, which was succeeded by the long-running, gently nostalgic and hugely popular country veterinarian comedy series *All Creatures Great and Small*), followed by feature films (on this occasion the British television première of Peter Bogdanovich's 1973 depression-era sentimental film comedy *Paper Moon*). In September 1978, on ITV, the competition consisted of *The Return of the Saint*, period drama *Lillie*, the wrestling sitcom *The Losers* (starring Leonard Rossiter and Alfred Molina, who nearly thirty years later played Touchstone in Kenneth Branagh's film version), *An Audience with Jasper Carrott* and *The South Bank Show*. On 17 December, *As You Like It* was part of a sequence of BBC Two evening programmes that began with an introductory talk by the novelist Brigid Brophy, part of the *Shakespeare in Perspective* series, in which picturesque West Wycombe Park provided the setting for her to spell out the play's debts to Lodge's *Rosalynd*, followed by the magazine programme *Assignment*, and a *World about Us* documentary about lumberjacks in British Columbia. The evening was to have ended with the late film, Paul Bogart's 1973 coming-of-age drama *Class of 44*, but strike action by BBC technicians meant that the film was pulled from the schedule and replaced with a programme of recorded music.

Those who opted to watch *As You Like It*, then, did so in preference to watching an evening of period drama, sexual intrigue, comedy wrestling and stand-up comedy (given most of its members' televisual preferences at the time, the Shaughnessy household that harboured my moody adolescent self was, I must report, not among their number). Who were these people, what were their expectations, and what did they make of the viewing experience? Some clues to the broader attitudes that might have shaped the size and composition of the *As You Like It* audience are provided by two contrasting articles, one in the UK's second-least-read newspaper, and the other in its second-most, both published on 2 December, the day before the screening of the first production in the series, *Romeo and Juliet*. In the *Guardian*, Peter Fiddick drew attention to the 'acting strength' of the first season and confessed that the series had 'already given me much pleasure, and without doubt will do as much for everyone else'; but he worried that the BBC 'is going to have to work very hard and subtly to convince its diverse audiences about quite a lot of the plays', and that the refusal to take risks would rule out 'those masterpieces of insight, usually from directors, which justify our national devotion to this single author'.

In the tabloid *Daily Mirror*, Ken Irwin offered a different perspective. Headlined 'A date with Bard's Birds', and illustrated with pictures of Janet Maw (the Queen in *Richard II*), Rebecca Saire (Juliet), Kate Nelligan (Isabella), Helen Mirren and Angharad Rees (captioned: 'just as we like it'), Irwin's two-page spread pictured the 'very beautiful young actresses lined up to appear in the plays', quoted BBC Head of Drama Shaun Sutton urging viewers to 'forget all about doing stuffy old Shakespeare at school', previewed *Romeo and Juliet* ('a wonderful production'), and asserted that 'there is no doubt at all that the Beeb's new Shakespearean plays will be superbly produced'. The attempt to find a *Mirror*-appropriate angle typifies the ambivalent, bemused tone of tabloid reporting on Shakespeare: not dismissive of high culture, but not at ease with it either, as Shakespeare is both differentiated from, and rather awkwardly co-opted by popular culture, here through a stab at mild titillation that is assumed to be the best means of attracting the *Mirror* readership's attention. A further symptom of the paper's divided attitude is the fact that Irwin actually adopts two positions on the series: running alongside the 'Bard's Birds' item is a by-line, 'What price Shakespeare v Soccer?', in which Irwin undermines his own claims in the main piece by asking how the BBC can afford to fund the series when 'they have lost all Football League matches to ITV over the next three years because they couldn't find enough money', and, no doubt guessing his readership's answer, '[W]hich is more important, to the great mass of viewers – football or Shakespeare?'

The oppositions are as familiar as the mischief-making is blatant: Shakespeare versus football, effeminate arts versus manly sport, elite versus popular taste. We need not take this too seriously. In one way, the *Mirror*'s perspective is as irrelevant to the BBC *As You Like It* as Shakespeare appears to have been to the *Mirror*'s readership, if the paper's priorities in any way reflect those of the men and women who bought it (which, with a sustained circulation in the late 1970s of over three million, 6 per cent of the UK population, seems quite likely). Once previewed, the series was mentioned again only in the television listings, and in this climate of indifference the plays were viewed (or, more likely, not viewed). Though the *Mirror* lost interest in the BBC Shakespeare once it had paraded its line-up of 'very beautiful young women', the *Guardian*, equally reflecting the priorities of a readership one-tenth the size of the *Mirror*'s, did not. Fiddick assumes that the venture was both televisually and culturally significant, and the first three productions in the series led the paper's Monday television review column. Nancy Banks-Smith was unimpressed by *Romeo and Juliet* and *Richard II* (10 December), but gave *As You Like It* a highly favourable review. Judging it 'perfectly lovely … marvellous', Banks-Smith singled out precisely the element that has earned the censure of subsequent commentators: the location shooting, she wrote, meant that '[n]ever did Under the Greenwood Tree seem so appropriate', with 'one particular hugely spreading chestnut tree whose boughs had touched the ground', and '[g]reen and red and gold leaves' that 'filtered and defused [sic] the light, dappling the lovers like deer' (18 December 1978). Though Mirren's Rosalind 'needed to swipe the flies away from her nose', she had 'a face like running water, transparent, changing and catching the light', and was strongly supported by 'Angharad Rees's Colin' [sic]. Given that the previous week she had written of *Richard II* that '[t]he only reason for doing the plays on television is to do them televisually' (*Guardian*, 11 December), it seemed that *As You Like It* achieved this aim rather better than the studio-bound productions that preceded and succeeded it; Banks-Smith concluded that the 'best' production of the first season was the location-shot *Henry VIII* (*Guardian*, 26 February 1979).

Banks-Smith's view is at odds with that of the majority of academic commentators on the production. As we have heard, Marshall claimed that the programme 'alienated viewers'; and 'for most viewers' the programme's efforts 'fell flat' (79–80). This accurately reflects the scholarly consensus, but it does not square with what can be known of the original viewing audience response to the programme; indeed, such evidence as exists appears to contradict Marshall's assertion. The BBC's audience research, based on the contributions of the volunteer members of its Viewing Panels and presented in the form of its Audience Research Reports, documents the programme's reception and indicates that Banks-Smith's response was broadly line with that of its first viewers.[5] The BBC's ranking system invited participants to score programmes on a scale ranging from A+ (outstanding) to C- (poor); quantitatively, at least, an overwhelming majority of respondents rated the programme very highly (39 per cent A+; 38 per cent A), which, aggregated, produced a 'very good' Reaction Index of 78. The report stated that many of the respondents 'found the production involved them closely and just over three-fifths of the total sample watched all of it', and that the programme 'gained a very good response from the sample audience who had thoroughly enjoyed the experience'. The author of the report identified in particular praise for 'the use of outside locations', which 'greatly enhanced enjoyment of the production for many, who described the combination of lovely locations and beautiful costumes as "visually perfect"'; a sentiment which appeared to resonate with reports that 'they liked this kind of production with "no gimmicks"'. Coleman's scenic choices and Messina's aesthetic priorities evidently satisfied those at whom the series was primarily targeted. As a piece of Sunday-night television, the BBC *As You Like It* evidently worked.

How representative were these views? The report notes that it is based on 72 questionnaires, representing 4 per cent of the Viewing Panel membership; the BBC's audience figures for the broadcast indicate that it was viewed by just under one-and-a-half million, or just less than 3 per cent of the UK population. This was rather less than what had been hoped for: at the season's outset, producer Shaun Sutton had said that he would be 'very happy' with 'a regular audience of three million' (*Daily Mirror*). It seems relatively small, when set against the figures for BBC One and ITV the same evening, with the 11 million and 9 million viewers, for, respectively, *Paper Moon* and *Lillie* (though it compares favourably with the audiences for BBC Two's rugby and cricket coverage earlier in the day). It was a quarter of the audience for the BBC's 1963 *As You Like It*, which pulled in nearly six million viewers (nearly half of ITV's audience share for that evening, though we should bear in mind that in the pre-BBC Two era there was nowhere else for viewers to go). To put these numbers in perspective, consider that, during the week of the broadcast, Trevor Nunn's RSC production of the *As You Like It* was also in repertoire at the 1,200-seat Aldwych Theatre in London. Opening on 5 September, it ran for 62 performances, closing on 8 March 1979. Even had it played to capacity, this production would have reached a total audience one-twentieth the size of that of the BBC version. To put it another way, to match the BBC audience, the RSC version would have needed a run of 1,175 performances, which in West End terms would mean daily shows for at least three years. Add to the first viewing figures the countless showings that have taken place worldwide in the decades that followed, and we have in the BBC *As You Like It* the version of the play that most non-Shakespeareans are most likely to have seen. Regardless of its merits as Shakespeare or as television, it for that reason cannot be ignored.

The meanings of Coleman's *As You Like It* are, of course, not confined to its first broadcast and the response of its first audience is, equally, far from definitive, but, as with Czinner's version, paying attention to that response and its circumstances is a way of allowing the production its historical due. More significantly, the audience response data also raise questions as to the criteria by which the BBC series continues to be judged, and by which it is usually found wanting. Shakespeare scholars agreed at an early stage that its prevailing adherence to realism was both wrong in principle and unsuccessful in practice, and that it produced versions of the plays that were conservative both formally and, in many cases, politically. For better or worse, however, this niche interest group was not the programme makers' target audience, and the evidence provided by the viewing panel (and by Banks-Smith) indicates that, at least on this occasion, Coleman and, behind him, Messina, got it broadly right. Pending a more extensive investigation of the audience response evidence, which could be extended to take into account the entire series, the question of how far this was representative must remain, for now, unanswered; but it is worth noting that when the far from artistically conservative Jonathan Miller succeeded Messina as producer of the third season, he knew his audience and his medium well enough to maintain the commitment to television realism; 'you are more or less obliged to present the thing as naturally as you can' (Hallinan 134). One way or another, the BBC *As You Like It* appears to have found favour with an audience that would, over the course of the harsh decade that followed, spend many Sunday evenings taking comfort in gentle pastoral comedy: not Shakespeare, but, in *All Creatures Great and Small*, the misadventures of a trio of veterinarians in the vanished green world of the Yorkshire Dales.

This desert city

The eternal summer of Coleman's studiedly retrograde production set it deliberately at odds not only with the contemporary Shakespearean theatre, but also with the contemporary world itself. Given the state of the UK at the time, a retreat into Arden seems all too understandable. By a number of measures, 1978 was a dismal year. Jim Callaghan's minority Labour government was in its terminal stages, with Margaret Thatcher biding her time before election victory the following spring. There was widespread industrial action in the public and private sectors that culminated in the notorious 'Winter of Discontent', and, starting in December, the severest actual winter, weather-wise, since 1962–63. It was also a year in which the continuing conflict in Northern Ireland claimed 17 lives. Commenting on the 'middle-aged Middle Ages studio production' of *Romeo and Juliet*, Banks-Smith speculated that it might have been productive to set the play 'in Northern Ireland, perhaps' (*Guardian*, 4 December 1978), the inference being that this would have provided the appropriate background of sectarian division and street violence. It was a timely point (though, given that she recognized that 'none of the plays will be done in modern dress', a moot one); on the day that *As You Like It* was broadcast, the Provisional IRA detonated bombs in five mainland UK cities, prompting fears that the organization was to embark on a Christmas bombing campaign (which did not, in the event, materialize).

Fourteen years later, the IRA and its loyalist opponents were still very much in business, on both sides of the Irish Sea. There were 35 terror-related deaths in 1992, and the IRA itself was responsible for dozens of bombings in London, culminating, on 30 October, in an explosion in Downing Street, home of Margaret Thatcher's successor as Prime Minister, John Major. The same day, Irish film-maker Neil Jordan's *The Crying Game* opened at Curzon West End. The film tells the story of IRA gunman Fergus (Stephen Rea), who falls out with his former comrades over the killing of a black British soldier, flees to London and becomes romantically involved with the soldier's girlfriend, Dil (Jaye Davidson) – who, to Fergus's horror, is revealed as male. Fergus subsequently both tentatively accepts Dil as his lover and renounces terrorism: the redemptive move poses gender-switching as a magic-realist resolution to the seemingly irreconcilable antagonisms of 'the Troubles'. The second of three British films released in 1992 to engage with androgyny and gender ambiguity (the others being Sally Potter's take on Virginia Woolf's fantasy *Orlando* and Christine Edzard's *As You Like It*), it was one of the more mainstream responses to the emergence of what *Sight and Sound* in August 1992 defined as the 'new queer cinema', a movement that included Derek Jarman's confrontational, contemporary Marlowe adaptation, *Edward II* (1991), Christopher Münch's *The Hours and the Times* (1991) and Gregg Araki's *The Living End* (1992); a cinema characterized by 'a common style ... of appropriation and pastiche, irony, as well as a reworking of history', that is 'irreverent, energetic, alternately minimalist and excessive' (B. Ruby Rich, *Sight and Sound*, August 1992).

The circumstances ought, then, to be have been propitious for Edzard's *As You Like It*, which opened at the Barbican Cinema on 9

October. Edzard had been acclaimed for her multi-award-winning 6-hour Dickens adaptation *Little Dorrit* (1987), a film notable for its visual richness and meticulous attention to period detail, and for the Victorian period drama *The Fool* (1990): *Dorrit* in particular was praised for its contemporary resonances, as Derek Malcolm (*Guardian*, 27 November 1987) affirmed: 'no other Dickens novel seems so relevant today – a portrait of a society that's both rich and poor, energetic and rotting at the same time'. Edzard and her cast were clearly claiming a similar relevance for their contemporary, London-set *As You Like It*, but this time, rather than allowing it to emerge, the film seemed determined to both capitalize and underline it. In interviews for the preview-screening press pack (which described the play, 'written 400 years ago', as 'a spoof on alternative living'), James Fox (Jaques) referred to the play 'worrying about "green issues"', Don Henderson (Dukes Frederick and Senior) stated that the 'desolate wasteland' of the contemporary Docklands setting 'is the 1992 equivalent of what it means to be in exile – living rough', and Emma Croft (Rosalind) injected the requisite note of 'edginess' by claiming that during filming, 'We were like the street kids of today, throwing stones, walking about in street gear – and yet, at the same time, the language we were using was Shakespeare'. Andrew Tiernan (Orlando and Oliver) elaborated: 'a rap record "Public Enemy" ... that's my music ... Chuck Dee [*sic*], his words are rhyming in pentameters ... [R]apping today is actually what Shakespeare was doing then, putting his message across in rhythm.' Arden, Tiernan enthused, was 'all derelict and full of this wasted human energy – and Orlando is a kid spraying his poems on the walls'.

Tiernan had the year before played Gaveston in Jarman's *Edward II*, a gleefully anachronistic, state-of-England film that, like the director's *The Tempest* (1980), combined visual flair and queer politics with a distinct pop sensibility. Here, the cack-handed attempt to bom-Bard *As You Like It* with youth culture, black music and style sounded like a wicked parody of the well-intentioned efforts of educators and theatre-makers to get Shakespeare down with the kids, but it was meant in earnest. Edzard unconvincingly promised 'a truly cheerful film'. Unfortunately, but unsurprisingly, the majority of reviewers did not see it that way. With a few exceptions, such as the hip music weekly *NME*'s Nick Hasted, who found the film 'more Mike Leigh than Sir Larry ... a relaxed, romantic ad for Bill S, more alive here than he has been for decades' (10 October), and the *Guardian*'s Derek Malcolm, who thought that 'Edzard shows that she understands the dangerous forest of Arden better than most' (8 October), they concurred with Michael Billington's verdict that it was 'a dead-as-mutton film that is poor Shakespeare and even worse cinema' (*Guardian*, 24 October). Philip French (*Observer*, 11 October) described it as 'listless ... fuzzy, unfocused, turning on the simplistic notion that some Londoners get rich while others sleep rough'; Adam Mars-Jones, while more willing to give Edzard the benefit of the doubt, still regretted 'an extraordinarily limited notion of what film can do' (*Independent*, 9 October). Others were more forthright: 'This was obviously made for an audience of three people called Julian, Tristan and Charlotte who all live in Hampstead', fumed Sue Heal in *Today* (9 October), 'I sincerely hope they enjoy it more than I did.' Andrew Pulver (*City Limits*, 8 October) saw it as '[e]ntirely stage-bound in conception', concluding that 'it would have made lousy theatre, and makes *appalling* cinema', a point echoed by Nigel Andrews: 'we feel like the victims of a mobile theatre experiment, moving our camp stools from one daft venue to the next as we follow a bunch of under-rehearsed actors belting it out in the void' (*Financial Times*, 8 October). 'The sheer misery of the experience', lamented Neil Norman (*Evening Standard*, 8 October) was 'enough to give any relatively literate viewer the screaming hab-dabs.'

Edzard's *As You Like It* had the ill luck to be released in the same week as the 'restored' print of Orson Welles's 1952 *Othello*, and the opportunities for comparison did not work to its advantage. 'All *Othello* has in common with the Edzard film', wrote Philip French, 'is the muffled soundtrack' (*Observer*); for Billington, the point that 'fidelity, patience, adherence to Shakespearean structure by themselves get you nowhere' was confirmed both by Edzard's film and by the fact that 'by chopping up the text, eliding scenes, shooting on the wing, Welles's film takes us to the heart of the play's vertiginous madness' (*Guardian*). Reviewers would have noticed the distance between Welles and Edzard right from the opening moments. *Othello* opens, stunningly, with a time-bending flash-forward to the aftermath of the tragedy, with a shot of the protagonist's inverted face framed in darkness, and moved through a wordless, hallucinatory montage of images of the funeral cross-cut with Iago being hauled skywards in a cage. Dizzying juxtapositions of scale and shifts of camera angle and perspective create a dreamlike world in which the narrative is experienced through the fractured consciousness of the hero. *As You Like It* begins with the credits (accompanied by a whimsically angular, folk-tinged woodwind score) superimposed on the image of what appears to be an open window through which can be glimpsed the outlines of a mist-shrouded forest; the promise, initially, seems to be of traditional pastoral. James Fox, smartly turned out in a long black cashmere coat, comes into shot and he begins 'All the world's a stage', straight to camera. On 'His acts being seven ages' (2.7.143) a *trompe l'oeil* shift of camera angle reveals the window to be a mirror, and as Fox continues he is intermittently flanked by his screen double. There may be a nod here to Fox's iconic performance in Donald Cammell and Nicolas Roeg's 1970 cult movie *Performance*, which makes extensive use of mirror shots to suggest doubled and divided identities; the sequence announces one of the film's key devices, as Oliver and Orlando, and the Dukes, are both doubled (as are various court and forest lords and ladies), and another in its signature imagery of mirroring and transparency (the court is dominated by clear and reflective glass, Arden by water and polythene). Duke Frederick's court is simultaneously flashily affluent and dispiritingly drab, a city bank or corporate headquarters, all plate-glass, marble flooring and stone columns, inhabited by hard-faced young men and women in sharp suits and designer spectacles. Among them is Tiernan's striped-shirted, gelled-haired Oliver, who briefs Charles (Tony Armatrading) at a pretentiously appointed mahogany desk in an echoing lobby that thrums to the sound of passing traffic and bursts of pneumatic drilling. As Orlando, Tiernan is styled at the opening as a hoodie-clad, knapsack-carrying outcast, possibly already living on the streets, hovering at the entrance to Frederick's domain, to which Cyril Cusack's long-suffering, cardigan-clad Adam acts as doorkeeper. The confrontation between Oliver and Orlando becomes an exercise in tricksy camerawork, since Tiernan has to argue, shot-reverse shot, with himself.

The dividing lines between the haves and have-nots in post-Thatcherite early 1990s London are clearly drawn, and further underscored when, at Charles's report of the 'old news' (1.1.86–91) of Duke Senior's banishment, a dissolve takes us forward to 2.1 and to the puddle-ridden wasteland of Arden, where the Duke casually delivers his opening homily surrounded by the abandoned detritus of city life: cardboard, polythene, scraps of wood and metal that his followers are attempting to fashion into shelter. A benevolent lot, the Duke's companions are evidently a group of the urban dispossessed miraculously unaffected by drug, alcohol or mental health problems; the style of verbal delivery is downbeat, prosaic; and the 'venison' that the Duke hopes to 'go kill' (2.1.21) is shrink-wrapped supermarket meat. The film likewise jumps between the court and Arden at the end of 1.2, when the dialogue between Orlando and Le Beau (an extravagantly fey Roger Hammond) is followed by Jaques and Amiens (John Tams), a pub singer with a Zapata moustache, in 2.5, who perch on an abandoned electricity cable drum beside another huge puddle, dilapidated sheds and scrap metal in the background; Jaques's 'I'll go sleep if I can …' (2.5.51–2) prompts a dissolve to Rosalind and Celia, whose dialogue in the first part of 1.3 takes place across a plush crimson sofa inexplicably parked in the Duke's lobby. The final part of the scene (the banishment is a separate interlude) is set in Celia's vast walk-in wardrobe, a space crammed with expensive worn-once outfits (which Croft and Bannerman spend some time aimlessly throwing about) and the odd empty champagne bottle. The moral of the cut from this ostentation, triviality and waste, on 'To liberty, and not to banishment' (1.3.134), to the open ground of Arden, is unmistakable. When, towards the end of 2.4, the narrative cuts from Corin's (Hammond again, accompanied by a lone sheep) hangout (a cosy wooden cabbie's shelter, the greenest space in the film) back to the mirrors, gilt pillars and marbled floor of the court for 2.2, the contrast between the glowing intimacy of the one and the cold emptiness of the other is even sharper. The gesture is repeated again in 2.7, where the final lines of 'All the world's a stage', spoken over the image of Adam tucking into a plate of the Duke's food, are followed by a jump to Duke Frederick and Oliver's dialogue in 3.1.

The contrast between the two worlds is also reflected in the first appearance of Rosalind and the somewhat older Celia (Celia Bannerman) in 1.2: decked out in black-and-white skirt and jacket and statement-making pink hat, the latter is the impeccably spoken, effortlessly confident essence of Sloane-Ranger sophistication, and far more at home at the canapé-and-champers do in Duke Frederick's lobby than Croft's vulnerable, diffident, red-frocked Rosalind, who spends most of the scene (and most of the film) looking thoroughly fed up. The class differences between Celia, Rosalind and Touchstone (Griff Rhys Jones) are marked:

he is a spivvy cockney-accented interloper, a chancer skulking surreptitiously around a party to which he has probably not been invited, who spends the film trying to milk what comedy he can from his part by alternately pulling long faces, putting on voices, and sniggering at his own jokes. In Arden, where Audrey (Miriam Margolyes, first seen hovering slyly on the fringes of the court) runs a greasy-spoon roadside café, he is accompanied by a jaunty, sitcom-style brass and woodwind theme that reminds us how funny he is. Perhaps in keeping with the film's particular mode of realism, there is the quasi-Brechtian moment of what seems to be an unscripted glitch during the 'pancakes' routine, when Rhys Jones taps his chest on 'by his honor' (1.2.68), catches his concealed microphone with an audible clunk, and briefly corpses.

As in Czinner's version, Rosalind and Celia are initially reluctant, flinching spectators of the wrestling, which, oddly, takes place entirely off screen; but by the end of a short sequence of mimed reactions to the bout, Rosalind smiles briefly for the first time. Perhaps, given that a wrestling match in this setting is incongruous enough as it is, actually showing it would have made it seem even more preposterous; the ugly responses of the court suggest that, beneath the moneyed veneer, there is an element of street-level brutality. The casting of Don Henderson as a snarling wide-boy Duke Frederick reinforces this: trading on the actor's long-established persona as a screen heavy, he signals his bad-guy status by greedily smoking throughout, tries to hit on Orlando on 'thou art a gallant youth' (1.2.198; gay shades of Ronnie Kray or of Richard Burton's sadistic Vic Dakin in the 1971 gangster film *Villain*) and generally brings to the 1990s setting a touch of the 1970s.

Croft spends much of the film's first act in the shadow of Bannerman, whose Celia is emotionally dominant and clearly Rosalind's social superior. It might be hoped that becoming Ganymede and escaping to Arden would bring Rosalind into her own. It does not. This in part because her 'man's apparel' – jeans, hoodie and black beanie – is unisex rather than boyish, but perhaps more because Croft makes little effort to masquerade as male, and thus the question of whether Orlando thinks Ganymede is a he or a she becomes irrelevant. Of the two, Celia appears to travel further: ditching her first-act hauteur, her designer wardrobe for a Barbour, headscarf, big sweaters and a checked skirt, and her long tipped cigarettes for messy roll-ups, Bannerman softens and blossoms as the film progresses, and when the transformed and dishevelled

Oliver turns up at the cab shelter, her face lights up with instant and totally persuasive joy. In contrast, Rosalind and Orlando's first encounter in Arden seems contrived to emphasize the distance between them: frequently seen in long shot, they have to bellow their dialogue across the bleak landscape, and when Rosalind tries to engage the stone-chucking Orlando in the 'Time' duet (3.2.288–307), she is forced to bob about and stalk him like a pestering nuisance; as she lands him a playful 'manly' punch on 'With a thief to the gallows' (l. 302), he raises his fist to retaliate. The scowl with which Tiernan delivers 'Where dwell you, pretty youth?' (l. 308) epitomizes his default setting of self-absorbed anger and resentment: Rosalind gamely does her best to catch his attention, but it is hard to see why she bothers. During their second wooing scene, he is a little more forthcoming, but the exchange still seems edged with sarcasm ('Forever and a day' (4.1.126) is virtually a sneer), and is oddly heated, even hostile. For the mock-wedding they clamber (together, awkwardly, with Celia, who is absent from 3.2) into a makeshift wood and polythene shelter, and just for a moment (on 'Then love me, Rosalind' (l. 100)), they seem to make genuine contact. It is just as quickly broken: Rosalind plants a quick, impetuous kiss on his lips on 'I do take thee, Orlando, for my husband' (l. 119–20), and he looks appalled, wipes it off in disgust, then appears to forget all about it. When he exits at a run to 'attend the Duke at dinner' (l. 157), Croft follows in seemingly desperate pursuit; as they shrink, in long shot, into the distance, her warning about promise-breaking is yelled, breathlessly, at his retreating back; Orlando's conciliatory response ('With no less religion than if thou wert indeed my Rosalind' (l. 172–3)) is cut, and poor Rosalind is left shouting 'Time is the old justice …' (l. 174) into the wind.

The strangely ambivalent and tentative quality of Rosalind and Orlando's wooing is at odds with Edzard's claim that hers is a 'truly cheerful' film, and it is difficult to determine whether this is intentional. The uncertainty of tone is most evident in the final scene, which returns the lovers and exiles to the space of the court, now transformed by draped polythene sheeting, fairy lights and orangey-yellow wash into a place of slightly dreamlike, festive reconciliation. The mood is partially lightened by the merging of 5.4 with Touchstone and Audrey's encounter with the pages in 5.3 (here a pair of wheezing, elderly, booze-toting, down-and-out buskers) and by Rhys Jones being given full rein to mug and gabble his way through the 'seven degrees' routine; but the atmosphere of this most awkward English wedding imaginable is strained. The entrance of Rosalind and Celia in bridal gowns, flanked by see-through curtains and descending a staircase through a cloud of dry ice, seems indeterminately situated between earnestness and kitsch. Arden's dwellers stand in a line as they approach, and on 'I'll have no husband, if you be not he' (5.4.114), Croft repeats the rabbit-punch that she had performed as Ganymede; it produces no response. The final credits are interspersed with a montage of exchanged looks between the mirrored members of the two courts, which includes the spectacle of Tiernan, coupled as Oliver with Celia and as Orlando with Rosalind, sharing with himself a cheesy grin. The film ends with the image of Jaques making his way back to Arden.

She's got the look

Edzard's *As You Like It* ran for a week at a handful of London cinemas and was released on VHS in 1993 and on DVD in 1998. Kenneth Branagh's film of the play similarly managed only a limited theatrical release when in premièred in the UK and United States in 2007; its first public showing was on American cable television, at 9.00 p.m. on HBO on 21 August 2007. Widely praised as the director responsible for reviving the fortunes of Shakespearean cinema in the 1980s and 1990s, Branagh's last Shakespeare film, the golden-age musical homage *Love's Labour's Lost* (2000), had flopped badly, and *As You Like It* took 15 years, from the moment he first had the idea, 'sitting in a stone garden [in Kyoto] for a couple of hours mostly on my own one spring day in 1990' (Burnett 160), to complete. As in his previous films, Branagh cast bankable American actors (Bryce Dallas Howard as Rosalind, Kevin Kline as Jaques) with British ones (Romola Garai, Celia; Adrian Lester, Oliver; David Oyelowo, Orlando) and old friends (Richard Briers, Adam); and, as before, he opted to locate the play in a distinct fantasy world (late nineteenth-century Japan). Critical reaction, as has often been the case with Branagh's productions, was mixed. Reviewing the network première, Matthew Gilbert of the *Boston Globe* (21 August) described it as 'likeable' and Howard's Rosalind as 'a pleasure from start to finish'; in London a month later, Laurence Phelan wrote in the *Independent* that it was 'quite delightful' (22 September), and Peter

Bradshaw (*Guardian*, 21 September) that this 'attractive, intelligent reading ... deserves a look'. Few went as far as *Daily Mail*'s Christopher Tookey, who described it as 'a creative and commercial catastrophe' (21 September), but Trevor Johnston's two-star *Time Out* review is representative: 'you can see what he's getting at, but the idea [of the Japanese setting] proves more distracting than liberating, especially when the paucity of oriental faces and the obviously English locations make it more *Mikado* than Kurosawa' (19 September). Not altogether unsympathetic to Branagh's conception, Mark Thornton Burnett offers a more detailed critique: acknowledging that the director was 'keen to dissociate himself from the recent commodification of the Orient', the film nonetheless 'caters to pre-conceived fantasies that bespeak the west more eloquently than the east' (Burnett 158).

Of all the full-length screen versions, Branagh's is the deftest in its adjustment of the text to the conventions of film narrative. As with the other feature films, Branagh centres his half-hour first act on the court, with the move to Arden marking the transition to the second act. This film introduces its benign, white-haired Duke Senior (Brian Blessed, who doubles as black-clad Duke Frederick) at the beginning, in a pre-credit sequence that stages the act of usurpation (described by Branagh in the press pack as a 'palace coup'), and that aims 'to keep that danger alive and to keep a kind of disturbing energy underneath the comedy and the romance'. It also allows early sightings of key figures, the establishment of back-stories, and the anticipation of plotlines that are taken up later. The Anglo-Sino hybridity of this world is signalled by captions which establish the time and setting, and the dramatis personae as expat English 'merchant adventurers', their families and their followers, living 'in enclaves round the "treaty ports"' and creating 'private mini-empires where they tried to embrace this extraordinary culture, it beauties and its dangers'. Announced as 'A dream of Japan', the film promises to reveal 'Love and nature in disguise' and to demonstrate that 'All the world's a stage.' These preoccupations are artfully merged in the opening shot, as a wigged and kimono-clad male actor appears against the flat backdrop of a delicate watercolour rendering of trees; this is a performance on a Kabuki stage taking place in a low-ceilinged chamber hung with paper lanterns, before Duke Senior's court. Seated to his right are Rosalind and Celia, both rapt spectators of this manifestly high-artifice act of gender masquerade, and a detached and indifferent Touchstone (Alfred Molina), practising origami and living up to his name by touching up one of the serving women (Janet McTeer, later revealed as Audrey). Oliver lurks in the shadows at the edge of the room. Elsewhere in the Duke's residence Jaques sits alone, cross-legged at a low writing desk. Shots of the Kabuki performance and its audience are intercut with shots of heavily armoured, black Samurai advancing stealthily outside, and it is Jaques who catches the first sign of trouble when he hears a footfall on the roof (the *New York Sun*'s Brendan Bernhard likened this to 'a campy assassination scene in an Inspector Clouseau movie' (21 August)). Moments later, the genteelly orientalized world of these Englishmen abroad is shattered, in an action sequence that evokes *Crouching Tiger, Hidden Dragon* (2000) and *House of Flying Daggers* (2004), by the warriors who come crashing through the paper-thin walls and ceiling of the Duke's chamber. As Duke Senior, Touchstone, Celia and Rosalind are rounded up, a noirishly extreme low-angle shot sees Duke Frederick stride into the room, visor-masked, to come face-to-face with his brother; we watch the banished Duke and his followers scurrying to escape and the usurper Duke's henchmen committing random acts of 12-rated mayhem (Blessed claims in his press-pack interview that 'In the first two pages he and his men kill over a thousand people', which seems a little overstated). The sequence ends, five minutes in, with the film's first brief snatch of dialogue, between Oliver and Charles: 'What's the news?'; 'The old Duke is banished by his younger brother the new Duke'; 'So where will the old Duke live?'; 'They say he is already in the Forest of Arden' (1.1.84–100). The film cuts to the Duke and his men, Jaques among them, who flee into darkened woodland, and then, with much bowing, encounter a mysterious seated, bald-headed figure – a Buddhist monk, the 'old religious man' (5.4.151) who later engineers the other Duke's conversion (Rosalind, Celia and Touchstone also meet the monk on their arrival).

The set-up is almost novelistic in its elaboration, and it typifies the film's expository mode: as well as affording the banishment a violent immediacy it generally lacks, the sequence affords cogency to Celia's attempts to cajole her cousin out of her misery in 1.2 (Rosalind is genuinely traumatised by the events of the coup). It is not surprising that the film satisfies audience expectations by allowing a glimpse of Kevin Kline in the first five minutes, but, more interestingly and unusually, it also gives more weight to the

Touchstone–Audrey subplot by allocating both characters some early, quite high-profile screen time (which includes keeping him in shot during Orlando and Rosalind's dialogue towards the end of 1.2), compensating for the fact that almost all of his lines in the first act are cut. Audrey's affectionate reaction to Touchstone's goosing suggests that they already have some kind of history, and McTeer establishes a strong presence which, as is subsequently confirmed, proves her to be anything but his docile plaything. It is Audrey who provides Duke Senior with provisions for his escape, and Branagh extends and also darkens her journey by having her dragged off, screaming, by the new Duke's men, quite possibly, it is implied, to be raped. When the action moves to Arden, Audrey appears in a wordless sequence that has her discovered, dirty-faced and dishevelled, by William (Chinese-American Paul Chan, one of the film's handful of credited ethnic actors), who, again with much smiling and bowing, takes her into his awkward care.

Branagh's reordering of the opening scenes means that the first Rosalind–Celia exchange and the rain-lashed initial confrontation between Orlando (David Oyelowo) and Oliver are both framed by the primary narrative of usurpation, and both are conducted in an atmosphere of oppression and fear. There is no chance, in this context, of Rosalind deciding to 'devise sports' or thinking of 'falling in love' (1.2.20–1), and Oliver is evidently a beneficiary of regime change; as their 'Wilt thou lay hands on me, villain' tussle (1.1.147) demonstrates, both brothers are accomplished martial arts practitioners. Lester nonetheless manages to suggest that, even at this stage, Oliver is conflicted over his treatment of Orlando: having plotted with Charles (Nobuyuki Takano), a mute Sumo wrestler whose lines are allocated to Denis (Gerard Horan), he is left fighting back tears, turning over a totally sincere 'Yet he's gentle, never schooled and yet learned' (1.1.143) as if trying to fathom his own malevolence. Previewed well in advance, his conversion seems all the more plausibly imminent at the end of his lachrymose, guilt-stricken stand-off with Duke Frederick, whose own darkly ruminative response to 'I never loved my brother in my life' – 'More villain thou' (3.1.14–15) – is a moment of self-realization directed more at himself than at his sobbing interlocutor, and one that presages his own moral volte-face. Frederick's demons have been in evidence since at least the banishment scene, where thundering bullying gives way to unexpected moments of tenderness: responding to Celia's declaration of loyalty to Rosalind, his 'You are a fool' (1.3.83) is spoken not in anger but in sorrow, surprise and deep regret.

Staged as a Sumo bout, broodingly watched by Duke Frederick and shot, sinisterly, from below, the wrestling match epitomizes the brutalism of the new court, an environment in which the Japanese fan-toting Rosalind and Celia are clearly on edge. Their fan etiquette, while in keeping with the film's late-Victorian-oriental milieu, bespeaks a certain guardedness (and is set sharply against Oyelowo's Sumo near-nakedness, which ensures that Rosalind in this scene really does not know where to look), but it also reiterates the idea of social and gender performance as half-masked: during Rosalind's first exchange with Orlando, the lower part of her face is completely covered, she speaks but we do not see her lips move (Branagh thought the image sufficiently eloquent to have it dominate the film poster, DVD sleeve and main menu). In this sequence (on, significantly, 'your fair ... eyes' (1.2.159)) Branagh also introduces a note quite alien to the minor-key, drum-dominated acoustic world of Frederick's court, in the shape of the wistful (or, for David Jays in *Sight and Sound* (October 2007), 'ruinously syrupy') woodwind and strings motif (composed by Patrick Doyle, who also plays Amiens) that is heard over the title credits and that is later to become Arden's tune and the film's love theme; there is, it signals, a world elsewhere ('Arden', Branagh stated in the press pack, 'is a mythical place, a state of mind'). In this arena of furtive glances, the fans stay aloft for the wrestling; as in Czinner's and Edzard's renderings, Rosalind can hardly bear to watch, while the less squeamish ladies of the court whoop and cheer the combatants on. When Orlando succeeds in throwing Charles, Rosalind's fan is back in place so that on 'O excellent young man' (1.3.183), one's attention is entirely upon her act of pleasurable looking. Observing her gaze, Celia drops her own fan, open-mouthed in shock. Following the Duke's exit, the fan serves as Rosalind's central prop in a courtship dance of advance and retreat, of facial exposure and concealment, and, most of all, of looks proffered, deflected, and coyly downcast.

Who looks, how and where, and how it relates to acts of speech and silencing, is also key to the banishment scene. It begins with Celia insistently drawing Rosalind back into the room by locking her gaze full on; 'Some of it is for my child's father' (1.3.11) prompts Celia suddenly to glance screen leftwards, mindful of the malign off-screen presence of her father. The move is repeated later, on

8 Rosalind (Bryce Dallas Howard) and Orlando (David Oyelowo), BBC Films/HBO Films/Shakespeare Film Company, 2006

'Know'st thou not the Duke/Hath banished me, his daughter' (1.3.90–1), and anticipated by Orlando in the previous scene, who shoots a look rightwards, on 'tyrant Duke' (1.2.257); the Duke remains central within the diegesis even when not on screen. In this context, it is entirely appropriate that the last two words of 'all points like a man' (1.3.112) are mouthed, not said: for the moment, at least, the transformative possibility of masculinity is so transgressively thrilling as to be literally unspeakable (Rosalind similarly mouths 'Orlando' when she responds to Celia's 'I' faith, coz, 'tis he' (3.2.198–9)). Their flight is intercut with the Duke's bearlike prowling and Oliver's torching of Orlando's lodging: in another role-enhancing moment for Touchstone, Celia's final lines in this scene are spoken, reassuringly, not to Rosalind, but to him as the three of them pose nervously on the threshold of the palace, a cowardly lion flanked by a pair of Dorothys.

The camerawork during the film's first act is dominated by tightly framed interior shots and close ups, creating a sense of claustrophobic enclosure and entrapment. With the move to Arden, the perspective noticeably broadens. Dawn breaks over a long-shot panorama of russet and green woodland, Arden's theme swells, and Rosalind as Ganymede (styled as a Dickensian urchin-gamine in flat cap, knee-length boots, breeches and camel-coloured jacket), leads the fugitives through woodland; elsewhere, Duke Senior and his followers gather firewood. If the cinematic styling of the first act just about manages to sustain the fantasy of a colour-blind enclave of nineteenth-century expats abroad, the second act embraces a location-shot realism that fails (and perhaps does not really try) to convince even in its own terms. Despite the presence of a few wooden bridges, a torii (gate), a sand garden (in which Jaques squats in Zen meditation, Rosalind receives Phoebe's letter, and Oliver and Celia fall in love), and some tai chi moves, this is a home-counties Arden (filming took place at Wakehurst Place, West Sussex, and at Kew Gardens), where Silvius (Alexander Wyndham) and Phoebe (Jade Jefferies), rather problematically, are white actors in understated yellow-face. If the first half-hour shows Branagh at his more inventive and cinematically adventurous, the middle section of the film is leisurely, and more theatrical in its framing and pacing, as the shots lengthen while the verbal text unfurls. 'Now my co-mates …' (2.1.1–17) establishes the pattern, filmed in one continuous 80-second tracking shot that cuts on 'good in everything' from the Duke's glance sideways to Jaques himself, who is given Amiens's response, 'I would not change it.' Jaques's 'I met a fool i' th' forest' (2.7.13–61), here an ostentatious, pedantically illustrative star turn, is given a similar (two-minute plus) one-tracking-shot treatment, forcing both camera and court-in-exile to follow Kline as he preens and cavorts his way through undergrowth and 50 lines of text. The trick is repeated for the 2½ minutes of 'All the world's stage', during which Branagh's restlessly circling steadicam finally settles on Kline's deep-contemplative face as he excruciatingly strings out the pause-punctuated final lines. Arden, we see, is where word-heavy 'serious' acting is given space to breathe.

Extended actor-indulging takes are also the rule in the wooing scenes. The first of these takes place on and around a lengthy wooden bridge, and its connotations of journeying, passing and crossover are far stronger than the faint-to-non-existent signals of sexual ambiguity emitted by Dallas Howard's resolutely unmasculine turn as Ganymede. Indeed, Branagh seems determined to keep Rosalind's, or Dallas Howard's, femininity very much in view, to the extent of staging 5.2.16–23 as an opportunity for mild sex-comedy jeopardy by having Orlando catch Rosalind skinny-dipping in a forest pool. Rosalind and Orlando's dialogue from 'Do you hear, forester?' (3.2.275) to 'Fair youth, I would I could make you believe I love ' (l. 352) is delivered as they walk the bridge's entire length, from Corin's dwelling, across marshland, and onto a shadowed forest path, in an Altmanesque continuous tracking shot lasting nearly three minutes. This is followed by a shot following their progress through the forest which lasts just as long and ends the scene on 'Nay, you must call me Rosalind' (3.2.392; Celia drops out of sight half-way through the previous shot). The walking-while-talking allows Rosalind to lead and Orlando to follow, and it develops the film's economy of looks granted, averted, exchanged and withheld, since Dallas Howard plays much of the scene not looking at Oleyewo, who in turn spends his time trying, and failing, to catch her eye (see Figure 8).

Introduced, as mentioned, in the opening scene, the Touchstone–Audrey courtship is afforded considerably more weight than in any of the other screen versions. It is helped in this respect by Molina's likeably droll and doleful performance: in the dialogue with Corin (3.2.11–74), for example, bemusement and exasperation are conveyed by a subtle pantomime of raised eyebrows and interrupted gestures as he tries, and fails, to trim his moustache with a pair of tweezers. Even here, the film's fondness for previously undisclosed subtext and back-stories is in evidence: on 'Wast ever in court, shepherd?' (3.2.28–9), Touchstone surreptitiously roots through Corin's personal belongings, discovers a bible, opens it, and pulls out an old photograph of Corin, wearing clerical dress, apparently at a graduation ceremony. The whole 'court' dialogue becomes unexpectedly loaded; a look passes between them, and 'I am a true labourer' (3.2.64) is the plea of a man who fears his cover has been blown. Yuill explains in the press pack: 'he has been a missionary ... For whatever reason, Corin lost his faith and stayed on in the forest.'

It is as good a reason as any to make Corin Martext in 3.3, where he turns up, apparently drunk, and pretends to pass out before the wedding ceremony can take place (cleaned and sobered up, Corin reappears as Hymen, here a presiding minister, for the final matches). Although it is evident that Touchstone is desperate to cajole a heavily sexualized, cleavage-heaving Audrey into quick roll in the hay, the groundwork makes this less cynical than usual: Audrey and Touchstone's meeting in Arden (interpolated into 3.2, immediately following 'Come, shepherd, let us make an honourable retreat' (l. 148)) is a reunion, and in the scene she gives as good as she gets: her response to his tactless musings on 'sluttishness' (3.3.30–3) is to land him two almighty and well-deserved slaps. Yet she meets his proposal with delight, and 'We must be married' (l. 83) is her line. Branagh completes the arc of their courtship by shifting the confrontation with William in 5.1 to follow the first Silvius–Phoebe scene (3.5): Touchstone's tirade becomes both a display of commitment and a demonstration of prowess, and it works, as Audrey becomes visibly more gleeful and aroused as the scene progresses. Unfortunately, the fact that he directs the tirade at the diminutive and disconcerted Paul Chan means that the humour seems more like racist bullying than amusing repartee; here, the film's orientalism is particularly charmless.

It is a measure of Audrey's prominence that she is afforded a reunion moment with Duke Senior in the final scene ('Audrey!' he interjects with delight; she curtsies in return as he kisses her hand), thereby resolving the banishment plot within the frame of the four marriages. Branagh's third act, which begins with Oliver and Orlando's reconciliation, moves relatively briskly, via a montage of shots of spring flowers, to a festive, unambiguously joyous finale, staged as an open-air multiple wedding festooned with fluttering banners. All but 40 of 5.4's 141 lines up to the entrance of Jaques de Boys (Jotham Annan) are cut (no seven degrees of the lie here); but Frederick's forest invasion and conversion is shown in full (in a neat segue, on 'all their lands restored' (l. 160), Blessed as Frederick hands Jaques de Boys a folded paper which, via a dissolve, he in turn hands to Blessed as Senior). As Duke Senior welcomes de Boys and addresses the guests, a tracking shot describes an inclusionary circuit around them: 'in true delights' (5.4.189) is the cue for 'It was a lover and his lass' and a hey-nonny-nonny hoedown that takes the frolicking party through the forest (past Duke Frederick, serenely posed in Zen posture beneath a tree) and, in a move that magically collapses the spatial distinctions made at the film's start, through the arch of the torii which appears to have been placed there solely for the dancers to run beneath, and into the Duke's palace, which turns out to have been adjacent to Arden all along. As Jaques settles beside Frederick in the forest, Branagh concludes with an act of homage both to the golden-age musical and to his own oeuvre, in the form of a classic Busby Berkeley overhead shot of wheeling couples.

That's not quite all. The final credits are interrupted by the reappearance of Howard, once again as Ganymede, to deliver the epilogue. She steps from behind a tree, as if from the wings, and as the camera tracks her movement it brings into shot the film's cast and crew, parked trailers, on-set caterers, a pair of hi-vis-jacketed policemen, and, briefly, Branagh himself. Delivering the final line, she steps into a trailer and closes the door, and Branagh, off camera, announces: 'and ... cut'. The Brechtian 'exposure of the mechanisms' of film-making is, of course, light-hearted (though the brief revelation of the sheer numbers of personnel involved, as well as the amount of kit and heavy technology on display, serves as a salutary reminder of how much time, labour and expense are involved even on a small-scale British film such as this), but it serves the text and the film well in that it refuses to take both too seriously.

Notes

1. The almost total disappearance of Czinner's *As You Like It* from cinemas can be compared with the trajectory of Olivier's *Henry V*, which ran for nearly three years following its release in 1944. In London alone, it was screened again in 1950, and in 1954, thereafter reappearing at the Academy cinema annually or biannually until 1963. It had brief runs again in 1966, 1968, 1970, 1971, 1973 and 1977; it premièred on British network television on Christmas Day, 1972, and was screened again in 1986 and (marking Olivier's death) 1989. In 1978, it was one of the first Shakespeare films to be released on video.
2. This is a shockingly callow and uninformed comment on a theatre career that spanned five decades and that included appearances on Broadway as Laertes (1904), Horatio and Malvolio (1930), as well as two seasons at the Shakespeare Memorial Theatre (1949–50), in which he played Banquo, Cymbeline, Gloucester and Buckingham in *Henry VIII*.
3. Jorgens saw the production on PBS on 28 February 1979, more than six months after the BBC showing. The American broadcasts were a in slightly different sequence from the British one: *As You Like It* followed *Julius Caesar* (14 February), and was followed by *Romeo and Juliet* (14 March), *Richard II* (28 March), *Measure for Measure* (11 April) and *Henry VIII* (25 April).
4. These include *Romeo and Juliet*, 3 December 1967; *The Tempest*, 12 May 1968; *Julius Caesar*, 13 April 1969; *Macbeth*, 20 September 1970; *A Midsummer Night's Dream*, 26 September 1971; *The Merchant of Venice*, 16 April 1972; *King Lear*, 23 March 1975 and *Love's Labour's Lost*, 14 December 1975. All had a running time of 120 minutes.
5. Authored by 'JRT/DJC', the Audience Research report is dated 8 February 1979, and includes data from the Survey of Listening and Viewing and a sample of audience reactions. The reaction index of 78 aggregates the ratings as follows: A+ (39 per cent), A (38 per cent), B (21 per cent), C (0 per cent), and C- (2 per cent). It notes that the figures for *Romeo and Juliet* and *Richard II* are 75 and 79, respectively.

CHAPTER VII

As we like it

It is just before 2.00 p.m. on the afternoon of Thursday, 3 September 2015. I am at Shakespeare's Globe in Southwark again, my second visit this year, for one of the final performances of this season's *As You Like It*. Although I avoided reading the reviews (with the hope, for the purposes of this very chapter, of coming to the show fresh), I have a sense that the production has been generally well received; one of my University of Kent colleagues, Mary McNulty (who also works as a Globe Education practitioner, and whose judgement generally concurs with mine), reported briefly but positively on it when she saw it in preview. It was very good, she told me some time back in May, but cautioned that, at nearly three hours, it was very long – perhaps too long for a Globe show, quite probably too long for a comedy. I buy a £5 standing ticket from the box office (cash only, it is stated; I wonder whether this is to preserve a real-money connection with the penny-admission original Globe?) before eating lunch sitting on the balustrade opposite the Globe's riverside entrance. I have arranged to meet a colleague and friend: Amy Cook, who is on a flying visit from New York to catch the new piece by Dreamthinkspeak, and who had emailed a few weeks earlier to suggest that we meet up.[1] She warned me that she might be running late and be a little spaced out with jet lag (her flight arrived that morning). I try the mobile number she gave me in an email but it doesn't connect, so I hang around the Globe lobby; we meet up around a quarter to two by the glass doors leading onto the piazza and make our way into the yard.

Amy, in denim and sensible shoes, is, I think, better dressed for the event than I, wearing as I am the cream jacket and chinos combination that (my older son says) makes me look like a slave trader. Optimistically, I have my battered sun-shielding panama-style straw hat crushed in my rucksack; my optimism proves to be misplaced. As I write this, exactly two weeks later (2.55 pm on a far warmer and sunnier Thursday 17 September) I speculate

9 Amy Cook and Robert Shaughnessy at Shakespeare's Globe, 2015

that, as characters in this book's narrative, we were unwittingly paying homage to Eileen Atkins and Richard Pasco in Buzz Goodbody's 1973 RSC production (see Chapter III). Amy seems not in the least jet-lagged, and we chat about our summers, vacations, work projects and families as we take up position as close as we can get to the stage-right side of the platform, which extends into the yard via two crab-claw-like sloping wooden gangways. The yard and galleries are pretty full, and the crowd seems cheerful, predisposed to have a good time, but rather quieter than I have come to expect. As usually happens in this place, I catch a familiar face: on this occasion, it is that of Andrea Walker, one of my former Shakespeare students, who is standing in prime position right at the front edge of the stage. She smiles and waves and we exchange a look of slightly self-conscious mutual amusement (*fancy seeing you here*). I wonder about that self-consciousness: does it register a sense of Globe performance as a guilty pleasure, or as a rather odd one? 'Let's get a picture', I say to Amy, and I hand my phone to one of the ever-vigilant stewards, who obliges while warning us not to take photos during the performance (*I know that*, I don't say) (see Figure 9).

The performance begins with the tolling of a bell and a roll of drums (a bit sombre for *As You Like It*, I think; four weddings *and* a funeral) and an interpolated prologue sequence. As surreptitiously as possible I retrieve my pad and pen from my bag and begin to scribble (mostly one-word) notes. This is not my usual habit (as I have recorded elsewhere ['One Piece'], I find the act of writing about performance while attending to it almost impossible to manage), but I am here partly to gather material for the book on *As You Like It* which I am hoping to finish a few months from now, so I make an exception. I don't really know what I am looking for, what I am expecting the production to reveal or to prove (if anything); when Amy asks after the show what I was making notes about, I reply: 'Whatever seemed worth making a note of at the time: stage business, the delivery of a line, the behaviour of both the audience and the weather.'[2] The opening sequence prompts me to scribble 'black', 'beat', bell' and 'funeral cortège', as we watch a draped coffin processed through the yard and onto the stage, accompanied by a slow tolling. Three young men are in attendance; it is, I surmise, the funeral of Sir Roland de Boys, a reasonable enough way of establishing the fraternal relationships (and a way of introducing Jaques de Boys somewhat earlier than his *deus ex machina* arrival in the text allows), though it does further complicate the already amorphous time-scheme of the play's opening events. Just as there are conflicting messages concerning the timing of Duke Senior's banishment, the sequence raises the unanswered question of how long Sir Roland has been dead, and how long Orlando under Oliver's charge, considerations which surely must feed into the playing of their first scene in particular.

These are not, however, thoughts that occur to me at the time, for my notes tell me that I am more bothered by the distraction of a woman in a dark cagoule positioned just in front of me who spends the first minutes of the show checking and rechecking her phone, and who, I am dreading, will serve as a constant source of irritation for the next three hours (thankfully, she soon pockets the phone and does not look at it again). During the first scene I note that the first short laugh from this attentive audience comes when Orlando seizes Oliver by the throat (1.1.46); the next on 'Call him in!' (l. 81) and then, as one would expect, 'I speak but brotherly of him' (l. 133). Onwards to the second scene and a pacey treatment of the exchanges between Rosalind, Celia and Touchstone: the 'pancakes' routine earns an inexplicably hearty laugh that confirms for me the audience's basic goodwill (it is no funnier than usual, but the crowd are prepared to behave as if it is). With the wrestling, things start to warm up (despite an ominous scattering of drops from a grey sky): Orlando removes his shirt to reveal an impressively toned torso that tangibly thrills both the audience and Rosalind: her first words to him, *'Young man'* (l. 143), somewhere between a gasp, a purr and a growl of arousal, brings the house down. I already like Rosalind very much for this, and it earns the show's first big roar of laughter. It is only afterwards that I remember that this is the second time I have admired a Michelle Terry performance this year, the first having been her Rosaline in *Love's Labour's Lost* in Stratford in February. The wrestling ends with the first round of applause, as the mountainous figure of Charles (Gary Shelford, I later learn from the programme, who doubles as a rather panto-dame Hymen in the final scene) is carried off. 'He calls us back' (l.221) is similarly milked for all it is worth (Orlando, of course, does nothing of the kind), and to good effect; by the end of the scene Rosalind, Celia (Ellie Piercy) and, in his slightly bemused way, Orlando (Simon Harrison, to my eye something of a Benedict Cumberbatch lookalike) already have the audience in their pockets.

For the next few scenes, my notes are sporadic, recording simply that blue sky breaks through the clouds during 2.1 (perhaps offsetting 'The season's difference ... the icy fang/And churlish chiding of the winter's wind' [ll.6–7], and that in 2.2 the attendant 'lords' are actually ladies, in keeping with the Globe's commitment to equal-opportunity casting (I half-expect 'Hisperia, the Princess' gentlewoman' (2.2.10) to be among them, but she is not). The production as a whole is a relatively small-cast one (William Mannering, for example, plays both Oliver and Amiens), and not all the doubling is credited: Phil Whitchurch is Sir Oliver Martext as well as Adam, but the programme doesn't tell us this (unless the idea is that Martext is Adam in disguise, which seems a bit odd). One doubling which doesn't do anything for me is that of David Beames as Dukes Frederick and Senior. It economizes on actors but makes no obvious dramaturgic or thematic point (unlike, for example, the doubling in Adrian Noble's RSC production of 1985, where Senior was Frederick's alter ego [see Chapter III]), and seems to force the actor to italicize the red-faced malevolence of Frederick just in order to differentiate him from the avuncular benevolence of Senior. In the same scene, somewhere in the audience a baby starts quietly chuntering, which causes some ripples of amusement around the yard, and I recall the report of a similar incident in the 2006 Globe *Coriolanus*, when a baby 'started to cry in 2.1', at the moment when Sicinius refers to 'Your prattling nurse' who 'Into a rapture lets her baby cry/While she chats him' (194–6); 'Frank McCusker's Sicinius referred, with a gesture, to the baby that had actually cried and the line got a big laugh' (Escolme 512). On this occasion, no such ironies are available: 'the infant/ Mewling and puking in the nurse's arms' [2.7.143–4] lies several scenes ahead, and by the time we get to it the young spectator has fallen silent. Nonetheless, the very possibility of such serendipity is enough to briefly remind me of the importance of the aleatoric in Globe performance.

Extradiegetic everydayness also makes itself known in 2.4. Rosalind and Celia have made their entrance from the yard, the former clutching a large unfolded Ordnance Survey map, which lies on the floor for the remainder of the scene (the production is Globe-style original practices in terms of costuming, which adheres to a restrained palette of rust-red, subdued green and black, but incorporates various jokey contemporary props, including the map and, later, Audrey's bicycle). During Rosalind's dialogue with Corin, the breeze picks up and the map stirs, threatening to drift across the stage. Touchstone (Daniel Crossley), perched casually on the base of the pillar stage right, discreetly traps it with his foot while shooting a look at Ellie Piercy, and for a moment I wonder who is who and what is being communicated in this exchange of glances: is Crossley in or out of role, and is Piercy? It looks more like two actors communicating than two characters, and I rather like the glimpse of colleagues at work, professional, attentive, connected. The precautionary manoeuvre is executed by the actor, but how does it map onto the gestural repertoire of the character? As it turns out, we will discover later that fancy footwork is Touchstone's, or Crossley's, forte, in the form of the virtuoso tap-dancing routine that transforms 'A lover and his lass' into a full-blown eleven o'clock number. For the moment, Touchstone is amused, restrained, more comedian than clown. A different kind of comic presence is introduced in the following scene (2.5), in the form of James Garnon's Jaques (this is the one Globe actor I recognize without referring to the programme). Clad from head to foot in black, and possessed of a glare that freezes the blood, Garnon reacts to Amiens's 'Under the greenwood tree' with ferocious sarcasm; physically and temperamentally he reminds me of stand-up comedian Eddie Izzard at his sharpest. Garnon is a performer who carries a palpable aura of danger, and I find myself slipping my notepad out of sight behind my back: I am suddenly acutely conscious, in this mutually exposed space, of how distracting and annoying the activity of note-taking can be, and I have no wish to become the target of this actor's disapproval. As has increasingly happened during my viewing of performances for this book, I start to anticipate the gags, wondering during this scene whether the 'Greek invocation to call fools into a circle' (2.5.51) will, as on numerous previous occasions, refer to the lords that have gathered in formation around Jaques in the course of his song. It does not: the circle of fools, Garnon indicates with a sweep of his arm, is the Globe audience. In his next scene, the 'ladies ... young and fair' (2.7.37) are identified in the yard; in 3.3, a gesture from Touchstone conscripts us as Audrey's goats.

I make no notes during 2.6 other than 'Adam + Orlando' (I think it dragged a little), but things pick up again in 2.7 with Jaques back on. His energy and attack propel the scene, and the opening line of 'All the world's a stage' is a delight, at once entirely within this Jaques's character and delightfully metatheatrical. 'All the world's a ... *stage?*': Garnon shoots the line at Duke Senior as a disbelieving riposte to his clunky set-up, as if to say, *I can't believe you are asking me to say this – that cliché? You've got to be kidding!* The delivery is assured, nimble and committed, and Jaques concludes with 'sans everything' on the gangway deep into the yard, in the midst of an audience that has taken him to its heart. The scene ends, the interval begins, and I am more than ready for it.

Amy and I find a bench in the café and talk about the show, and about the play. Amy reflects on how so many of the characters seem preoccupied to the point of obsession with time; I turn over the phrase 'this desert city' (2.1.23), whose oxymoronic force and oddness I have never really registered before. What, I wonder, is the reference point, the anchor, for this paradoxical image in this place, at this time, among these people? What – and where, and when – is 'this' city, this 'desert' city? At one level it is the temporarily unseen but still very much heard brick, steel, glass and concrete landscape of contemporary London, the London of nearly nine million citizens and nearly twice as many annual visitors; at another it is a remembered London of some 200,000 persons, a London whose southernmost limits, where the metropolis gave way to countryside, were marked by the playhouse in which these words were, possibly, first spoken. At yet another it is a place where shepherds speak like courtiers, men turn into women who, in turn, turn to men, and where the Forest of Arden appears and disappears according to the direction of the wind and the angle of the light. These cities, and others, real and unreal, we inhabit in our experience of this performance, this play; a play that, even as it promises to take us to the heart of the pastoral dream, gently but insistently reminds us of its impossibility.

None of this is consciously formulated in our conversation or in my thoughts; yet it is in a way already imprinted upon our bodies, in the ache of standing still on concrete, and in the early September chill that, try as we do to tough it out, suffuses our bones and shapes our responses to this show. Returning to the yard, I catch another friendly face. It is Paul Edmondson, Head of Learning and Research at the Birthplace Trust. As I meet Paul's eye I know that we have the same thought. This is Thursday; on Monday I had received the news of the passing, on 25 August, of John Russell Brown, a man who had, amongst a great deal else, been not only one of the founding figures of performance-centred Shakespeare studies but also, for me, a friend and mentor; the man who had written the reader's report on my first Shakespeare-related book, who had continued to challenge, to cajole and to encourage, and who had been an academic father to me as he had been to many others. *Sad news about John*, or words to that effect, I say to Paul, or possibly says Paul to me; I say that I am going to the funeral (just over a week away, on Monday 14 September), and Paul says yes, *we were wondering if you might like to say a few words*. I am both flattered and daunted, mumble something to the effect of *I'd love to, I'll see what I can do*, and rejoin Amy at 'our' spot in the yard. I recount my brief conversation with Paul as I wonder who the 'we' who thought I *might like to say a few words* might be, and the second half is under way.

Duke Frederick bullies Oliver; 'I never loved my brother in my life/More villain thou' (3.1.14–15) earns a big laugh; Orlando appears with his verses and pins them – as he must – to the pillars. So far, so predictable, if satisfying, but what follows – Touchstone's dialogue with Corin – is a beautiful demonstration of what the Globe can offer that most other venues cannot. Touchstone and Corin are placed forward on the promontories, so that the to and fro of their exchange operates across the heads of the standing audience, who swivel *en masse* from one speaker to the other; it is irresistibly reminiscent, from where I am standing, of the audience at a Wimbledon tennis match, and their visibly embodied attentiveness energizes my own. I am involved in this dialogue, this relationship, because I see other spectators physically invested in it, involuntarily committed to it; I am I but in this situation 'I' am also 'we', both observer and participant (Amy also remarks on this moment afterwards). There's a neat gag when Corin overhears Rosalind reading Orlando's poetry (3.2.77–84): 'Who's Rosalind?' asks Corin (not an unreasonable question); 'No idea', is her quick-fire response. The wooing that follows is vigorous, affecting – and yet, as I remember it, strangely bereft of memorable detail. A note, made just after the interval, prompts me to reflect on just how long Rosalind and Orlando are, in this play, kept separate: they barely know each other at the start of the second half and yet around half an hour later Orlando is somehow the man with whom Rosalind is 'fathom deep in love' (4.1.180). Simon Harrison as Orlando is a winning, attractive and very amiable presence, but the suspicion remains that, once he has shown his stuff in the wrestling, Orlando has nothing particularly interesting to say or do; not for the first time, I wonder what Rosalind (and especially a Rosalind as smart and alive as Michelle Terry's) sees in him.[3] Jaques, for one, has little patience with this Orlando: when the latter responds to the query about his love's stature by indicating 'Just as high as my heart' with a 'this high' palm held to his chest, Jaques looks aghast at the winsomeness. Symptomatically, at the end of the scene, Rosalind's 'Will you go?' (3.2.393) is directed not at Celia, but at him. Charming as he is, Orlando is rather slow on the uptake.

Touchstone and Audrey steer the proceedings even more firmly into the realms of broad farce: Audrey (Sophia Nomvete) is twice Touchstone's size, and clearly even readier for sex than he is (3.3.24, 'Would you not have me honest', reads 'Would you not have me? Honest?'); Sir Oliver makes his entrance as Touchstone drops his breeches to his ankles and Audrey falls to her knees ready to administer her own take on 'the gods give us joy' (l.39). It all gets

[201]

big laughs, but I suspect that I am not the only one starting to flag; the applause at the end of the scene seems more ragged, less spontaneous than before. Silvius and Phoebe's scene feels very long; it is not helped by the intrusion of a particularly insistent helicopter (the first half of the show had been uncharacteristically free of air traffic, but the second is proving much harder going), nor by the decision to give Phoebe a heavy stage-Welsh accent. I can't tell whether this is put on, and am slightly troubled by the stereotyping it invokes: the fickle, ever-so-slightly crazed Welsh sex kitten is a British comedy standard (checking afterwards, I discover that Gwyneth Keyworth is, indeed, a Welsh-born actor; I am not sure whether this makes the portrayal okay or not).

The second wooing scene and mock-wedding are, again, well done and there is nothing out of the ordinary here (I note that 'Say "a day" without the "ever"' [4.1.127] is offered as a helpful instruction), but 'O coz, coz, coz ...' (l. 179) is heartfelt, deeply affecting (my notes say: 'I want to cry'). A few more moments stand out as the production ambles towards its close: following Rosalind's faint, there is no doubt that Oliver has seen through the disguise, and it is equally clear in 5.2 that Orlando too knows the truth; the 'what 'tis to love' quartet (ll. 74–98) is, I simply record, a knockout; and 'It Was a Lover and His Lass' becomes, as mentioned earlier, an all-singing, all-dancing, shimmying, toe-tapping, crowd-pleasing show-stopper. The applause and, for the first time, cheers, that erupt at the end of this scene embody the goodwill and rewarded patience of an audience that, after nearly three hours under a now steadily darkening sky and quickening breeze, is more than ready for a feelgood ending. And so it proves: there is for me a moving simplicity in Rosalind's promise 'To make these doubts all even' (5.4.25), and when Hymen (barrel-bare-chested, skirted, and equipped with a very silly headdress) is trundled out of the discovery space on a makeshift truck, the effect is at once absurdly childish, touching and magical. Such is the crude, knocked-up, everyday stuff from which matches and marriages are made. Phoebe accepts poor, dippy Silvius without reservation and with a tight hug (a huge 'aaah' goes up), and I feel more strongly than ever that Touchstone and Audrey do not deserve Jaques's spite.

The show ends, Globe-fashion, with a vigorous jig, to which we dutifully clap along; a few encores, and we are out of the yard and onto the streets. My summery outfit by now feels deeply misjudged, and on our way to the pub, Amy and I mull over the afternoon.

Not least because it had involved a degree of commitment and had cost us something in terms of physical comfort, we agreed that we had rather enjoyed the production, although we also agreed that there was little that was innovative or distinctive about it. Over a beer I ask Amy if she will share her own impressions of the production for me to somehow work them into this chapter as a counterpoint to my own. Two weeks later, on Wednesday 16 September, an email (subject: As we liked it) lands on my phone as I am standing on a wet train station platform. I resolve not to read it until I have completed a draft of this chapter, and on Friday 25 September I finally open it:

> I was exhausted from a night of travel across an ocean and then across London and then from the flat I was staying along the Thames to The Globe. I was also thrilled to be meeting Robert to get to see *As You Like It*. We find a place in the yard and the place fills with people. I loved moving among the people to shift my perspective. There was a father near us who seemed to be explaining the entire play to his daughter (or so I hoped) as it went along. This was annoying but also more acceptable than I would have thought. The actors seemed so strong and in control of their story and world that I didn't worry about this rudeness stumbling them. Sometimes it didn't bother me to watch the backs of actors and other times I needed a new view. Some of the actors played with us, involved us. Actually, it was character based: some of the characters remained in the story world—like Duke Senior and Rosalind and Orlando—while others were our guides in to the story world and thus worked with us—like Touchstone and Jacques. Anachronistic pieces are slipped in as another way of playing with the audience: Touchstone's sunglasses, Martext's grocery cart, Audrey's bike, Rosalind's map of London. Amiens plays a contemporary guitar lick on his period instrument. Jacques references the annoying helicopters. Throughout the show I get colder, searching for places to put my hands to warm them. It rains and people put on raincoats. Despite this, I don't feel jet-lagged and it feels good to be there.
>
> At the end, during her epilogue, Rosalind pulls off her skirt, revealing a male hose/pants to match her wedding dress top. I'm not sure what this was supposed to mean: does she identify with being a man in a contemporary gender-fluid way? Is she supposed to be a man? Is the actor commenting on the history of performance? Not clear to me, but the audience laughed—though I thought maybe they just laughed because it seemed like they should. The Dukes were double cast and I'm not sure why. Music wasn't upstaged by the action; we listened to music together and

the story world and the audience world collapsed. It started with Old Sir Roland's funeral so we saw all 3 brothers at the start and the banners/heralds of the houses. This way we can see the relationship and know there is someone named Jaques who we then see again later.

Jacques starts his 'All the world's a stage' speech as if it is the cliché we've come to hear it as—he rolls his eyes and seems to make fun of Duke Senior for referencing the cliché. But then he goes through it, pulling out the entailments and falling deeper into it.

I feel my memory of the performance shifting as I read. I am struck by the ways in which our accounts resonate with each other, and pleased by the sense that this was a shared experience: like me, Amy notices the bicycle and the map, although she reads the latter as an item of urban cartography (a map of *London*), whereas for me it is an instrument of rural navigation, a city-dweller's must-have accessory that, as Rosalind quickly realises, is no help at all. Like me, Amy remembers the funereal prologue and 'All the world's a stage', observing Jaques, or Garnon, 'pulling out the entailments and falling deeper into it'. I wasn't aware of the annoying commentator-parent, and Amy's discrimination between those performers who remained within the fiction and those who inhabited a more flexible space between play and audience is something that I now remember us discussing in the pub. Amy reminds me of Jaques casting a furious eye skyward in frustration with the helicopters, his colouring of his next line, and the sympathetic laugh this solicited, though I have to search the text to place it (it *might* have been on 'a melancholy of my own, extracted from many *objects*' [4.1.15–16], which would have been perfect, but I can't be sure), and of the exposed hose during the Epilogue. I share her doubts, and can add that, at the end of the last full production of this play at the Globe (in 2009), Naomi Frederick performed exactly the same trick, and to much the same uncertain effect.

This *As You Like It*, however routine and unexceptional it may have been in some ways, served as an opportunity to spend some time in the company both of a play that I have come to care more about than I would have ever expected, and of a friend whose company I value and whose work I admire. In a follow-up email on 8 October, Amy responds to my draft, observing that 'It feels perfect that the production is unextraordinary – it simply *was* and that's often plenty.' Does this warrant its inclusion in this book? Possibly not, if the grounds for such consideration are, say, lasting theatrical significance, originality or distinctiveness. Yet there is another sense in which the amiable ordinariness of this production is worth preserving because, in common with all of the events reimagined in the preceding pages, it offered opportunities for encounter, for discovery and for connection that inhere within the essential sociality of theatregoing as an activity. During a run of 51 performances that began on 15 May and ended on 5 September, the Globe *As You Like It* would have been seen by up to 50,000 men, women and children. For some, this might have been their first, last or only encounter with the play, with the theatre or with Shakespeare. For others, it might have been their fifth or their fiftieth. But for all of them, for all of us, *As You Like It* will occupy a greater or lesser place in the ongoing, and for the time being unfinished, narratives of our lives.

I looked for Paul Edmondson on the way out but he was nowhere to be seen. A few days after the performance, I received the answer to my question as to who 'we' were. Paul doubles his role as a Shakespeare scholar with that of an Anglican minister, and an email from the Brown family confirmed that he was to officiate at John's funeral service. To my relief (for it would have been quite a challenge), the idea that I might like to say a few words has been forgotten, and on the afternoon of Monday 14 September my wife and I make our way down to deepest Sussex to a country church in the village of Hooe, not far from John's home, Court Lodge, to bid him farewell. As a vision of deep England it can hardly be bettered, and it is, I reflect afterwards, another site of and occasion for open-air performance, celebration and commemoration, reckoning with the legacy of a much-loved father, and laying to rest. At the end of the funeral service, in which the talk has been of the joy of a life lived to the full, we follow the pallbearers into the churchyard. John's grave lies open beside a huge, spreading tree, and when my wife catches sight of it she quietly gasps and slips her hand into mine. She tells me later that it reminds her of the resting place of her own father, much loved, deeply mourned. *Under the greenwood tree/Who loves to lie with me* ... I think of those productions of *As You Like It* that mark the end of the first half of the play with the death of Adam, and thus also with the end of winter and the arrival of spring. It is a day of brilliant sunshine and sharp, sudden showers, and at the exact moment that the burial rite ends, believe it or not, a rainbow appears; collectively, we sigh. The Shakespeare and the theatre establishments are out in force today (John's memorial service, which follows, begins with a eulogy by Stanley Wells and ends with a tribute from Terry Hands), and later we find ourselves in an oak-panelled room at Court Lodge with Paul, Stanley, Paul Prescott and Michael Dobson.[4] Paul Edmondson and I swap impressions of the Globe production (he didn't care for the doubled Dukes either), and the conversation turns to *As You Like It*: Paul tells me of a poem by Wendy Cope, pinned up in the reading room of the Shakespeare Birthplace Trust, that speaks of seeing Max Adrian as Jaques in the 1961 RSC production, which he softly recites from memory:

> It's sad that the actor never knew
> About the teenage girl who saw him play
> In *As You Like It* long ago and who
> Can still recall his face and voice today:
> His Jaques dignified, aloof and dry –
> No bellowing, no sawing of the air,
> Nothing that could offend the author's eye
> Or ear, if you imagined he was there.
> More than fifty years have passed since then
> But when I read the text it's him I see,
> And when I watch it on the stage again
> Jaques doesn't stand a chance with me.
> Max nailed the part and no-one else will do.
> And that, it's possible to hope, he knew.[5]

I mention the recording of the BBC television version that I watched in Stratford back in June, and my elation at discovering that I shared the original reviewers' enraptured response to Vanessa Redgrave's performance. Michael Dobson warmly agrees: 'It's as fresh', he says, 'as if it had been filmed yesterday.' And Stanley, the only one among us to have experienced it as a young man, in the flesh, remembers: 'Vanessa', he muses, luminous in recollection, 'was *wonderful*.'

Notes

1 Amy Cook is Associate Professor in English and Theatre Arts, and author of *Shakespearean Neuroplay* (2010).
2 There is nothing unusual in this: from the earliest days of writing about Shakespeare's Globe, the semi-autobiographical approach, which keeps one eye on the stage and the other on the auditorium, has been almost *de rigueur*: see Worthen, *Shakespeare and the Force of Modern Performance*. During the writing of this chapter I was particularly mindful of the formidable example set by Rob Conkie in his essay 'Red Button Shakespeare',

first published in *Shakespeare Survey* 62 (2009) and subsequently included in his *Writing Performative Shakespeares* (2016).

3 Rereading this in early November, having written elsewhere about how being rude about Orlando is a critical commonplace, I am embarrassed. A middle-aged Shakespeare professor gazes at a good-looking, fit, highly personable young man and claims to wonder what Rosalind sees in him?

4 Stanley Wells is former Director of the Shakespeare Institute, Emeritus Professor of Shakespeare and General Editor of the Oxford Shakespeare, and author of (most recently), *Great Shakespeare Actors* (2015). Terry Hands was Artistic Director of the RSC from 1978 to 1997. Paul Prescott is Reader in English at the University of Warwick and author of *Reviewing Shakespeare* (2013); Michael Dobson is Professor of Shakespeare Studies and Director of the Shakespeare Institute, and author of *Shakespeare and Amateur Performance* (2011).

5 'In Memory of Max Adrian 1903–1973.' See Edmondson's *Blogging Shakespeare*, http://bloggingshakespeare.com/wendy-copes-reads-her-shakespeare-poem.

APPENDIX

Major actors and staff for productions discussed in this volume

Shakespeare Memorial Theatre, Stratford-upon-Avon, 1919

Director: Nigel Playfair

Rosalind	Athene Seyler	*Silvius*	Clement Charles
Orlando	Geoffrey Kerr	*Phoebe*	Faith Faber
Celia	Marjory Holman	*Corin*	Stafford Hilliard
Touchstone	Nigel Playfair	*Duke Frederick*	Herbert Marshall
Jaques	Herbert Marshall	*Adam*	Gilbert Hare
Oliver	Lionel Watts	*Amiens*	Bertram Binyon
Duke Senior	Kinsey Peile	*Audrey*	Betty Chester

Théâtre de l'Atelier, Paris, 1934

Director: Jacques Copeau

Rosalind	Madeleine Lambert	*Silvius*	Lucien Arnaud
Orlando	Daniel Lecourtois	*Phoebe*	Madeleine Lauzun
Celia	Marie-Louise Delby	*Corin*	Guy Favières
Touchstone	Arthur Devère	*Duke Frederick*	Raymond Destac
Jaques	Jacques Copeau	*Adam*	Léonce Corne
Oliver	Jean Gournac	*Amiens*	Marcel d'Orval
Duke Senior	Geymond Vital	*Audrey*	Raymone Duchâteau

Inter-Allied Film, London, 1936

Director: Paul Czinner

Rosalind	Elisabeth Bergner	*Silvius*	Richard Ainley
Orlando	Laurence Olivier	*Phoebe*	Joan White
Celia	Sophie Stewart	*Corin*	Aubrey Mather
Touchstone	Mackenzie Ward	*Duke Frederick*	Felix Aylme
Jaques	Leon Quartermaine	*Adam*	J. Fisher White
Oliver	John Laurie	*Amiens*	Stuart Robinson
Duke Senior	Henry Ainley	*Audrey*	Dorice Fordred

Royal Shakespeare Company, Stratford-upon-Avon and London, 1962–63

Director: Michael Elliott

Rosalind	Vanessa Redgrave	*Silvius*	Peter McEnery
Orlando	Ian Bannen	*Phoebe*	Jill Dixon
Celia	Rosalind Knight	*Corin*	Russell Hunter
Touchstone	Colin Blakeley	*Duke Frederick*	Tony Church
Jaques	Max Adrian	*Adam*	Clifford Rose
Oliver	David Buck	*Amiens*	Eric Flynn
Duke Senior	Redmond Phillips	*Audrey*	Patsy Byrne

British Broadcasting Corporation, London, 1964

Director: Ronald Eyre

Rosalind	Vanessa Redgrave	*Silvius*	Peter Gill
Orlando	Patrick Allen	*Phoebe*	Jeanne Hepple
Celia	Rosalind Knight	*Corin*	Russell Hunter
Touchstone	Patrick Wymark	*Duke Frederick*	Tony Church
Jaques	Max Adrian	*Adam*	Clifford Rose
Oliver	David Buck	*Amiens*	Eric Flynn
Duke Senior	Paul Hardwick	*Audrey*	Patsy Byrne

National Theatre, London, 1967–69

Director: Clifford Williams

Rosalind	Ronald Pickup	*Silvius*	John McEnery
Orlando	Jeremy Brett	*Phoebe*	Richard Kay
Celia	Charles Kay	*Corin*	Gerald James
Touchstone	Derek Jacobi	*Duke Frederick*	Frank Wylie
Jaques	Robert Stephens	*Adam*	Harry Lomax
Oliver	Neil Fitzpatrick	*Amiens*	Roderick Horn
Duke Senior	Paul Curra	*Audrey*	Anthony Hopkins

Royal Shakespeare Company, Stratford-upon-Avon, 1973

Director: Buzz Goodbody

Rosalind	Eileen Atkins	*Silvius*	Peter Machin
Orlando	David Suchet	*Phoebe*	Janet Cappell
Celia	Maureen Lipman	*Corin*	Jeffrey Dench
Touchstone	Derek Smith	*Duke Frederick*	Clement McCallin
Jaques	Richard Pasco	*Adam*	Sydney Bromley
Oliver	Charles Keating	*Amiens*	Ray Armstrong
Duke Senior	Tony Church	*Audrey*	Annette Badland

Schaubühne, Berlin, 1977

Director: Peter Stein

Rosalind	Jutta Lampe	*Silvius*	Wolf Redl
Orlando	Michael König	*Phoebe*	Elke Petri
Celia	Tina Engel	*Corin*	Otto Mächtlinger
Touchstone	Werner Rehm	*Duke Frederick*	Otto Sander
Jaques	Peter Fitz	*Adam*	Gerd David
Oliver	Eberhard Feik	*Amiens*	Gerd Wameling
Duke Senior	Günter Lampe	*Audrey*	Libgart Schwartz

British Broadcasting Corporation, London, 1978

Director: Basil Coleman

Rosalind	Helen Mirren	*Silvius*	Maynard Williams
Orlando	Brian Stirner	*Phoebe*	Victoria Plucknett
Celia	Angharad Rees	*Corin*	David Lloyd Meredith
Touchstone	James Bolam	*Duke Frederick*	Richard Easton
Jaques	Richard Pasco	*Adam*	Arthur Hewett
Oliver	Clive Francis	*Amiens*	Tom McDonnell
Duke Senior	Tony Church	*Audrey*	Marilyn Le Conte

Royal Shakespeare Company, Stratford-upon-Avon and London, 1985–86

Director: Adrian Noble

Rosalind	Juliet Stevenson	*Silvius*	Roger Hyams
Orlando	Hilton McCrae	*Phoebe*	Lesley Manville
Celia	Fiona Shaw	*Corin*	Colin Douglas
Touchstone	Nicky Henson	*Duke Frederick*	Joseph O'Conor
Jaques	Alan Rickman	*Adam*	Mark Dignam
Oliver	Bruce Alexander	*Amiens*	Andrew Yeats
Duke Senior	Joseph O'Conor	*Audrey*	Mary Jo Randle

Cheek by Jowl, London and tour, 1991

Director: Declan Donnellan

Rosalind	Adrian Lester	*Silvius*	Mark Benton
Orlando	Patrick Toomey	*Phoebe*	Sam Graham
Celia	Tom Hollander	*Corin*	Mike Afford
Touchstone	Peter Needham	*Duke Frederick*	David Hobbs
Jaques	Joe Dixon	*Adam*	Sam Graham
Oliver	Mark Bannister	*Amiens*	Conrad Nelson
Duke Senior	David Hobbs	*Audrey*	Richard Cant

Sands Films, London, 1992

Director: Christine Edzard

Rosalind	Emma Croft	*Silvius*	Ewen Bremner
Orlando	Andrew Tiernan	*Phoebe*	Valerie Groga
Celia	Celia Bannerman	*Corin*	Roger Hammond
Touchstone	Griff Rhys Jones	*Duke Frederick*	Don Henderson
Jaques	James Fox	*Adam*	Cyril Cusack
Oliver	Andrew Tiernan	*Amiens*	John Tams
Duke Senior	Don Henderson	*Audrey*	Miriam Margolyes

Cheek by Jowl, London and tour, 1994–95

Director: Declan Donnellan

Rosalind	Adrian Lester	*Silvius*	Gavin Abbott
Orlando	Scott Handy	*Phoebe*	Wayne Cater
Celia	Simon Coates	*Corin*	Paul Kissaun
Touchstone	Peter Needham	*Duke Frederick*	David Hobbs
Jaques	Michael Gardiner	*Adam*	Richard Cant
Oliver	Jonathan Chesterman	*Amiens*	Rhashan Stone
Duke Senior	David Hobbs	*Audrey*	Richard Cant

BBC Films/HBO Films/Shakespeare Film Company, UK and USA, 2006

Director: Kenneth Branagh

Rosalind	Bryce Dallas Howard	*Silvius*	Alex Wyndham
Orlando	David Oyelowo	*Phoebe*	Jade Jefferie
Celia	Romola Garai	*Corin*	Jimmy Yuill
Touchstone	Alfred Molina	*Duke Frederick*	Brian Blessed
Jaques	Kevin Kline	*Adam*	Richard Briers
Oliver	Adrian Lester	*Amiens*	Patrick Doyle
Duke Senior	Brian Blessed	*Audrey*	Janet McTeer

Shakespeare's Globe, London, 2015

Director: Blanche McIntyre

Rosalind	Michelle Terry	*Silvius*	Jack Monagha
Orlando	Simon Harrison	*Phoebe*	Gwyneth Keyworth
Celia	Ellie Piercy	*Corin*	Patrick Driver
Touchstone	Daniel Crossley	*Duke Frederick*	David Beame
Jaques	James Garnon	*Adam*	Phil Whitchurch
Oliver	William Mannering	*Amiens*	William Mannering
Duke Senior	David Beames	*Audrey*	Sophia Nomvete

REFERENCES

Addenbrooke, David. *The Royal Shakespeare Company: The Peter Hall Years.* London: William Kimber, 1974.
Allentuck, Marcia. 'Sir Thomas Hanmer Instructs Francis Hayman: Illustrations of Shakespeare.' *Shakespeare Quarterly* 9 (1958). 141–7.
Bate, Jonathan, and Eric Rasmussen, eds. *As You Like It.* The RSC Shakespeare. Basingstoke: Palgrave Macmillan, 2010.
Baumgärtel, Stephen. 'Body Politics Between Sublimation and Subversion: Critical Perspectives on Twentieth-Century All-Male Performances of Shakespeare's *As You Like It.*' *Shakespearean International Yearbook* 9 (2009). 248–69.
Beauman, Sally. *The Royal Shakespeare Company: A History of Ten Decades.* Oxford: Oxford University Press, 1982.
Belsey, Catherine. 'Disrupting Sexual Difference: Meaning and Gender in the Comedies.' In John Drakakis, ed. *Alternative Shakespeares.* London: Methuen, 1985. 166–90.
Berger, John. *Ways of Seeing.* Harmondsworth: Penguin, 1972.
Blayney, Peter. *The Texts of King Lear and their Origins, Volume 1: Nicholas Okes and the First Quarto.* Cambridge: Cambridge University Press, 1982.
— 'The Publication of Playbooks.' In John D. Cox and David Scott Kastan, eds. *A New History of Early English Drama.* New York: Columbia University Press, 1997. 383–422.
Boaden, James. *The Life of Mrs Jordan.* 2 vols. New York: Athenaeum Press, 1831.
Bradley, David. *From Text to Performance in the Elizabethan Theatre: Preparing the Play for the Stage.* Cambridge: Cambridge University Press, 1992.
Brook, Peter. *The Empty Space.* Harmondsworth: Penguin, 1968.
Brown, John Russell. *Free Shakespeare.* London: Heinemann, 1974.
Bulman, James C. 'Queering the Audience: All-Male Casts in Recent Productions of Shakespeare.' In Barbara Hodgdon and W. B. Worthen, eds. *A Companion to Shakespeare and Performance.* Oxford: Blackwell, 2005. 564–87.
Burnett, Mark Thornton. *Filming Shakespeare in the Global Marketplace.* Basingstoke: Palgrave Macmillan, 2007.
Callaghan, Dympna. 'Buzz Goodbody: Directing for Change.' In Jean I. Marsden, ed. *The Appropriation of Shakespeare: Post-Renaissance Reconstructions of the Works and Myth.* Hemel Hempstead: Harvester Wheatsheaf, 1991. 163–81.

Callow, Simon. *Being an Actor.* Harmondsworth: Penguin, 1985.
Chambers, Colin. *Other Spaces: New Theatre and the RSC.* London: Methuen, 1980.
— *Inside the Royal Shakespeare Company: Creativity and the Institution.* London and New York: Routledge, 2004.
Coleman, John. *Players and Playwrights I Have Known: A Review of the English Stage from 1840 to 1880.* 2 vols. Philadelphia, PA: Gebbie, 1890.
Conkie, Rob. *Writing Performative Shakespeares: New Forms for Performance Criticism.* Cambridge: Cambridge University Press, 2016.
Copeau, Jacques. *Texts on Theatre.* Ed. and trans. John Rudlin and Norman H. Paul. London and New York: Routledge, 1990.
Crowl, Samuel. *Shakespeare Observed: Studies in Performance on Stage and Screen.* Athens: Ohio University Press, 1992.
David, Richard. *Shakespeare in the Theatre.* Cambridge: Cambridge University Press, 1978.
Déprats, Jean-Michel. 'Translating Shakespeare for the Theatre.' *Shakespeare Yearbook* 5 (2005). 345–58.
Derrida, Jacques. *Archive Fever: A Freudian Impression.* Trans. Eric Prenowitz. Chicago, IL and London: University of Chicago Press, 1996.
Dobson, Michael. 'Shakespeare Performances in England, 2000.' *Shakespeare Survey* 54 (2001). 246–82.
— 'Shakespeare Performances in England, 2003.' *Shakespeare Survey* 57 (2004). 258–89.
Dollimore, Jonathan. 'Subjectivity, Sexuality, and Transgression: the Jacobean Connection.' *Renaissance Drama*, new series, 17 (1986). 53–81.
Dusinberre, Juliet, ed. *As You Like It.* The Arden Shakespeare, third series. London: Arden Shakespeare, 2006.
Erne, Lukas. *Shakespeare as Literary Dramatist.* Second edition. Cambridge: Cambridge University Press, 2013.
Escolme, Bridget. 'Shakespeare, Rehearsal and the Site-Specific.' *Shakespeare Bulletin* 30 (2012). 505–22.
Fenwick, Henry. 'The Production.' In *As You Like It.* London: BBC Publications, 1978. 20–6.
Frye, Northrop. *A Natural Perspective: The Development of Shakespearean Comedy and Romance.* New York and London: Columbia University Press, 1965.
Furnivall, F. J., ed. *Phillip Stubbes' Anatomie of the Abuses in England of Shakespeare's Youth.* 3 vols. London: New Shakespere Society, 1877–79.
Garber, Marjorie. *Vested Interests: Cross-Dressing and Cultural Anxiety.* New York: Routledge, 1992.
Gay, Penny. *As She Likes It: Shakespeare's Unruly Women.* London: Routledge, 1994.

Goodwin, John ed. *Royal Shakespeare Company 1960–63*. London: Max Reinhardt, 1964.
Greene, Graham. *The Pleasure Dome: The Collected Film Criticism, 1935–40*, ed. John Russell Taylor. London: Secker & Warburg, 1972.
Griffin, Emma. *Blood Sport: Hunting in Britain Since 1066*. New Haven, CT, and London: Yale University Press, 2007.
Gunaratne, Anthony R. *Shakespeare, Film Studies, and the Visual Cultures of Modernity*. New York: Palgrave Macmilllan, 2008.
Habicht, Werner. 'Shakespeare in West Germany.' *Shakespeare Quarterly* 29 (1978). 296–9.
Hall, Peter. 'Shakespeare and the Modern Director.' In John Goodwin, ed. *Royal Shakespeare Theatre Company 1960–1963*. London: Max Reinhardt, 1964. 41–8.
Hallinan, Tim. 'Jonathan Miller on The Shakespeare Plays.' *Shakespeare Quarterly* 32 (1981). 134–45.
Hancock, Sheila. *Ramblings of an Actress*. London: Hutchinson, 1987.
Herrmann, Karl-Ernst, ed. *Schaubühne am Halleschen Ufer/am Lehiner Platz 1962–1987*. Berlin: Propyläen Verlag, 1987.
Heywood, Thomas. *An Apology for Actors*. London: Shakespeare Society, 1841.
Hodgdon, Barbara. 'Sexual Disguise and the Theatre of Gender.' In Alexander Leggatt, ed. *The Cambridge Companion to Shakespearean Comedy*. Cambridge: Cambridge University Press, 2002. 179–97.
— *Shakespeare, Performance and the Archive*. London: Routledge, 2016.
Holland, Peter. *English Shakespeares: Shakespeare on the English Stage in the 1990s*. Cambridge: Cambridge University Press, 1997.
— '*The Lost Workers*: Process, Performance, and the Archive.' *Shakespeare Bulletin* 28 (2010). 7–18.
Hortmann, Wilhelm. *Shakespeare on the German Stage: The Twentieth Century*. Cambridge: Cambridge University Press, 1998.
Iyengar, Sujata. 'Colorblind Casting in Single-Sex Shakespeare.' In Ayanna Thompson, ed. *Colorblind Shakespeare: New Perspectives on Race and Performance*. New York and London: Routledge, 2006. 47–68.
Jackson, Russell. 'Shakespeare in Stratford-upon-Avon: The Royal Shakespeare Company's "Half Season", April-September 1996.' *Shakespeare Quarterly* 48 (1997). 208–15.
— 'Remembering Bergner's Rosalind: *As You Like It* on Film in 1936.' In Peter Holland, ed. *Shakespeare, Memory and Performance*. Cambridge: Cambridge University Press, 2006. 237–55.
Jacquot, Jean. 'Copeau et *Comme Il Vous Plaira*: De l'Atelier aux Jardins Boboli.' *Revue d'Histoire du Théâtre* 16 (1965). 119–37.
Jardine, Lisa. *Still Harping on Daughters: Women and Drama in the Age of Shakespeare*. Brighton: Harvester, 1983.

Jorgens, Jack J. 'The BBC-TV Shakespeare Series.' *Shakespeare Quarterly* 30 (1979). 411–14.
— 'Realising Shakespeare on Film.' In Robert Shaughnessy, ed. *Shakespeare on Film*. Basingstoke: Macmillan, 1998. 18–42.
Jung, C. J. *Memories, Dreams, Reflections*. Trans. Richard Winston and Clara Winston. Glasgow: Fontana, 1967.
— *Collected Works, Volume 9: The Archetypes and the Collective Unconscious*. Trans. R. F. C. Hull, ed. Herbert Read, Michael Fordham and Gerhard Adler. London: Routledge, 2014.
Kellen, Konrad. 'Ideology and Rebellion: Terrorism in West Germany.' In Walter Reich, ed. *Origins of Terrorism: Psychologies, Ideologies, Theologies, States of Mind*. Baltimore, MD and London: Johns Hopkins University Press, 1998. 43–58.
Kennedy, Dennis. *Looking at Shakespeare: A Visual History of Twentieth-Century Performance*. Cambridge: Cambridge University Press, 1993.
King, T. J. *Casting Shakespeare's Plays: London Actors and their Roles, 1590–1642*. Cambridge: Cambridge University Press, 2009.
Knowles, Richard, ed. *As You Like It*. New Variorum Edition. New York: Modern Languages Association, 1977.
Knutson, Roslyn Lander. *The Repertory of Shakespeare's Company, 1594–1613*. Fayetteville: University of Arkansas Press, 1991.
Kott, Jan. *Shakespeare Our Contemporary*. Trans. Boleslaw Taborski. London: Methuen, 1965.
Kurtz, Maurice. *Jacques Copeau: Biography of a Theatre*. Carbondale: Southern Illinois University Press, 1999.
Lackner, Peter. 'Stein's Path to Shakespeare.' *Drama Review* 21 (1977). 79–102.
Laris, Katie. 'As You Like It.' *Theatre Journal* 47 (1995). 300–2.
Latham, Agnes, ed. *As You Like It*. The Arden Shakespeare, Second Series. London: Methuen, 1975.
McLuskie, Kate. *Renaissance Dramatists*. Hemel Hempstead: Harvester Wheatsheaf, 1989.
McMillin, Scott. 'The Sharer and His Boy: Rehearsing Shakespeare's Women.' In Peter Holland and Stephen Orgel, eds. *From Script to Stage in Early Modern England*. Basingstoke: Palgrave Macmillan, 2004. 231–44.
Marshall, Cynthia, ed. *As You Like It*. Shakespeare in Production. Cambridge: Cambridge University Press, 2004.
Mazer, Cary M. 'Rosalind's Breast.' In James C. Bulman, ed. *Shakespeare Re-Dressed: Cross-Gender Casting in Contemporary Performance*. Madison, WI: Farleigh Dickinson University Press, 2008. 96–115.
— 'Sense/Memory/Sense-Memory: Reading Narratives of Shakespearian Rehearsals.' *Shakespeare Survey* 62 (2009). 328–48.

Miola, Robert S., ed. *Every Man in his Humour*. The Revels Plays. Manchester: Manchester University Press, 2000.
Mohrt, Michel. 'Jaques Copeau, Charles Dullin.' *Yale French Studies*, 5 (1950). 105-6.
Munro, Lucy. *Children of the Queen's Revels: A Jacobean Theatre Repertory*. Cambridge: Cambridge University Press, 2005.
Noble, Adrian. '"Well, This Is the Forest of Arden": An Informal Address.' In Werner Habicht, D. J. Palmer and Roger Pringle, eds. *Images of Shakespeare: Proceedings of the Third Congress of the International Shakespeare Association, 1986*. London and Toronto: Associated University Presses, 1988. 335-42.
Orgel, Stephen. *Impersonations: The Performance of Gender in Shakespeare's England*. Cambridge: Cambridge University Press, 1996.
Palfrey, Simon, and Tiffany Stern. *Shakespeare in Parts*. Oxford: Oxford University Press, 2007.
Patterson, Michael. *Peter Stein: Germany's Leading Theatre Director*. Cambridge: Cambridge University Press, 1981.
Pemble, John. *Shakespeare Goes to Paris: How the Bard Conquered France*. London and New York: Hambledon & London, 2005.
Phelan, Peggy. *Unmarked: The Politics of Performance*. London: Routledge, 1993.
Playfair, Nigel. *The Story of the Lyric Theatre Hammersmith*. London: Chatto & Windus, 1925.
— *Hammersmith Hoy: A Book of Minor Revelations*. London: Faber, 1930.
Pollard, Tanya, ed. *Shakespeare's Theater: A Sourcebook*. Malden, MA: Blackwell, 2004.
Ponge, Francis. *Le parti pris des choses*. Paris: Gallimard, 1967.
Redgrave, Vanessa. *An Autobiography*. London: Hutchinson, 1991.
Rickman, Alan. 'Jaques in *As You Like It*.' In Russell Jackson and Robert Smallwood, eds. *Players of Shakespeare 2*. Cambridge: Cambridge University Press, 1988. 73-80.
Rischbieter, Henning. 'Wie es euch zerfeil.' *Theater Heute* 18 (1977). 11-16.
Rosenthal, Daniel. *100 Shakespeare Films*. London: British Film Institute, 2007.
— *The National Theatre Story*. London: Oberon, 2013.
Rothwell, Kenneth. *A History of Shakespeare on Screen: A Century of Film and Television*. Cambridge and New York: Cambridge University Press, 1999.
Rowell, George. *Queen Victoria Goes to the Theatre*. London: Paul Elek, 1978.
Rudlin, John. *Jaques Copeau*. Cambridge: Cambridge University Press, 1986.
Rutter, Carol Chillington. 'Maverick Shakespeare.' In Barbara Hodgdon and W. B. Worthen, eds. *A Companion to Shakespeare and Performance*. Oxford: Blackwell, 2005, 335-58.

— 'Shakespeare Performances in England 2009.' *Shakespeare Survey* 63 (2010). 338–75.
— 'Shakespeare Performances in England 2013.' *Shakespeare Survey* 67 (2014). 396–438.
Scheil, Katherine West. 'Early Georgian Politics and Shakespeare: the Black Act and Johnson's *Love in a Forest.*' *Shakespeare Survey* 51 (1998). 45–56.
Schücking, L. L., ed. *Wie es euch gefällt.* In *Shakespeares Werke, Englisch und Deutsch*, Dritter Band. Berlin and Darmstadt: Tempel-Verlag, 1965. 491–565.
Senelick, Laurence. *The Changing Room: Sex, Drag and Theatre.* London and New York: Routledge, 2000.
Shaughnessy, Robert. 'On Location.' In Barbara Hodgdon and W. B. Worthen, eds. *A Companion to Shakespeare and Performance.* Oxford: Blackwell, 2005. 79–100.
— 'One Piece at a Time.' *Shakespeare Bulletin* 25 (2007). 11–26.
Shaw, Fiona and Juliet Stevenson. 'Celia and Rosalind in *As You Like It.*' In Russell Jackson and Robert Smallwood, eds. *Players of Shakespeare 2.* Cambridge: Cambridge University Press, 1988. 55–72.
Shaw, George Bernard. *Shaw on Shakespeare: An Anthology of Bernard Shaw's Writings on the Plays and Production of Shakespeare.* Ed. Edwin Wilson. London: Cassell, 1961.
Sinfield, Alan. *Out On Stage: Lesbian and Gay Theatre in the Twentieth Century.* New Haven, CT, and London: Yale University Press, 1999.
Slaughter, Helena Robin. 'Jacques Copeau, Metteur en Scène de Shakespeare et des Élisabéthains.' *Études Anglaises* 13 (1960). 176–91.
Smallwood, Robert. 'Shakespeare at Stratford-upon-Avon, 1992.' *Shakespeare Quarterly* 44 (1993). 343–62.
— 'Shakespeare Performances in England, 1996.' *Shakespeare Survey* 50 (1997). 191–206.
— *As You Like It.* Shakespeare at Stratford. London: Arden Shakespeare, 2003.
Soliman, Alisa. *Re-dressing the Canon: Essays on Theatre and Gender.* London and New York: Routledge, 1997.
Speaight, Robert. 'The Old Vic and Stratford-upon-Avon, 1960–61.' *Shakespeare Quarterly* 12 (1961). 425–41.
— *Shakespeare on the Stage.* London: Collins, 1973.
— 'The Stratford-upon-Avon Season.' *Shakespeare Quarterly* 24 (1973). 400–4.
Stern, Tiffany. *Rehearsal from Shakespeare to Sheridan.* Oxford: Clarendon Press, 2000.
Styan, J. L. *The Shakespeare Revolution: Criticism and Performance in the Twentieth Century.* Cambridge: Cambridge University Press, 1977.

Tennant, David. 'Touchstone in *As You Like It*.' In Robert Smallwood, ed. *Players of Shakespeare 4*. Cambridge: Cambridge University Press, 1998. 30–44.

Thomson, Peter. 'Shakespeare Straight and Crooked: A Review of the 1973 Season at Stratford.' *Shakespeare Survey* 24 (1974). 117–26.

Trewin, J. C. *Benson and the Bensonians*. London: Barrie & Rockliff, 1960.

Tribble, Evelyn B. *Cognition in the Globe: Attention and Memory in Shakespeare's Theatre*. New York: Palgrave Macmillan, 2011.

Wales, Katie. 'An A–Z of rhetorical terms.' In Sylvia Adamson, Lynette Hunter, Lynne Magnusson, Ann Thompson and Katie Wales, eds. *Reading Shakespeare's Dramatic Language: A Guide*. London: Arden Shakespeare, 2001. 271–301.

Warren, Roger. 'Shakespeare in Britain, 1985.' *Shakespeare Quarterly* 37 (1986), 114–20.

Webber, Andrew J. *Berlin in the Twentieth Century: A Cultural Topography*. Cambridge: Cambridge University Press, 2008.

Wells, Stanley, and Gary Taylor. *William Shakespeare: A Textual Companion*. Oxford: Clarendon Press, 1987.

Williams, Raymond. *The Country and the City*. St Albans: Paladin, 1975.

— *Television: Technology and Cultural Form*. London: Routledge, 2004.

Worthen, W. B. *Shakespeare and the Force of Modern Performance*. Cambridge: Cambridge University Press, 2003.

Young, David. *The Heart's Forest: A Study of Shakespeare's Pastoral Plays*. New Haven, CT and London: Yale University Press, 1972.

INDEX

A Larum for London 12, 33
Abbott, Gavin 156
Aberg, Maria 93, 95
Adrian, Max 54, 58, 206
Ainley, Henry 163, 164
Alexander, Bruce 77
Alexander, George 143
All Creatures Great and Small 171, 176
Allen, Patrick 56–9
Alleyn, Edward 18, 27
Altman, Robert 191
Annabella (Susanne Charpentier) 99, 110–11
Annan, Jotham 192
Anouilh, Jean 100
Araki, Gregg
    The Living End 177
Armatrading, Tony 180
Armin, Robert 13
Arne, Thomas 106
Artaud, Antoinin 100
Asche, Oscar 168
Ashcroft, Peggy 47, 60, 73
Atkins, Eileen 60, 61, 65–6, 68, 71–3, 95, 195
Aumont, Jean-Pierre 99
Auric, Georges 106–7, 113, 128
Aylmer, Felix 162

Baader, Andreas 115–16
Baker, Josephine 100
Balanchine, George 100
Balthus (Balthasar Klossowski de Rola) 99
Banks-Smith, Nancy 173–4, 176–7
Bannen, Ian 47, 53–4, 58
Bannerman, Celia 181–3
Barker, Harley Granville 42, 101–2, 110
Barnes, Clive 142
Barnowsky, Victor 99–101, 109–11
Barrault, Jean-Louis 100, 108, 128
Barrie, J. M. 159
    The Little Minister 166
    Peter Pan 160–1
Barton, Anne 67–8
Barton, John 47, 60, 61, 71
Bate, Jonathan 6, 26, 39, 50
Baty, Gaston 100
BBC/Time-Life Shakespeare Series 8, 64, 166–76
Beames, David 197–8
Beauman, Sally 39, 46
Beeston, Christopher 28
Belsey, Catherine 17–18, 23
Benson, Constance 59
Benson, Frank 36, 41–2, 59
Berger, John 67, 76
Bergner, Elisabeth 99, 159–66
Berkeley, Busby 192
Berkeley, Michael
    Or Shall We Die? 76
Berliner Ensemble 46
Berliner Schaubühne 7, 114–28
Billington, Kevin 167
Billington, Michael 62–5, 68–9, 73, 80–1, 91–4, 97, 150–1, 153–6, 179
Blair, Tony 90
Blayney, Peter 12–13, 35
Blessed, Brian 185–6, 192
Boaden, James 5
Boboli Gardens 112–14
Bogart, Paul
    Class of 44 172

Bogdanov, Michael 69, 158
Bogdanovich, Peter
    Paper Moon 171, 175
Bolam, James 167, 169
Bond, Edward
    Saved 117
Bond, Samantha 89
Bourdeaux, Henri 102
Bowie, David 93
Boyd, Michael 26, 50, 91–3, 95
Bradley, David 26–7, 33
Branagh, Kenneth 8, 95, 144, 172, 184–93
Bread and Puppet Theatre 116
Brecht, Bertolt 72, 117, 125, 149, 193
Brett, Jeremy 131, 139–40, 157
Bridges-Adams, William 42, 44
Briers, Richard 184
Bristol Old Vic 158
British Broadcasting Corporation 8, 54–9, 64, 98, 166–76
    An Age of Kings 56
    The Wars of the Roses 98, 171
Brook, Peter 44–5, 65, 68, 75, 158
Brooke, Ralph 9
Brophy, Brigid 172
Brown, John Russell 72, 200, 205–6
Bruce, Brenda 60
Bryden, Ronald 130, 134, 137–9
Bulman, James C. 18, 147, 150, 152–4, 168
Burbage, Richard 21, 27–8, 30, 32–3
Burnett, Cliff 93
Burnett, Mark Thornton 184–5
Burton, Richard 182
Burton, William 9
Butler, Jim 123
Byam Shaw, Glen 45–6
Byron, (Lord) George Gordon 93

Caird, John 89
Callaghan, Dympna 70–1
Callaghan, Jim 176
Callow, Simon 81, 88
Cammell, Donald 180
Campion, Thomas 76
Cant, Brian 157
Cant, Richard 145, 149, 155–7
Cater, Wayne 149, 155
Chambers, Colin 47, 61, 68, 70, 71
Chan, Paul 187, 192
Chaplin, Charles 81
Cheek by Jowl 7–8, 143–58
Chekhov, Anton 55, 63
Chevalier, Maurice 100
Chorus of Splinters 129
Chuck D (Carlton Douglas Ridenhour) 178
Church, Tony 62, 167
Cibber, Colley 3
Clive, Kitty 3
Cloth Breeches and Velvet Hose 13, 33
Coates, Simon 149, 155
Cocteau, Jean 100
Coleman, Basil 167–76
Comédie-Française 100, 114
Condell, Henry 14, 28, 32
Conkie, Rob 206–7
Cook, Amy 194–204
Cooke, Dominic, 91
Cope, Wendy 206
Copeau, Jacques 7, 99–114, 119, 128
Cory, William 14
Coward, Noel 159
Crane, Ralph 10
Crispin, Janine 99
Croft, Emma 178, 181–4
Crossley, Daniel 198–9
Crouching Tiger, Hidden Dragon 186
Crowl, Samuel 160–1
Crowley, Bob 83, 86

Cukor, George 159
Cumberbatch, Benedict 197
Cunningham, Liam 90
Curtis, Tony 129
Cusack, Cyril 180
Cusack, Niamh 90
Cushman, Charlotte 6
Czinner, Paul 8, 159–66, 175, 188, 193

Dallas Howard, Bryce 184–93
Daly, Augustin 6
David, Gerd 127
David, Richard 108–9
Davidson, Jaye 177
Davis, Bette 129
Dawson, Les 156
de Jongh, Nicholas 89, 90, 97, 148, 152, 155
de Régnier, Henri 111
Dekker, Thomas 12
  The Roaring Girl 15
  The Shoemaker's Holiday 28–9
Delacre, Jules 103–6, 128
Déprats, Jean-Michel 104
Dering, Edward 13, 35
Derrida, Jacques 96
Devère, Arthur 108–9
Devereux, Robert, Earl of Essex 10–11
Devillier, Catherine 106
Dexter, John 130–2, 156
Diaghilev, Sergei 106
Dietrich, Marlene 129
Dixon, Joe 146, 151
Dobson, Michael 43–4, 90, 97, 206, 207
Dollimore, Jonathan 16
Donat, Robert 159
Donnellan, Declan 7, 143–58
Donovan (Philips Leitch) 156
Doran, Gregory 90–1, 98
Dostoevsky, Fyodor 63
Doyle, Patrick 188
Drake, Nick 93

Duke, John 28
Dullin, Charles 100, 102
Dusinberre, Juliet 13–14
Dylan, Bob 156

Edmondson, Paul 200, 205–7
Edwardes, Jane 147, 148, 155
Edzard, Christine 8, 177–84, 188
Eld, George 13
Elgar, Edward 134
Eliot, T. S. 76, 78
Elizabeth I, Queen 10, 14, 118
Elliott, Michael 7, 47–54
Elsom, John 62, 64, 68, 97
Engel, Tina 122
Engels, Johan 89
English Shakespeare Company 158
Erne, Lukas 11
Eschenburg, Johann Joachim 124
Esslin, Martin 138
Evans, Edith 60
Eyre, Ronald 55

Fagan, J. B. 36
Farquhar, George
  The Constant Couple 3
  The Recruiting Officer 3
Fassbinder, Rainer Werner 116
Fassett, Kaffe 90–1
Favyn, André 9
Fiddick, Peter 172–3
Field, Kate 40
Fields, Gracie 159
Fiennes, Joseph 90
Fitz, Peter 121
Fleetwood, Charles 3
Fleetwood, Susan 73, 93
Flower, Archie 39
Floy, Gregory 141–2
Forsyth, Bruce 144–5, 157
Fox, James 178, 180
Francis, Clive 168
Francis, Sean 151

Frederick, Naomi 91, 204
Freshwater, Geoffrey 50
Froissart, Jean 6
Frost, Robert 76, 78
Frye, Northrop 123

Gabor, Zsa Zsa 129
Gale, Mariah 92
Garai, Romola 95, 184
Garber, Marjorie 133, 151
Garnon, James 199, 204
Gascoigne, Bamber 48, 49, 53
Gay, Penny 50, 66, 68–70, 73
The Generation Game 144
Genet, Jean 131
Gielgud, John 45, 47
Gilbreath, Alexandra 91
Gilder, Jeanette 6
Gill, Peter 71
Giradoux, Jean 99
Glover, Brian 62
Goodbody, Buzz 61–74, 93, 97, 108–9, 151, 167, 195
Gorky, Maxim 117–18
Graham, Sam 149, 155–6
Gray, Simon
    Wise Child 132
The Great Ziegfeld 163
Green, Dorothy 61
Greene, Graham 160, 161
Greene, Robert 13, 75
    Orlando Furioso 18–19
Griffiths, Trevor 61
Grock (Charles Adrien Wettach) 108
Guinness, Alec 129, 132
Guneratne, Anthony R. 161
Guthrie, Tyrone 46

Habicht, Werner 119, 121, 127
Hagerty, Bill 147
Hall, Peter 43, 46–7, 69
Hamilton, Victoria 90, 97
Hammer, Ellen 124
Hammond, Roger 180

Hancock, Sheila 68, 97
Handke, Peter 116
Hands, Terry 73, 206
Hanmer, Thomas 2, 4
Hare, John 6
Harington, John 10
Harrison, Simon 197, 201
Harvey, David M. 82–4, 86
Harvey, Laurence 95
Hayman, Francis 2, 4
Heinrichs, Benjamin 119, 121, 126
Heminges, John 13, 14, 28
Hemingway, Ernest 100
Henderson, Don 178, 182
Henslowe, Philip 136
Henson, Nicky 78, 80
Hepburn, Audrey 51, 142
Herbert, William 14
Herrick, Robert 76
Herrman, Karl-Ernst 120, 121
Hewlett, Arthur 168
Heywood, Thomas 16
Higgins, John 138–9
Hinge and Bracket (George Logan and Patrick Fyffe) 77–8
Hobbs, David 150
Hodgdon, Barbara 96, 150
Holland, Peter 82, 153, 154, 157
Hollander, Tom 146, 148–9, 155
Holloway, Balliol 44
Hopkins, Anthony 129, 131, 133, 135, 137
Horan, Gerard 187
Hordern, Michael 46
Hortmann, Wilhelm 117–18
House of Flying Daggers 186
Howerd, Frankie 143
Hyams, Roger 79

Ibsen, Henrik 117–18
Iden-Payne, Ben 44
Ifeachor, Tracy 158
Ihering, Herbert 162

Irwin, Ken 172–3
Iyengar, Sujita 151–2
Izzard, Eddie 199

Jackson, Barry 44–5
Jackson, Russell 89–90, 162, 164
Jacobi, Derek 134, 135, 143–4
Jacquot, Jean 103–9, 113, 128
Jaggard, William 9
Jagger, Mick 81
James I, King 14
Jardine, Lisa 16
Jared, Chris 93
Jarman, Derek
   Edward II 177, 178
   The Tempest 178
Jefferies, Jade 190
Johnson, Charles
   Love in a Forest 3
Jones, David 49
Jones, Griffith 79
Jones, Tom 93
Jonson, Ben 10, 11, 12, 35
   The Alchemist 19
   Every Man in his Humour 28–9
   Every Man Out of his Humour 33
Jordan, Dora 5
Jordan, Neil
   The Crying Game 177
Jorgens, Jack J. 160, 168, 193
Jouvet, Louis 100
Joyce, James 100
Jumbo, Cush 158
Jung, C. J. 76, 78

Kaiser, Joachim 114–15, 126
Katz, Richard 95
Kay, Charles 129, 133, 136, 138, 140
Kay, Richard 129, 133, 138, 140
Kellen, Konrad 116
Kemble, Charles 5
Kempe, Will 13, 28

Kendal, W. H. 6
Kennedy, Dennis 7, 39–40, 42, 118, 127
Keyworth, Gwyneth 202
Killigrew, Thomas 3, 14
Kind Hearts and Coronets 129
King, T. J. 27
Kingsley, Ben 151
Kingston, Jeremy 62, 63, 65, 73–4, 130, 139, 155
Kline, Kevin 184, 186, 190
Knight, Rosalind 54, 58
Knutson, Roslyn Lander 34
Koltai, Ralph 61, 131, 134, 139
König, Michael 119–20
Kott, Jan 76, 123, 131–3
Kray, Ronnie 182
Kushner, Tony
   Angels in America 145–6
Kyd, Thomas
   The Spanish Tragedy 27
Kynaston, Edward 129

La Rue, Danny 129–30, 136
Labiche, Eugène Marin
   The Piggy Bank 117
Lambert, J. W. 49, 54
Lambert, Madeleine 100, 107, 109
Lampe, Jutta 119, 122, 125–6
Langham, Michael 47
Lascaris, Théodore 103
Latham, Agnes 9, 123
Lecourtois, Daniel 100, 107, 109
Led Zeppelin 120
Leggatt, Alexander 30
Leigh, Mike 178
Leighton, Margaret 45–6, 95
Lemmon, Jack 129
Lester, Adrian 93, 145, 147–56, 184, 187
Letts, Quentin 92
Levin, Bernard 50–1
Lewis, Matthew 123
The Likely Lads 167
Lillie 171, 175

Lipman, Maureen 60, 62, 73–4
Living Theatre 116
Lloyd, Bernard 71
Lodge, Thomas 75
   Rosalynd 172
The Losers 171
Lovat Fraser, Claud 36–7, 41
Lucy, Spencer 40–1
Luther, Martin 66
Lyly, John 12, 15
   Campaspe 25
Lyric Hammersmith 36, 90, 158

Macready, William Charles 5–6
Major, John 177
Mannering, William 197
Manville, Lesley 79, 85
Margolyes, Miriam 182
Marilyn (Peter Robinson) 76
Marling, Laura 93
Marlowe, Christopher 27, 29, 132–3, 177
   Hero and Leander 133
Marshall, Cynthia 4, 7, 42–3, 168, 170, 174
Masi, Rosanna 113
Masson, Forbes 93
Maw, Janet 172
May, Steven 14
Mayes, Richard 62
Mazer, Cary M. 85, 152
McCallin, Clement 62
McCartney, Paul
   Sgt. Pepper's Lonely Hearts Club Band 131, 134
McCrae, Hilton 60, 77–9
McEnery, John 138
McEnery, Peter 47
McEwan, Geraldine 60
McEwan, Ian 76, 78
McGowran, Jack 47
McIntyre, Blanche 8, 194–206
McLuskie, Kate 16
McMillin, Scott 18–20, 23, 30–1, 34

McNulty, Mary 194
McTeer, Janet 186–7, 191–2
Meerson, Lazare 163
Mei Lanfang 129
Meinhof, Ulrike 115–16
Meister, Georg 123
Messina, Cedric 166–8, 175, 176
Middleton, Thomas 12
   The Roaring Girl 15
Miller, Jonathan 176
Miola, Robert S. 35
Mirren, Helen 167–70, 172, 174
Mohrt, Michel 103
Molina, Alfred 171–2, 186, 191–2
Moll Cutpurse (Mary Frith) 15
Moodie, Tanya 158
Morley, Christopher 61–2
Morley, Thomas 106
Moscow Art Theatre 46
Mozart, Wolfgang Amadeus 99
Muggeridge, Malcolm 64, 97
Münch, Christopher
   The Hours and the Times 177
Munro, Lucy 35
Mussolini, Benito 112
Myett, Sarah 84

Napier, John 73
Nathan, David 62, 63, 134, 139, 152
National Theatre 7–8, 61, 66, 94, 129–42, 156
Needham, Peter 144–5
Negri, Richard, 91
Nelligan, Kate 73, 172
Nelson, Conrad 154
Newth, Jonathan 91
Nicholas, Paul 169
Nightingale, Benedict 62, 66, 68, 92, 97, 144, 147–8, 154
Nisbett, Louisa 6
Nixon, Pippa 93, 95
Noble, Adrian 7, 8, 73–89, 91, 97, 98, 198
Nobuyuki Takano 187

Nomvete, Sophia 201
Nordhoff, Günter 120
Nunn, Trevor 70, 71–3, 98, 175

O'Conor, Joseph 78
O'Toole, Peter 47
Oh Calcutta! 132
Olivier, Laurence 47, 129–30, 131, 144, 159–66, 178, 193
Omere, Ivy 158
Orgel, Stephen 16
Ormerod, Nick 145, 154
Osborne, John
    The Entertainer 144
Owen, Alison 84, 85
Oyelowo, David 184, 187, 188, 189

Palfrey, Simon 18, 20–1, 31
Pasco, Richard 61, 63–4, 69, 167, 195
Patterson, Michael 119, 126–8
Pavier, Thomas 11
Peele, George, 118
Peking Opera 129
Pemble, John 111
Performance 180
Petri, Elke 118
Phelan, Laurence 184
Phelan, Peggy 94
Phelps, Samuel 6
Philips, Augustine 28
Phillips, Robin 65
Picasso, Pablo 99
Pickup, Ronald 129–31, 133, 135, 138–42, 157
Piercy, Ellie 197, 198
Pimlott, Stephen 89, 143
Pitoëff, Georges 100
Pizzetti, Ildebrando 113
Planché, James Robinson 5
Plant, Robert 120
Playfair, Nigel 7, 36–42, 44
Pointon, Andrew 95
Poldark 167, 169

Ponge, Francis 127–8
Pope, Thomas 28
Potter, Sally
    Orlando 177
Prentice, Herbert 44
Prescott, Paul 206, 207
Pritchard, Hannah 3–4
Proops, Marjorie 138
Proust, Marcel 54
Public Enemy 178
Punt, Dacre 131

Quartermaine, Leon 160–1, 166, 193
Quayle, Anthony 45
Queen Victoria 5–6
Quin, James 3

Rainoldes, John 16
Raleigh, Sir Walter 118
Ramsey, Peter H. 67
Rappresentazione di Santa Uliva 112
Rasmussen, Eric 6, 26, 39, 50
Rea, Stephen 177
Redgrave, Michael 47, 53
Redgrave, Vanessa 7, 47, 50–60, 66, 68, 73, 89, 93, 95, 97, 138, 171, 206
Rees, Angharad 167, 169, 172
Rehan, Ada 6
Rehm, Werner 120, 122
Reinhardt, Max 112–13
Rhys Jones, Griff 181–4
Richardson, Ian 47, 60
Richardson, Ralph 45
Rickman, Alan 74, 81, 84, 87–8
Ringler, William 14
Roberts, James 10, 12–13, 33, 35
Robinson, Edward G. 159
Roeg, Nicolas 180
Ronson, Mick 93
Rosenthal, Daniel 131, 132, 156, 160, 161, 166
Rossiter, Leonard 171

Rothwell, Kenneth 161, 165–6
Royal Court 144
Royal Shakespeare Company
    7–8, 47–54, 61–98, 126, 158,
    167, 171, 175, 195, 198
  Aldwych Theatre 46, 52, 54,
    71, 167, 175
  Barbican Theatre 84, 98
  Courtyard Theatre 92
  The Other Place 60, 61,
    69–70, 91, 97, 98, 151
  The Place 61
  The Romans 61
  Royal Shakespeare Theatre
    46–7, 60, 70, 71, 84, 89
  The Swan 91
  Theatregoround 61
  The Wars of the Roses 98, 171
Rubinstein, Arthur 110
Rutter, Carol Chillington 50,
    92–3, 153
Ryan, Oliver 93

Sackler, Howard 54
Saire, Rebecca 172
Schlegel, Karl Wilhelm Friedrich
    124
Schleyer, Hans Martin 115
Schwartz, Libgart 121
Scott, Margaretta 44
Sedgwick, John 159–60
Senelick, Laurence 150–1
Shakespeare Birthplace Trust 55
Shakespeare in Love 90
Shakespeare in Perspective 172
Shakespeare Memorial Theatre
    7, 36–46, 193
Shakespeare Recording Society
    54
Shakespeare, William
  All's Well that Ends Well 60
  Antony and Cleopatra, 19–20,
    34, 98
  The Comedy of Errors 12, 70,
    98

Coriolanus 24, 36, 47, 100, 198
Cymbeline 15, 17, 193
Hamlet, 11, 12, 33, 35, 47, 53,
    60, 97, 98, 117–18, 151
Henry IV, Part One 35, 98
Henry IV, Part Two 10, 13, 35,
    98
Henry V 10, 11, 19–20, 33–4,
    35, 193
Henry VI, Part One 12, 29, 167
Henry VI, Part Two, 12, 29,
    167
Henry VI, Part Three, 12, 29,
    167
Henry VIII 167, 174, 193
Julius Caesar 12, 24, 33–4, 193
King John 5, 12, 30, 71, 117
King Lear 11, 12, 24, 97, 193
Love's Labour's Lost 12, 30, 44,
    98, 158, 167, 184, 193, 197
Lucrece 11
Macbeth 24, 71, 98, 193
Measure for Measure 45, 158,
    172
The Merchant of Venice 3, 10,
    12, 15, 17, 30, 34, 47, 117,
    158, 165, 193
The Merry Wives of Windsor
    11, 12, 30, 34, 36
A Midsummer Night's Dream
    1, 3, 12, 34, 47, 65, 68, 75,
    97, 98, 112, 158, 193
Much Ado about Nothing, 10,
    12, 13, 30, 34, 47, 60, 97, 98
Othello 19–20, 28, 47, 60, 98,
    117, 179–80
Pericles 11
Richard II 35, 56, 60, 98,
    172–4, 193
Richard III 27, 35, 47, 56, 102,
    171
Romeo and Juliet 24, 30, 47,
    60, 90, 159, 172–3, 176–7,
    193
The Taming of the Shrew 12,

29, 47, 60, 69, 130, 158
The Tempest 24, 167, 178, 193
Timon of Athens 83
Titus Andronicus 11, 12, 27, 29, 35, 45
Troilus and Cressida 11, 13, 47, 60
Twelfth Night 3, 12, 15, 17–18, 23, 36, 47, 61, 71, 101, 103, 114, 148
The Two Gentlemen of Verona 12, 15, 17, 30, 47, 65, 98
The Two Noble Kinsmen 167
Venus and Adonis 11
The Winter's Tale 47, 98, 102
Shakespeare's Globe 8, 194–205
Shaw, George Bernard 36, 143, 162
Shaw, Fiona 74, 77–81, 84–7
Shelford, Gary 197
Shepherd, Thomas H. 5
Sher, Antony 98
Shulman, Milton 135–6, 138, 139, 143
Siddons, Sarah 5
Sidney, Mary, Countess of Pembroke 14
Simon, Josette 152, 158
Sinfield, Alan 132
Sly, Will 28
Smallwood, Robert 43–4, 54, 74, 89–90
Smith, Rae 91
Sokoloff, Lisa 106
Some Like it Hot 129
Sosanya, Nina 91, 158
Speaight, Robert 47, 54, 66, 103, 114
Spencer, Charles 89–92, 144, 147–9, 151, 155–6
Stavisky, Alexander 100
Stein, Gertrude 100
Stein, Peter 7, 114–28
   Shakespeare's Memory 118–19, 120

Stephens, Katy 92, 95
Stephens, Robert 134
Stern, Tiffany 18, 20–1, 27, 31
Stevenson, Juliet 60, 74, 77–81, 84–7
Stewart, Sophie 162, 165
Stirner, Brian 168
Stone, Rashan 151, 154
Stoppard, Tom
   Rosencrantz and Guildenstern are Dead 131
Stravinsky, Igor 100
Street, Stephanie 158
Stride, John 131, 133, 137
Stubbes, Philip 13, 15–16
Sturm, Dieter 124
Styan, J. L. 36–9
Suchet, David 60, 65, 95
Sullivan, Barry 7, 37
Sunday Night at the London Palladium 144
Supervielle, Jules 99, 105
Sutton, Shaun 172–3, 175

Tams, John 180
Tennant, David 90, 98, 143
Terry, Michelle 197, 201–4
Thacker, David 43, 89
Thalberg, Irving 159
Thatcher, Margaret 146, 176–7, 180
Théâtre de l'Atelier 7, 99–111, 113, 133
Théâtre des Champs Élysees 99, 110–11
Théâtre du Vieux-Colombier 101–3, 107, 110
Théâtre National Populaire 46
Thompson, Gregory 91
Thompson, Sophie 89
Thomson, Peter 62–4, 69
Tieck, Johann Ludwig 124
Tiernan, Andrew 178, 180, 183–4
Tilley, Danielle 95

Tinker, Jack 80, 81, 94, 143, 148, 151
Toomey, Patrick 148, 154
Tornadoes 134
Trevis, Di 97
Trewin, J. C. 53, 62
Tribble, Evelyn 18, 21–2, 24, 32, 84
Tutin, Dorothy 47, 60, 139
Tynan, Kenneth 54, 131, 132
Tzara, Tristan 100

Villain 182
Villard-Giles, Jean 101
Vincent, Augustine 9
Vitrac, Roger 100

Waldmann, Alex 93, 95
Wales, Katie 26
Walker, Andrea 195–6
Waller, David 65
Walter, Harriet 98
Walton, William 159, 163
Ward, Mackenzie 162–3
Wardle, Irving 49, 62–3, 66, 89, 94, 137–9, 144, 151, 156
Warner, Marina 76

Warren, Roger 74
Wedekind, Frank 162
Welles, Orson
    Othello 179–80
Wells, Stanley 206, 207
Whatever Happened to the Likely Lads? 167
Whitchurch, Phil 197
Williams, Clifford 7–8, 131–42
Williams, Kenneth 144
Williams, Lia 91–2
Williams, Raymond 5, 170
Wilson, Alexander 83
The Wizard of Oz 114, 189
Woffington, Margaret 4
Wolfenden, Guy 63
Wood, Peter 47
Woolf, Virginia 67, 177
Worthen, W. B. 206
Wylie, Frank 134
Wyndham, Alexander 190

Young, David 67
Yuill, Jimmy 191

Zadek, Peter 117–18
Zeffirelli, Franco 47

EU authorised representative for GPSR:
Easy Access System Europe, Mustamäe tee 50,
10621 Tallinn, Estonia
gpsr.requests@easproject.com

www.ingramcontent.com/pod-product-compliance
Lightning Source LLC
Chambersburg PA
CBHW070237240426
43673CB00044B/1831